SOTHEBY'S
ART AT AUCTION 1989–90

SOTHEBY'S
ART AT AUCTION 1989-90

SOTHEBY'S PUBLICATIONS

© Sotheby's 1990

First published for Sotheby's Publications by
Philip Wilson Publishers Ltd,
26 Litchfield Street, London WC2H 9NJ
and
Sotheby's Publications,
Rizzoli International Publications, Inc.,
300 Park Avenue South
New York, NY 10010

ISBN 0 85667 363 8
ISSN 0084–6783
Library of Congress Catalog Card Number 67–30652

Editor: Sally Prideaux
Assistant Editors: Louise Rogers; Jean-Louis Morisot (London);
                    Lynn Stowell Pearson; Bronwyn Albrecht (New York)

Design: Andrew Shoolbred
Printed in England by Jolly & Barber Ltd, Rugby, Warwickshire,
and bound by BPCC Hazell Books Ltd, Aylesbury, Buckinghamshire

Note
Prices given throughout this book include the buyer's premium applicable in the saleroom concerned.
These prices are shown in the currency in which they were realized. The sterling and dollar equivalent
figures, shown in brackets, are based on the rates of exchange on the day of sale.

Frontispiece
Federico Zuccaro
HALF-LENGTH FIGURE OF A MAN LOOKING OVER HIS LEFT
SHOULDER IN AN ATTITUDE OF SURPRISE
Black chalk on pink-washed paper, $7\frac{1}{4}$in by $6\frac{3}{4}$in (18.5cm by 17.2cm)
New York $154,000 (£92,771). 11.I.90
From the collection of the British Rail Pension Fund

Contents illustration
Pascal-Xavier Coste
A hand-coloured lithograph depicting the sanctuary of the Mosque of El Moyed from *Architecture Arabe ou
monuments du Kaire*, first edition, Firmin Didot, 1839
London £17,050 ($28,303). 11.X.89
From the library of Henry M. Blackmer II

Endpapers, front
Joseph Mallord William Turner, RA
DARTMOUTH COVE, DEVONSHIRE
Watercolour heightened with bodycolour and scratching out, *circa* 1825–26, $10\frac{5}{8}$in by $15\frac{1}{2}$in
(27cm by 39.5cm)
London £332,200 ($554,774). 16.XI.89
From the collection of Mr and Mrs Ernest Gaskell

Back
Joseph Mallord William Turner, RA
HAMPTON COURT PALACE
Watercolour with scratching out and stopping out, and some gum arabic, $11\frac{3}{8}$in by $15\frac{7}{8}$in
(28.8cm by 40.5cm)
London £473,000 ($804,100). 15.III.90

Contents

Preface

A. Alfred Taubman
Chairman, Sotheby's Holdings, Inc.

The 1989–90 season marks the culmination of a remarkable decade in the development of the art market, one characterized by tremendous growth and international expansion. During the period, auction sales increased more than five-fold from $573 million in 1978–80 to the record $3.2 billion reported this season. Sotheby's is the first auction house to reach this historic level, an achievement that reflects the dedication and skill of our senior international management team and our expert and administrative staff worldwide.

The season saw record sales in fields as diverse as books and manuscripts, photographs, tribal art, antiquities, Latin American art and Impressionist paintings. Certainly the high point was the New York sale of Renoir's masterpiece *Au Moulin de la Galette* from the collection of Mr and Mrs John Hay Whitney. This timeless image of Paris at play brought $78.1 million, the highest price ever paid for a Renoir or for the work of any Impressionist painter.

During the 1989–90 season, we offered a particularly distinguished group of private collections. Among the most notable were those of John T. Dorrance Jr, the Count and Countess Guy du Boisrouvray, Martine, Comtesse de Béhague, Lydia Winston Malbin, Nelson Bunker Hunt and William Herbert Hunt. The on-going dispersal of the holdings of the British Rail Pension Fund brought an exceptional group of Chinese ceramics, old master drawings and Victorian paintings to the market. Unique to the year were the fine libraries presented, those of George Abrams, Henry M. Blackmer II, H. Bradley Martin and The Garden Ltd.

Sotheby's remains committed to strategic global expansion. During the past season we conducted two auctions in Tokyo in conjunction with the Seibu Group and, in response to growing collecting interest in Korea, we have opened an office in Seoul. Our relationship with the USSR was furthered by signing a historic Protocol of Intent with the Cultural Foundation in December. According to this document, Sotheby's will act as consultants to the Cultural Foundation, advising them on all aspects of the international art market and bringing to their attention any items of Russian heritage which are to be sold in the West. In return, the Cultural Foundation will advise Sotheby's regarding the firm's work within the USSR. We plan to open a new office in Berlin in October to improve our service to the German market, and we will continue to develop relationships in the new Eastern European democracies.

Recognizing the achievements and success of the 1989–90 season, I congratulate, on behalf of the Board of Directors, the senior management of Sotheby's: Michael L. Ainslie, President and Chief Executive Officer, Sotheby's Holdings, Inc.; for the UK, Europe and Asia, The Rt Hon. the Earl of Gowrie, Chairman, and his colleagues Julian Thompson, Deputy Chairman, Asia, Simon de Pury, Deputy Chairman, Europe, and Timothy D. Llewellyn, Managing Director; for North America, John L. Marion, Chairman, and Diana D. Brooks, President; and for Financial Services, Mitchell Zuckerman, President.

A Roman marble statue of Dionysos, *circa* 1st century AD, height 82½in (209.5cm) New York $220,000 (£127,168). 20.VI.90

Formerly in the Hope Collection, this statue is now in the Metropolitan Museum of Art, New York.

Introduction

Wendell Garrett

Horace's motto – *Littera scripta manet* ('the written word remains') – could well serve as the epigraph of the annual editions of *Art at Auction*. This ingathering in published form of individual works of art and collections of objects sold in the international salerooms of Sotheby's, like a museum or library is a model of the memory – a repository of past images, a chamber of living dreams, a glass for visions of the future. The articles by specialists celebrate artists and craftsmen, collectors and patrons, curators and scholars, those who make and those who study and those of us who creatively meander; they honour collectors of books and aesthetic objects, custodians of the past, whose urge to gather in and preserve is almost as deep as the primary hunger and thirst human beings have to express, to make, to create in the forge of the spirit a tangible shape.

That exuberant theatricality and dynamic speculative capitalism are both to be found in the salerooms is undeniable; the record prices are the staple of front-page news. But an auction house is more than simply a market place: it is in part culture's archive, in part a gallery of works of art – an act of faith in the power of the human imagination to make ourselves whole, an expression of man's best hopes in sustaining that most ennobling part of common life we call civilization. And as we have depended on those past who created works of art, who gathered them, who cared for them, so the future depends on us.

Established in Hanoverian England in a consumer revolution – which altered eighteenth-century life as much as the industrial revolution changed nineteenth-century society – Sotheby's was founded at a time when more men and women than ever before enjoyed the experience of acquiring material possessions. 'Fashion is infinitely superior to merit,' wrote the Staffordshire potter Josiah Wedgwood and, in so doing, spoke for his age. The desire to be in fashion and to consume was not an eighteenth-century novelty; but it was the more widespread ability to do so that was new – the maturity, in the words of W. W. Rostow, of 'a society of high mass consumption'. Changes in attitude and thought, greater prosperity and improved standards of living, (at least for the leisured classes), commercial techniques and promotional skills were all necessary attendants to the birth of a consumer society. Objects which for centuries had been the privileged possessions of the very rich came within the reach of a larger and more confident mercantile group. Needs were transformed into fashions. All these changes were taking place as Sotheby's was founded, and their impact on those engaged in making and selling objects was revolutionary.

Thomas Gainsborough, RA
THE BLUE PAGE
65in by 44½in (165cm by 113cm)
London £1,100,000
($1,826,000). 6.XII.89
From the collection of
Sir Joseph Robinson, Bt

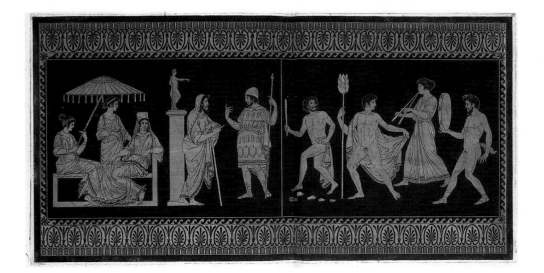

As J. H. Plumb has pointed out in his work on the commercialization of leisure in the eighteenth century, Joseph Addison and Richard Steele's *The Spectator* was the first English periodical to discover and exploit the new, leisured middle-class readership of eighteenth-century London. The astonishing success of this effort set the model for a particular kind of popular journalism encompassing the arts, manners and morals as well as politics. In another sense – the sense implied by its name – *The Spectator* took a position outside this bewildering array of goods and services in order to offer itself as a judicious, confident and charming arbiter of value. This role was new enough in the early 1700s for English writers to borrow the word 'connoisseur' from the French in order to describe and legitimate it. The word 'taste' ran throughout the pages of *The Spectator* and its imitators as a mark of their belletristic ambitions, although the term itself had acquired its association with aesthetic discrimination only after the restoration of Charles II. In the years between 1725 and 1775, the resolutely genial and cosmopolitan style of Addison and Steele was followed by the Scottish Enlightenment, a school of thought that celebrated Common Sense and assured its many adherents of the adequacy of man's senses, the efficacy of his intuitions, the rationality of his judgements, the immediacy of his sympathies, and the mutuality of his relations with others.

As the eighteenth century advanced, those who embraced the Scottish Enlightenment and Common Sense viewed property less as the timeless prerogative of rank and more as a timely prerequisite of trade and free markets. Commerce – 'a world of moving objects' in J. G. A. Pocock's phrase – was developed into a full-blown theory of self-interest and economic motivation in Adam Smith's *Wealth of Nations* (1776). In the opening pages, he wrote, 'It is not from the benevolence of the butcher, the brewer, or the baker, that we expect our dinner, but from their regard to their own interest.' Then he continued, 'We address ourselves, not to their humanity but to their self-love, and never talk to them of our necessities but of their advantages.' Smith's functionalist and materialist inquiry into the wealth of nations and the ideological division of labour that he fostered was based on man's 'propensity to truck, barter, and exchange' in a hard world of limited supply and limitless demand.

Despite the generations that separate eighteenth-century society from our own contemporary mass market culture, there are material contrasts and figurative parallels in the lives and efforts of those busy, inventive, profit-seeking entrepreneurs of Hanoverian England and colonial America: they established the roots of modern capitalism. Their eager advertising, active marketing and inspired salesmanship inaugurated a new economy and structure of demand in the English-speaking world.

The auction house is a reflection of that spirit, a link between the world of commerce and the world of aesthetics that brings together in an open market place rare and beautiful objects for competition among all those interested and able to participate. Like universities, libraries and museums, auction houses are expressions of the conviction that the future is not only possible but also accessible; and not only accessible, but noble. Acting as agent for seller and buyer is a way of making a living connection between what we are and what we want to be, for we believe that a work of art is an affirmation of that portion of us that resists the acid of time, that overcomes the rush to ruin and decay, that wills endurance. To foster the imagination in the service of both the spirit and the market place is what Sotheby's has been doing for two and a half centuries; it is what, at our best, we will always attempt to do as we affirm, through the cycles of crisis and renewal, the continuity and durability of civilization.

Opposite and above
Pierre-François Hugues d'Hancarville
Collection of Etruscan, Greek and Roman Antiquities from the Cabinet of Sir William Hamilton, British ambassador in Naples, first edition, four volumes, 183 hand-coloured plates, proofs of which were lent to Josiah Wedgwood who, in June 1769, celebrated the opening of his new factory by throwing six black vases decorated with figures taken from this work, François Morelli, Naples, 1766–67
London £39,600 ($65,736). 12.X.89
From the library of Henry M. Blackmer II

Country house sales

West Green House, Hartley Wintney, Hampshire.

Right
One of a pair of George II panel-back settees, in the
manner of William Kent, *circa* 1745,
width 6ft 3in (190.5cm)
West Green House £50,600 ($84,957). 16.V.90
From the collection of Lord McAlpine

The contents of West Green House, Hartley Wintney, were sold
on 16th and 17th May. The collection realized £1,703,225, and
particular interest was generated by a large collection of early
agricultural and gardening implements. An evening sale of wine
from the cellars was the first occasion on which Sotheby's had
offered a cellar as part of a country house sale. The contents of
Wherwell Priory, Andover, were sold on 2nd May by direction
of the executors of the late Countess of Brecknock, DBE. The
sale realized £649,328.

The sale at Colstoun, near Haddington, East Lothian, arose from the proposed reduction of the house to its earlier proportions. It was unusual in that it was not a dispersal of the entire contents, nor a residuary sale, but a disposal of the part contents which well reflected the variety of the whole.

The nucleus of the sale was undoubtedly the collection formed by the Marquess of Dalhousie when Governor-General of India (1847–1856), including an assemblage of Indian arms and armour, together with Indo-European and Chinese furniture and ceramics, most notably a portrait of Duleep Singh, a splendidly-carved ivory centre table, and a Chinese export nine-fold lacquer screen with the arms of Lord Dalhousie (£14,850). Scottish furniture included an elaborate walnut display cabinet by John Taylor of Edinburgh, *circa* 1850 (£33,000). Exceptional interest was also shown in a group of Maltese inlaid furniture of which a bureau cabinet sold for £27,500.

For reason of alterations to the house the two-day sale was both viewed and held in a marquee, and made a total of £1,430,465.

Above
George Beechey
PORTRAIT OF DULEEP SINGH
Approximately 36in by 29in (91.5cm by 73.6cm)
Colstoun £66,000 ($118,140). 21.V.90
From the collection of the late Marquess of Dalhousie

Right
An Indian ebony and ivory centre table, second quarter nineteenth century, width 2ft 10in (86cm)
Colstoun £37,400 ($66,946). 21.V.90
From the collection of the late Marquess of Dalhousie

Alexander Pope
The final page of an autograph letter, signed and dated *19th November 1713*, to Pope's patron Sir William Trumbull who encouraged him to translate Homer

John Donne
An autograph letter, signed and dated *10th September 1614*, to William Trumbull, British resident in Brussels from 1609 to 1625, unpublished

The Trumbull Papers, from the collection of the Most Honourable the Marquess of Downshire, were sold by private treaty through Sotheby's to the British Library.

Heritage sales

Timothy Sammons

Sotheby's continues to assist clients and their advisers in negotiating sales of various works of art to the nation under the special 'douceur' arrangements, whereby the taxpayer only incurs 75% of his tax liability and the nation acquires the work of art at a specially reduced price.

The most significant examples have been a *Still-life with Chinese Pottery* by James Ensor (1806–1949), sold by private treaty to the Fitzwilliam Museum, Cambridge, and a sketch by John Constable, *Farmcart with Horses in Harness*, sold in lieu of tax to the Tate Gallery. Of particular interest was *The Family of Henry VIII; An Allegory of the Tudor Succession* by Lucas de Heere. Accepted in lieu of tax and still remaining *in situ* at Sudeley Castle, this painting represents a good example of the flexibility of the current 'in lieu' arrangements (see following page). The most important negotiation, however, has been the sale of the Trumbull papers, by private treaty, to the British Library.

The Trumbull Papers are the archives of the related Trumbull and Weckherlin families which had descended to the present Marquess of Downshire. Comprising some 100,000 pages, including documents signed by such monarchs as Henry of Navarre, James I, Charles I and Charles II, they represent the most important collection of seventeenth-century state papers that has ever been offered at auction.

They were amassed principally by William Trumbull (*circa* 1580–1635), British Resident in Brussels; his daughter's father-in-law, Georg Rudolph Weckherlin (1584–1653), Charles I's Secretary and afterwards Latin Secretary to Parliament; and William Trumbull's grandson, Sir William Trumbull (1639–1716), Ambassador to Paris and Constantinople and Secretary of State. Besides throwing light on vast areas of British and European diplomatic affairs, and on numerous other aspects of seventeenth-century life, the papers include highlights such as a cache of unrecorded Royalist letters captured during the Civil War and partly read out in Parliament, and a highly important intercepted letter by Charles I, written when he was desperately thinking of playing his last card to save himself from defeat, by bringing over an army from Ireland (this alone would have cost him his head).

Letters by and relating to a host of literary and historical illuminati range from Francis Bacon to Alexander Pope, including such figures as Ben Jonson (the letter of introduction he carried to Trumbull, as well as Jonson's referee's confidential remarks sent later under separate cover: 'for the rest you shall soone make a discoverie thereof'), Shakespeare's patron the Earl of Southampton, Shakespeare's publisher Edward Blount, Sir Walter Ralegh, John Donne, Henry King, Thomas Lodge, John Dryden, John Locke and William Penn. Among the most striking and significant of

Below
William Trumbull
(*circa* 1580–1635).

the documents are the Privy Council order by which James I established his Licensers of the Press, the order for seizing the papers of William Prynne who afterwards had his ears cut off for criticizing the Royal Family's taste for the theatre, papers relating to early settlements in America, and a Parliamentary warrant by John Bradshaw ordering a large number of the documents now in the Trumbull archive to be handed over to the Commonwealth's new Latin Secretary, John Milton (an order evidently ignored).

Lucas de Heere
THE FAMILY OF HENRY VIII; AN ALLEGORY OF THE TUDOR SUCCESSION
Circa 1570–75, 51in by 71in (129.5cm by 180.3cm)
Negotiated in lieu of tax; to remain *in situ* at Sudeley Castle, Gloucestershire

With its mixed allegorical and historical subject matter, the basic theme of this painting is the glorification of the Protestant succession within the house of Tudor and the prosperity for the nation that came from this. The Roman Catholic Mary, Queen of Scots, and her husband Phillip II of Spain are shown with Mars, the God of War, to one side, while Elizabeth I leads Peace by the hand in the foreground.

Old master paintings

**Arcangelo di Ghese Vanni,
called Arcangelo di Cola da
Camerino**
THE ANNUNCIATION
One of a pair, tempera and gold
ground on panel, each 37in by 13½in
(94cm by 34.3cm)
New York $1,100,000 (£662,651).
11.I.90

Fig. 1
The Master of 1487
THE DEPARTURE OF THE ARGONAUTS
Oil on panel, dated *MCCCCLXXXVII*, 33in by 64½in (83.8cm by 163.8cm)
London £4,620,000 ($7,669,200). 6.XII.89
From the collection of Sir Joseph Robinson, Bt

Fig. 2
Bartolomeo di Giovanni
THE ARGONAUTS IN COLCHIS
Tempera and oil on panel, 32¾in by 64½in (83cm by 163.8cm)
London £5,060,000 ($8,399,600). 6.XII.89
From the collection of Sir Joseph Robinson, Bt

The Sir Joseph Robinson Collection

Peter Cannon-Brookes

All too often the questions as to when, how, and why an art collection was formed, are never asked until the collector and his associates are dead. Indeed, curiosity about the origins of a collection is rarely aroused until it is about to be broken up, and catalogues in consequence often take on the character of a memorial. Well-documented collecting activity is still something of a rarity, and detailed accounts by collectors of their policies and motivation are rarer still. The personality of the collector can therefore be glimpsed only through the works of art themselves, with the inevitable attendant difficulties of interpretation. After all, Francis Haskell observed of the 5th Earl of Exeter's collecting activities towards the close of the seventeenth century that the glaring contrasts between his paintings 'tell us much about the breadth – or inconsistency – of his taste'.

Two centuries later, the same problems of interpretation are experienced. Joseph Benjamin Robinson came late to the world of art collecting, and his early life as a pioneer in South Africa developed in him a fiercely independent, entrepreneurial spirit. Born in 1840 of British settler parents at Cradock in the Cape Colony, he discovered diamonds in the Vaal River in 1868 and subsequently played a key role in developing the diamond mines of Kimberley, being the first to export a parcel of these stones to Britain. Later he was elected Mayor and, in 1880, Kimberley's first M.P., but on receiving advance news of the discovery in March 1886 of gold-bearing 'banket' at Langlaagte on the Witwatersrand, some thirty miles north of Pretoria, he moved very fast indeed. After locating the reef outcrops and undertaking preliminary surveys, he purchased on behalf of the 'Robinson Syndicate' from November 1886 some forty thousand acres of farms, including ten miles of the reef. These properties were to form the core of the Randfontein Estates.

Robinson first visited London in 1889, and in December 1893 he announced that he and his family were settling in Britain. The enterprises in the Transvaal were to be managed by Jan Langerman and Robinson's brother-in-law, James Ferguson, while Robinson concentrated on raising capital in Europe. Thus the purchase of the lease of Dudley House in Park Lane, early in 1894, coincided with activity on the Paris market and close contact with Jules Porges and Rodolphe Kann. On 4th January 1895, however, the Jameson Raid took place and Robinson returned to the Transvaal to mediate between the mining houses and his old friend President Kruger. When the Boer War broke out in October 1899, with the mines flooded and shut down, Robinson returned to London.

The acquisition of Dudley House brought with it a magnificent but empty picture gallery, some 80 feet long, which had been created by Samuel Whitfield Daukes for the collection of the 11th Lord Ward. Robinson soon began to collect paintings, with the independence of mind and shrewdness which had made him such a powerful figure in the mining world. Notwithstanding his absence, an impressive start was achieved, both in terms of quality and quantity, and some of his most important acquisitions were made during the years 1894–99. If the empty gallery provided the immediate incentive for picture collecting, the model adopted for that collection is perhaps less obvious. Although Robinson played off his 'official' advisers – Sir George Donaldson and Charles Davis – against one another, the overall balance of the collection and the range of masters represented reveal remarkable parallels with the collections being built up from 1880 in Paris by Robinson's South African rival Rodolphe Kann and his brother, Maurice.

Amongst Robinson's earliest acquisitions, the most important were the Tornabuoni-Albizzi marriage panels by the Master of 1487 (Fig. 1) and Bartolomeo di Giovanni (Fig. 2) which Sir George Donaldson had purchased from the Ashburnham Collection through the New Gallery in 1894–95. These were accompanied by two further long panels of scenes from *The Story of St John the Baptist* by Francesco Granacci from the same source, and all share a provenance from the Tornabuoni family in Florence. The marriage of Lorenzo Tornabuoni to Giovanna degli Albizzi took place in 1486 and these panels, together with that *en suite* by Biagio d'Antonio in the Musée des Arts Décoratifs in Paris and those of *Apollo* and *Aphrodite* bearing the arms of the two families (private collection), almost certainly decorated a room in the Palazzo Tornabuoni in Florence. Most of the building, designed by Michelozzo, was demolished in 1875 during the widening of the Via Tornabuoni, but these panels would appear to have been removed long before then and may have been inherited by the Pandolfini family in the seventeenth century. Perhaps it is not just a coincidence that one of Rodolphe Kann's most prized possessions was the *Portrait of Giovanna Tornabuoni*, by Domenico Ghirlandaio (dated 1488), also believed to have passed from the Tornabuoni family to the Pandolfini before reaching Paris in the mid nineteenth century. This portrait, now in the Thyssen-Bornemisza Collection at Lugano, is, like the present marriage panels, in brilliantly fresh condition.

Fig. 3
Bartholomé Esteban Murillo
THE VISION OF ST FRANCIS OF PAOLA
74in by 57½in (188cm by 146cm)
London £1,485,000 ($2,465,100). 6.XII.89
From the collection of Sir Joseph Robinson, Bt

As with the Kann Collections, the Italian paintings acquired by Robinson were relatively few in number, though generally of the highest quality, and restricted to the fifteenth and eighteenth centuries. One of the earlier major purchases was the superb altarpiece by Giambattista Tiepolo: *The Madonna of the Rosary with Angels*. Also purchased from the Ashburnham Collection by way of Sir George Donaldson was Murillo's moving *Vision of St Francis of Paola* which dates from late in the artist's life (Fig. 3), but at the core of the Robinson Collection were the superb paintings by Dutch and Flemish masters of the seventeenth century, together with the eighteenth-century English paintings, above all the works by Thomas Gainsborough.

An important group of Dutch paintings was purchased from the Cornwall Legh Collection in 1895 – the same year as Van Dyck's *Elizabeth, Lady Herbert of Raglan* – and the pair of de Witte portraits by Van Dyck were purchased in 1899, at the same time as *A Family Party* by Gonzales Coques. After 1900 the number of new acquisitions was greatly reduced, despite the return of Robinson to London, and it is intensely frustrating that no buying records for this collection appear to have survived. The four large tapestry cartoons by Boucher, however, were not purchased until the Reginald Vaile sale of 1903, when Robinson's taste for French eighteenth-century painting would appear to have crystallized. After 1900 he also purchased Boucher's *Landscape with a Rustic Bridge* from Sir George Donaldson. On the other hand Gainsborough's ravishing *The Blue Page* (see page 10), was apparently purchased in 1898 from Wertheimer, and the same artist's portrait of *Mrs Drummond* was probably purchased from the Ames Collection in Boston during the course of the same year.

In 1908, Robinson was created a baronet in recognition of his public service and his role in developing the diamond and gold mining industries, but two years later he gave up Dudley House and purchased a property off the Bayswater Road in which to store the contents. Robinson returned to South Africa for the duration of the First World War, selling control of the Robinson Group to Solly Joel, chairman of Barnato Brothers of London and the Johannesburg Consolidated Investment Company, in 1916. The following year he moved into Hawthornden at Wynberg near Cape Town. At the end of the First World War when he was already nearly eighty, the contents of his London house were still in store. In 1923, Christie's were instructed to sell the paintings. A catalogue of 116 lots was published and widely distributed, but on the eve of the sale Sir Joseph arrived in his wheel-chair to bid the paintings farewell . . . only to fall in love with the collection again. It was too late to cancel the sale and instead he placed what he believed to be prohibitively high reserves on all the lots. Nevertheless, twelve paintings were sold, including portraits by Rembrandt, Frans Hals and Lawrence, the large John Constable sketch for the *Opening of Waterloo Bridge* (National Trust, Anglesey Abbey) and J. M. W. Turner's *Falls of the Clyde* (Lady Lever Art Gallery). The remaining 104 paintings were returned to store and after the death of Sir Joseph in 1929 they passed to his daughter, Ida, Princess Labia, who left them undisturbed in London until 1958 when 84 works were displayed in the Diploma Gallery of the Royal Academy. In the following year 108 paintings were exhibited at the National Gallery of South Africa, in Cape Town. Since then it has not proved possible to keep the collection intact, however, and the sale last December represented the last major group to be sold.

Eglon Hendrisz. van der Neer
FIGURES IN AN INTERIOR
Signed and dated *1678*,
33¾in by 27⅝in (85.7cm by 70.1cm)
London £924,000 ($1,533,840). 6.XII.89
From the collection of Sir Joseph Robinson, Bt

Luis Meléndez
STILL LIFE WITH ORANGES, BOXES OF SWEETS AND A VASE
Signed with monogram, 15⅜in by 13⅜in (39cm by 34cm)
Madrid Ptas 68,064,000 (£368,911:$631,978). 22.II.90

Juan de Zurbarán
A STILL LIFE OF FRUIT IN A BASKET, A WHITE FAIENCE JAR AND A PEWTER PLATE TO THE LEFT, POMEGRANATES
TO THE RIGHT, ALL UPON A STONE LEDGE
28⅜in by 37in (72cm by 94cm)
London £715,000 ($1,186,900). 6.XII.89

Zurbarán's promising career was cut short at the age of twenty-nine, by bubonic plague, and
our knowledge of his distinctive, sensous style is limited to three signed and dated works, in
the Lung Collection, Bordeaux, The Museum of Western and Oriental Art in Kiev, and the
Gösta Serlachius Fine Arts Foundation in Finland. One of the first Sevillian painters to
specialise in still life, his robust realism is quite distinct from the geometric style of his father,
Francisco de Zurbarán. Strong stylistic similarities between the present picture and the latter
of Juan's three surviving signed and dated works date it towards the end of his short life.

Joachim Wtewael
THE WEDDING OF PELEUS AND THETIS
Oil on copper, dated *1612*, 14⅜in by 16½in (36.5cm by 42cm)
London £770,000 ($1,339,800). 11.IV.90

Opposite
Ambrosius Bosschaert the Elder
A STILL LIFE OF TULIPS, NARCISSUS, FRITILLARY AND OTHER FLOWERS IN A ROEMER FLANKED BY A FLOWER
AND A SHELL, ALL ON A LEDGE
Oil on copper, signed with monogram, the reverse stamped with the marks of the Antwerp panel-makers
guild and the maker Peeter Stas, 9⅛in by 7in (23.3cm by 17.9cm)
London £814,000 ($1,416,360). 11.IV.90

Hubert Robert
LA PASSERELLE
18⅞in by 26in (48cm by 66cm)
Monte Carlo FF2,886,000 (£290,050:$506,316). 15.VI.90

The picture is first recorded in the collection of Ange-Laurent de La Live de Jully, one of the greatest collectors of French art of the eighteenth century. It was exhibited at the 'Salon de l'Académie Royale de Peinture' of 1767, with its pendant depicting the ruined gates of the temple of Balbec at Heliopolis. Both paintings were included in de La Live de Jully's sale of his collection in Paris, on 5th March 1770, where they fetched 360 *livres*.

Opposite
Joos de Momper
WINTER, A CART ON A WOODED ROAD WITH A VILLAGE UNDER SNOW BEYOND
Jan Brueghel the Younger
SUMMER, COWS CROSSING A FORD WITH A FARM BEYOND
A pair, oil on panel, each 18⅛in by 29½in (46cm by 75cm)
Amsterdam Dfl2,012,500 (£630,878:$986,520). 22.XI.89

Giovanni Antonio Canale, called Il Canaletto
A VIEW OF THE MOLO FROM THE BACINO DI SAN MARCO WITH THE PIAZZETTA AND PALAZZO DUCALE
A VIEW OF THE GRAND CANAL FACING EAST FROM THE CAMPO DI SAN VIO
A pair, each 19¼in by 31½in (48.9cm by 80cm)
New York $11,000,000 (£6,547,619). 1.VI.90

Francesco Guardi
A VIEW OF THE ISLAND OF
SAN CRISTOFORO WITH THE
ISLANDS OF SAN MICHELE
AND MURANO IN THE
DISTANCE
$24\frac{3}{4}$in by $37\frac{3}{4}$in
(62.9cm by 95.9cm)
New York $4,400,000
(£2,784,810). 27.X.89
From the collection of the
late Count and Countess
Guy du Boisrouvray

Francesco Guardi
A VIEW OF THE GIUDECCA CANAL AND THE ZATTERE, VENICE
$47\frac{1}{4}$in by $80\frac{3}{4}$in (120cm by 205cm)
Monte Carlo FF94,350,000 (£9,828,125 : $15,341,463). 1.XII.89
From the collection of the late Martine, Comtesse de Béhague

Jusepe de Ribera, called Lo Spagnoletto
THE MARTYRDOM OF ST BARTHOLOMEW
Signed, inscribed and dated *español F. 1634*, 41in by 44½in (104cm by 113cm)
London £2,750,000 ($5,225,000). 4.VII.90

Old master drawings

Above
Taddeo Zuccaro
A RIVER GOD
Pen and brown wash, heightened with white,
over black chalk on blue paper, 8in by 11¼in
(20.2cm by 28.6cm)
New York $137,500 (£82,831). 11.I.90
From the collection of the British Rail
Pension Fund.

Giorgio Vasari
A STUDY OF A SEATED MALE NUDE TURNED TO
THE RIGHT, AND A SEPARATE STUDY OF
DRAPERY AND OF HIS LEFT HAND
Red chalk, 14⅛in by 9½in (35.9cm by 24.1cm)
New York $110,000 (£65,089). 12.I.90

Fig. 1
Federico Zuccaro
TADDEO LEAVING HOME, ESCORTED BY TWO GUARDIAN-ANGELS
Pen and brown wash, with traces of black chalk underdrawing, 10¾in by 10¼in (27.4cm by 26cm), from
The Life of Taddeo Zuccaro, a series of twenty narrative and allegorical drawings
New York $2,530,000 (£1,524,096). 11.I.90
From the collection of the British Rail Pension Fund

The early life of Taddeo Zuccaro by his brother Federico Zuccaro

J. A. Gere

The famous series of drawings by Federico Zuccaro (1540–1609), illustrating the early tribulations and eventual triumph of his elder brother, the painter Taddeo Zuccaro (1529–66), was sold in New York in January 1990. The series had long been known from printed descriptions and from old copies, including some autograph versions, in the Uffizi and other collections, but the originals had hardly been seen since the middle of the last century. The catalogue of the New York sale is the first publication in which the series as a whole is reproduced.

Taddeo Zuccaro was born on the 1st September 1529, at S. Angelo in Vado, a small town in the Duchy of Urbino. His father was a painter and taught him all he could, but at the age of fourteen Taddeo insisted on completing his education in Rome. In the second drawing of the series (Fig. 1), we see him leaving home escorted by two guardian angels. We next see him being shown a prospect of Rome, by Minerva, entering the city bearing a yoke – a symbol of toil and slavery – and confronted by figures prophetically identified as *Servitude, Toil* and *Hardship*. In the fifth drawing, Taddeo introduces himself to a kinsman, Francesco il Sant'Angelo (described by Vasari as a journeyman specialist in grotesque decoration), only to be roughly turned away (Fig. 2). In the relatively haphazard conditions of artistic training in the Rome of the 1540s, Taddeo drifted unhappily from one obscure painter to another, supporting himself by doing odd jobs about the studio. An otherwise unrecorded painter named Giovanni Piero il Calabrese takes him in, but

Fig. 2
Federico Zuccaro
TADDEO REBUFFED BY
FRANCESCO IL SANT'AGNOLO
Pen and brown wash,
numbered *5*, 7in by 16⅜in
(17.9cm by 41.5cm)

Fig. 3
Federico Zuccaro
TADDEO IN THE HOUSE OF GIOVANNI PIERO CALABRESE
Pen and brown wash, with traces of red chalk underdrawing, numbered *7* and inscribed in pen on the
recto against the suspended basket *al suon del campanel, co[n]vie[n] che io viva*; against the figure of Taddeo
holding the lamp *tu mi privi di quel ch'io ta[n]to bramo*; in the lower left corner *giova[n] pietro Calavres no[n]
vol lasciarli vedere e...*, 10⅞in by 10½in (27.5cm by 26.6cm)

he is starved and forbidden to look at his master's Raphael drawings (Fig. 3). Subsequent drawings show him working as a servant during the day, and kept so busy that he is obliged to draw at night by the light of the moon, since even oil for a lamp is denied him. Nevertheless, he manages to follow the traditional course of artistic education in Rome, copying antique sculpture, the façade paintings of Polidoro da Caravaggio, the paintings of Raphael in the Vatican and in the Farnesina (where he is sometimes reduced to spending the night), and Michelangelo's *Last Judgement* in the Sistine Chapel. Of these various influences, Polidoro made the greatest impression, if we are to judge from the episode depicted in the fourteenth and fifteenth drawings in the series, which Federico recounted in a lengthy annotation. Made ill by all his hardships, Taddeo decides to return home. On his way to S. Angelo in Vado he lies down to sleep beside a river. Waking in a fever he fancies, deliriously, that the stones on the river bank are painted in the manner of Polidoro's façades. Having picked up as many as he can carry, he brings them home with him in a sack which he presents to his parents. After being nursed back to health, he returns to Rome, and is shown re-entering the city in happier circumstances – no longer a child, and escorted by the figures of *Disegno* and *Spirito* towards a vision of the Three Graces. The series culminates in the largest and most elaborate of the scenes, showing Taddeo engaged on his first independent commission, the decoration of the façade of the Palazzo Mattei (Fig. 4). This work, completed in 1548, established his reputation, and was hailed as a masterpiece by the leading artists in Rome at the time – Siciolante da Sermoneta, Daniele da Volterra, Vasari, Francesco Salviati and Michelangelo himself – all of whom are shown watching in admiration from the street below.

In addition to the sixteen scenes from Taddeo's life, the series comprises four drawings of pairs of figures symbolising *Virtues*, each pair flanking a circular space which in two of the drawings is occupied by Federico's device of a sugar loaf (*zucchero*) stuck with lilies. The twenty drawings vary in shape. Four are rectangular, the largest (Fig. 4), being oblong and the other three (Figs 1 and 3) almost square. The rest can best be described as dumb-bell shaped, eight being vertical and eight, including the four pairs of *Virtues*, horizontal (Fig. 2). The series originally consisted of twenty-four drawings, the additional four being symbolic portraits of Taddeo himself, and the three artists considered to have had the greatest influence on him – Michelangelo (in the pose of his *Moses* in S. Pietro in Vincoli), Raphael (in the pose of his *Isaiah* in S. Agostino) and Polidoro da Caravaggio (represented as a bearded man in Roman armour, holding a torch in one hand and a scroll in the other. The originals of the four portraits have disappeared, but there are copies of them in the Uffizi.

The earliest reference to this series of drawings is a note in the appendix to the third volume of Bottari's edition of Vasari, quoting a communication from P. J. Mariette (of which an amplified version was later published in his *Abecedario*). Mariette had seen them in 1735, when the portraits were still part of the series, and had recognised that they were by Federico, not Taddeo, to whom they had been attributed. In the absence of any contemporary or near-contemporary reference to the series, its purpose must be a matter of conjecture but the variety of shapes and sizes, and the fact that some of the 'dumb-bells' are horizontal and some upright, suggest that it was not intended simply as a set of drawings. The most likely explanation is that these are designs for an elaborate decorative scheme intended for the house which Federico began building in Rome in the 1590s.

The Palazzo Zuccaro, close to the church of SS. Trinita dei Monti in the angle of the Via Sistina and the Via Gregoriana, was designed to be more than a mere habitation for Federico and his family. In his will, made in 1603, six years before his death, Federico declared his intention of leaving the house in trust for the Accademia di S. Luca with the provision that part of it should be used as a hostel for the accommodation of poor but deserving young students of art who had come as strangers to Rome and had nowhere to live, adding that it had long been his wish to do something of the sort. He was clearly thinking of the hardships suffered by his brother fifty years before, and the story of Taddeo's eventual triumph over adversity would have made an ideal scheme for the decoration of a communal studio or meeting room.

The part of the palace intended for the hostel was still unfinished when Federico died in 1609. It was completed by his heirs, but there is no evidence that it was used for that purpose, and in 1615 the whole property was sold. Nevertheless, it does seem possible that the paintings of seven of the scenes on leather now in the Palazzo Venezia may have decorated a room in the palace. Six of these paintings, corresponding with numbers three, four, eight, nine, sixteen, and eighteen – all upright 'dumb-bells' – measure about $17\frac{3}{4}$ inches by $6\frac{1}{2}$ inches (45cm by 16cm); the seventh, which corresponds with number nineteen, is about $31\frac{1}{2}$ inches by 67 inches (80 cm by 171cm). It is true that they are not listed in the very full inventory of Federico's property made after his death, but if they had been built into the panelling or plasterwork of one of the rooms of the palace they could have been regarded as fixtures and not necessarily included in the inventory. Santangelo's statement, that there is a seal on the back of each panel with Federico Zuccaro's 'emblem' (presumably the sugar loaf or *zucchero*) is incorrect. There are seals, but the coat-of-arms on them is surmounted by a coronet, and in no way resembles Federico's arms as represented on the ceiling of the Sala del Disegno in the palace.

Mariette does not say where he saw the drawings in 1735, but at some time in the eighteenth century they were in the Paignon Dijonval Collection, in the catalogue of which, published in 1810, the series is described minus the four portraits but still incorrectly attributed to Taddeo. The disappearance of the portraits remains a mystery. In the interval between Paignon Dijonval's death in 1792 and the compilation of the catalogue nearly twenty years later they could have been accidentally separated from the rest and their connection overlooked, but no drawings identifiable with them are listed elsewhere in the catalogue.

In 1816 Paignon Dijonval's grandson sold the entire collection to the London art dealer Samuel Woodburn. Many of the best, including the Zuccaro series, were bought by the English collector Thomas Dimsdale, and after his death in 1823 by Sir Thomas Lawrence. After Lawrence's death in 1830 his great collection of drawings reverted to Woodburn, his principal creditor, who tried to dispose of it by organizing a series of exhibitions under the collective title 'The Lawrence Gallery'. The seventh exhibition, in April 1836, included 80 drawings by the two Zuccaros, among them the series of the Life of Taddeo, attributed correctly to Federico but described in exactly the same terms as in the Paignon Dijonval catalogue.

Fig. 4
Federico Zuccaro
TADDEO DECORATING THE
FAÇADE OF THE PALAZZO
MATTEI
Pen and brown wash, with
traces of black chalk
underdrawing, the
paintings on the façade and
the masonry of the lower
storey in black chalk only,
numbered *19* and inscribed
in ink on the *recto* against
the figures surrounding
Taddeo on the scaffold
grazie spirito fierezza; against
the onlookers in the street,
from left to right *[G]erolimo
[S]ermoneta, daniel da
volterra, michelangelo.b.rota,
urbino, giorgio vasari,
francesco salviati*, 9⅞in by
16⅝in (25cm by 42.2cm)

The eighty Zuccaro drawings failed to find a purchaser and when Woodburn died in 1853 the greater part of the Lawrence Collection was still on his hands. At some time in the interval he had had the twenty drawings of the Life of Taddeo mounted in an album together with fifty-three others by or attributed to Taddeo and Federico. When the Lawrence-Woodburn Collection was eventually dispersed at auction in the summer of 1860 this volume, 'handsomely bound in red morocco', caught the eye of the eccentric bibliophile Sir Thomas Phillipps and was bought by him for sixty guineas. Phillipps (1792–1872) devoted his long life to the amassing of a vast miscellaneous hoard of early printed books and manuscript material. He bought some 750 drawings at the Lawrence-Woodburn sale but immediately forgot about them, for when the bulk of his collection of drawings was acquired by the British Museum in 1946 most of them were still in the paper wrappers inscribed with lot numbers in which they had been offered for sale nearly a century before. His collections were inherited by his grandson, Thomas Fitzroy Fenwick (1856–1938), who in 1930 sold the Zuccaro album to the New York dealer in rare books and manuscripts, A. S. W. Rosenbach. It remained in the possession of the Rosenbach Company, and from 1950 in that of the Philip H. and A. S. W. Rosenbach Foundation in Philadelphia, until 1978 when its contents (less six drawings which had been bought by Mr Janos Scholz and now in the Pierpont Morgan Library) were acquired by the British Rail Pension Fund.

Leonardo da Vinci
DRAPERY STUDY: FIGURE
KNEELING TO THE LEFT
Drawn with the brush
in brown-grey wash,
heightened with white
bodycolour, on linen
prepared with grey
bodycolour, laid down
on paper, 11¾in by 7⅛in
(28.8cm by 18.1cm)
Monte Carlo FF35,520,000
(£3,700,000: $5,775,610).
1.XII.89
From the collection of the
late Martine, Comtesse de
Béhague

Left
Simon Vouet
STUDY OF A KNEELING WOMAN, WITH A DETAIL OF DRAPERY AND A FOOT
Black and white chalk on buff paper, 14⅛in by 9¾in (36cm by 24.7cm)
London £74,800 ($139,876). 2.VII.90
From the collection of the British Rail Pension Fund

Formerly in the collection of Pierre-Jean Mariette, this study is still on his distinctive mount.

Below, left
Jean-Honoré Fragonard
LA COQUETTE
Red chalk, 14⅜in by 8¼in (36.5cm by 21cm)
New York $297,000 (£175,740). 12.I.90

Below
Joseph Heintz the Elder
THE TOILET OF VENUS
Red and black chalk, signed and dated *1594* in black chalk, 8⅜in by 5⅞in (21.4cm by 15cm)
London £143,000 ($267,410). 2.VII.90

Jan van Goyen
A WINTER SCENE WITH FIGURES AND A HORSE-DRAWN SLEIGH ON A FROZEN RIVER
Black chalk and light grey wash with touches of dark grey wash, signed and dated *1627* in grey ink,
7⅝in by 12⅜in (19.3cm by 31.3cm)
Amsterdam Dfl 112,700 (£35,000:$54,976). 21.XI.89

Pierre-Antoine Quillard
ASSEMBLEE ELEGANTE
Red chalk, 6⅝in by 10¾in
(16.8cm by 27.4cm)
Monte Carlo FF283,050
(£28,447:$49,658).
15.VI.90

Hubert Robert
FIGURES ON A GRAND STAIR-
CASE LEADING TO A VILLA
Pen and black ink and two
shades of brown wash, 7⅛in
by 9in (18cm by 23cm)
Monte Carlo FF266,400
(£27,750:$43,317).
1.XII.89
From the collection of the
late Martine, Comtesse de
Béhague

British paintings and watercolours

Joseph Mallord William Turner, RA
SEASCAPE WITH SQUALL COMING UP
17⅞in by 24in (45.5cm by 61cm)
London £638,000 ($1,071,840). 15.XI.89

This composition was painted at the same time as larger seascapes such as *Fishermen on the Lee Shore*, *The Egremont Seascape*, both of 1802, and *Calais Pier*, 1803, which reflect the impact of the artist's first Channel crossing in that year. The unity of sky and sea and their effect on the activity of the fishing boats is powerfully demonstrated in *Seascape with Squall coming up*, where Turner harnessed his first hand experience of the elements with his understanding of the work of Dutch seventeenth-century painters. This painting is the best of the sea pictures produced on a more intimate scale.

John Constable, RA
CHILD'S HILL: HARROW IN THE DISTANCE
$23\frac{5}{8}$in by $29\frac{1}{2}$in (60cm by 75cm)
London £616,000 ($1,034,880). 15.XI.89
From the collection of the Westmoreland Museum of Art

Constable first took lodgings in Hampstead, then a small village in fairly rural surroundings, in 1819. Seven miles to the west lay the village of Harrow, and the prominent feature of its church was included by Constable in a number of sketches and drawings. Hampstead's position was ideal for the study of the skies, clouds and weather patterns that were to form such an original and important part of his practice, and a letter of 1st August 1825, describes this particular scene as '. . . Serene afternoon, with sunshine after rain, and heavy clouds passing off.' This composition is based on an open air sketch now in the Victoria and Albert Museum, dated by Reynolds to between 1820–23. It was exhibited at the Royal Academy in 1825 as a companion to *The Branch Hill Pond Hampstead*, now in the Virginia Museum of Fine Arts.

John Zoffany, RA
PORTRAIT OF GEORGE FITZGERALD WITH HIS SONS GEORGE AND CHARLES
39⅜in by 49⅜in (100cm by 125.5cm)
London £902,000 ($1,731,840). 11.VII.90

The Fitzgerald family came from County Mayo. George Fitzgerald had served as a Captain
in the Austrian army, and the relief profile of a Roman soldier, on the broken pedestal upon
which he is seated, probably alludes to his military career, now exchanged for family life.
The picture belies the unhappy fate of his eldest son George Robert, shown here flying a kite,
who was later convicted of murder and hanged in 1786. His younger brother, Charles Lionel,
depicted as the fond and dutiful son at his father's knee, inherited the estate at Turlough.

Opposite
Joseph Wright of Derby, ARA
PORTRAIT OF JOHN WHETHAM
50in by 40in (127cm by 101.5cm)
London £418,000 ($802,560). 11.VII.90

George Stubbs, ARA
'PROTECTOR' IN A LANDSCAPE
Signed and dated *1779*, 40in by 50in (101.6cm by 127cm)
New York $1,210,000 (£715,976). 8.VI.90
From the collection of Marcia Whitney Schott

Opposite
Thomas Gainsborough, RA
ROCKY WOODED LANDSCAPE WITH MOUNTED DROVER, HORSES WATERING AT A TROUGH AND DISTANT
VILLAGE AND MOUNTAINS
48¾in by 39in (123cm by 99cm)
London £715,000 ($1,201,200). 15.XI.89
From the collection of the British Rail Pension Fund

John Ward of Hull
THE OLD HARBOUR AND GARRISON
SIDE, KINGSTON-UPON-HULL
18¼in by 27⅜in (46.5cm by 69.5cm)
London £71,500 ($121,550). 14.111.90

Joseph Francis Nollekens
A MUSICAL PARTY
Oil on metal, 14in by 18in (35.5cm by
45.5cm)
London £154,000 ($258,720). 15.XI.89
From the collection of the late Lord
Chelwood

William Daniell, RA
A VIEW OF THE EUROPEAN FACTORIES AT CANTON IN CHINA
36in by 71¼in (91.5cm by 181cm)
London £704,000 ($1,182,720). 15.XI.89

Exhibited at the Royal Academy in 1808, this painting is possibly the finest of a small group
of ten known oil paintings of Chinese subjects by William Daniell and his uncle Thomas.
Thomas Daniell was granted permission by the East India Company to 'proceed to Bengal
to follow his profession of an engraver' on 1st December 1784, and took with him his young
nephew, William, as an assistant. They sailed from the Downs on 7th April 1785 in the East
Indiaman *Atlas*, bound for China under the command of Captain Allen Cooper, and
reached Whampoa on 23rd August 1785. They travelled up-river to Canton where they
spent several months sketching junks, local inhabitants and much of the local scenery before
proceeding to India. Apart from John Webber, who visited China in 1779–80, they were the
first British professional artists to come to South-East Asia. After spending seven years in
India, they left for England in 1793. The painting was commissioned by James Drummond,
6th Earl of Strathallan, President of the East India Company Committee in Canton from
1802–1806, and shows the hongs or 'factories' belonging to Denmark, Spain, France, the
United States of America, Sweden, Great Britain and Holland.

Alexander Cozens
THE PROPHET ELIJAH FED BY THE RAVENS
Brown and yellow washes over pencil heightened with white, 18⅞in by 25⅜in (48cm by 64.5cm)
London £90,200 ($153,340). 15.III.90

This dramatic image depicts the Old Testament biblical episode related in *I Kings 17:1-6*, in which Elijah went to live beside the brook of Cherith. The verses relate that the prophet was fed by ravens, who brought him meat and bread each morning and evening.

Richard Wilson, RA

THE VILLA BORGHESE, ROME

Pencil heightened with white, original mount signed with initials, inscribed and dated *f.Roma 1754/Villa Borg^esi. No. 2* and numbered *52* on the reverse, 11in by 16½in (28cm by 42cm)

London £48,400 ($82,280). 15.III.90

Commissioned by William Legge, 2nd Earl of Dartmouth, in 1754, this work is from a series of 68 drawings, much admired by eighteenth- and early nineteenth-century connoisseurs, including John Hoppner. Of the 25 surviving drawings, 19 depict views of Rome. The first of these is missing, and the present work is the second in the group. Describing the series, Hoppner wrote that 'they were such as the Greeks would have made & put all others at a distance.'

Fig. 1
Thomas Girtin
JEDBURGH ABBEY FROM THE SOUTH EAST
Watercolour over pencil with slight touches of
bodycolour, signed, 16⅝in by 21⅞in
(42.3cm by 55.4cm)
London £286,000 ($549,120). 11.VII.90

Left
Fig. 2
Thomas Girtin
VILLAGE OF JEDBURGH
Watercolour over pencil, signed and dated *1800*,
11⅞in by 20½in (30cm by 52cm)
(Reproduced courtesy of the National Gallery of
Scotland).

Two Girtin discoveries

Susan Morris

'If Tom had lived, I would have starved', Turner is said to have remarked. Tom Girtin's immense promise – and tangible achievements – as a watercolourist were cut short by his death in 1802 aged twenty-seven, removing Turner's major rival from the field. It is idle to speculate how Girtin would have developed, or whether his fame would have surpassed Turner's. What is certain is that by 1800, Girtin was a watercolourist of extraordinary brilliance, capable, like Turner, of transforming the medium from 'tinted drawing' into a powerful proto-Romantic art. Although about 800 works by Girtin survive, it is rare to find major late works in good condition, thanks to the Victorian mania for hanging watercolours in full sunlight. *Jedburgh Abbey* (Fig. 1) and *Lydford Castle, Devon* (Fig. 3), are remarkable for their artistic power, their superb condition, and the fact that they were entirely unknown until this year. They were discovered at the bottom of a linen chest in the house of a descendant of Sir John Ramsden (1755–1839), who is thought to have commissioned them.

Ramsden became an MP in 1780, and owned a house at Byram, West Yorkshire. He was connected by marriage to Lord Rockingham of Wentworth Woodhouse, and shared Rockingham's taste for the arts, employing both Robert Adam and Carr of York at Byram. Ramsden was also a neighbour of several Girtin patrons – the Horton-Fawkes at Otley, the Winns of Nostell Priory, and Edward Lascelles at Harewood House. Girtin probably visited Harewood in 1799, 1800 and 1801, sketching extensively in the area. He gave drawing lessons to Lascelles, either at Harewood or at Lascelles' house in London, and no doubt met Ramsden through this circle of Yorkshire patrons.

Ramsden owned two other Girtin watercolours, *Village of Jedburgh* (the companion to *Jedburgh Abbey*, now in the National Gallery of Scotland; Fig. 2) and *A View on the River Taw Looking from Braunton March towards Instow and Appledore* (private collection; Fig. 4). Both are important works, indicating that Sir John was prepared to buy major, large-scale paintings, probably paying about 20 guineas (Girtin's top price *circa* 1800). But whereas Edward Lascelles had commissioned Girtin to paint views of his house and the surrounding countryside, Ramsden seems to have had no obvious personal connection with the subjects of his pictures. He would have selected the subjects from compositional pencil sketches like those in Girtin's Shepherd Sketchbook

Fig. 3
Thomas Girtin
LYDFORD CASTLE, DEVON
Watercolour over pencil,
signed and dated *1800*,
12¾in by 20⅜in
(32.4cm by 52cm)
London £176,000
($337,920). 11.VII.90

Left
Fig. 4
Thomas Girtin
A VIEW ON THE RIVER TAW
LOOKING FROM BRAUNTON
MARCH TOWARDS INSTOW
AND APPLEDORE
Watercolour over
pencil, 1800, 11¾in by 20½in
(29.8cm by 52cm)

(Whitworth Art Gallery, Manchester). The watercolours were then worked up in the artist's London studio. *Lydford* is dated 1800, and *Jedburgh Abbey* probably also dates from that year, together with several other stylistically similar views of the same subject. *Village of Jedburgh* is also dated 1800, but derives from a pencil sketch made on Girtin's tour of 1796, when he first discovered the romantic scenery of the north of England.

Girtin visited the West Country in 1797, and there are enough mature watercolours to suggest that he returned in 1800 and perhaps again in 1801. The Shepherd Sketchbook (1799–1801) has a view of Mount Edgcumbe, Plymouth, and there is a view of Devonport dated 1801 in the National Gallery of New Zealand. A superb on-the-spot sketch (Yale Center for British Art), too fluent and sophisticated for a 1797 date, has been identified as *The Estuary of the River Taw*. Until the discovery of the two present Ramsden watercolours it seemed, however, as if the north of England had been the scene of Girtin's greatest triumphs in the medium, with fine works depicting Jedburgh, the Eildon Hills, Melrose and Kirkstall Abbey. *Lydford* proves that he could also rise to the challenge of the very different landscape of the south.

A village on the edge of Dartmoor, Lydford was famous for its rough justice, in the days when a stannary court was held there – 'I oft have heard of Lydford Law/How in the morn they hang and draw/And sit in judgement after.' Nearby was a picturesque waterfall, ignored by Girtin in favour of a view across Lydford Gorge to the rolling countryside beyond. The village is marked by St Petrock's church and the twelfth-century keep of the castle; beyond, Girtin depicts the barren slopes of Dartmoor, lashed by a sudden rainstorm. The panorama and naturalism of the work are breathtaking. The fitful light on a sheep-studded hillside, newly-ploughed brown furrows, the sweep of cloud along the horizon – all are observed with an acute eye for natural effects, and a profound engagement with the beauties of nature. The perfectly-preserved watercolour reveals a balanced palette of strong greens, indigo clouds and straw-coloured fields – colouring rarely observed in Girtin's work, where now indigo has often burnt to red, and green to brown. The attack and vivacity of *Lydford* demonstrates the strength of Girtin's challenge to landscapes in oil.

Jedburgh Abbey is a more serene, monumental picture, and a compositional type – ruins in a landscape – that Girtin had been producing from very early in his career. Here, he is at the height of his powers. The abbey is set on rising ground, and the curving lines of the picture sweep up to it. It is the most brightly lit object in the picture, backed by a swirling spiral of cumulus cloud. Unlike the Lydford scene, the weather here is benign. Girtin plays on the eighteenth-century fascination for medieval ruins, but sets the abbey firmly within a contemporary community, and within a landscape. Individual passages, such as the sunlight playing across the house at the far left, or the cloud shadows on the distant hills, are superbly painted. Girtin made several close-up views of the abbey, but this is undoubtedly the finest.

The fine condition of *Jedburgh Abbey* and *Lydford* is probably due to the fact that they were kept in portfolios, away from light. A few mysteries about them remain. Why were they not sold in 1932 with Sir John Ramsden's other Girtins? Whatever the reason, an accident of family history has provided us with two of the most exciting additions to the Girtin canon to appear for many years.

Joseph Mallord William Turner, RA
DARTMOUTH COVE, DEVONSHIRE
Watercolour heightened with bodycolour and scratching out, *circa* 1825–26, 10⅝in by 15½in
(27cm by 39.5cm)
London £332,200 ($554,774). 16.XI.89
From the collection of Mr and Mrs Ernest Gaskell

The last of four views of Dartmouth painted between about 1814 and 1826, this watercolour
was commissioned in 1825 by publisher Charles Heath for his engraved series, *Picturesque
Views in England and Wales*. Originally planned to include 120 pictures by the artist, the whole
rather ambitious project came to an end in 1837, when Longman, who then held publishing
rights, issued a two-volume set of 92 engravings taken from the 96 watercolours that Turner
had eventually produced. The revellers on the grassy bank probably allude to scenes
witnessed at Dartmouth during the Napoleonic wars, when naval shore leave was restricted
and often, on landing, mass marriages took place, sometimes at the rate of two or three
hundred ceremonies in a week.

Joseph Mallord William Turner, RA
HAMPTON COURT PALACE
Watercolour with scratching out and stopping out, and some gum arabic, 11⅜in by 15⅞in
(28.8cm by 40.5cm)
London £473,000 ($804,100). 15.III.90

Turner's south view of Hampton Court, showing the Banqueting House, the Pond Garden
and the Privy Garden, was painted for publisher Charles Heath's engraved series, *Picturesque
Views in England and Wales*, the most important of several such series to which Turner
contributed. Published in 1829, the engraving, by C. Westwood, included one extra staffage
figure and some feathers and pebbles scratched around the basket in the foreground, the
latter being added by Turner himself at second proof stage.

Jacob Jacobs

THE ARRIVAL OF SULTAN ABDULMEJID AT THE NUSRETIYE COMPLEX, THE GOLDEN HORN BEYOND

Signed, 18in by 26¾in (46cm by 68cm)

London £28,600 ($51,194). 15.II.90

This quintessential Orientalist scene shows Sultan Abdülmejid (1839–61) disembarking from his barge on the Golden Horn at Constantinople. The Sultan supervised the building of the Dolmabahce Palace, as well as the Medijidiye Mosque at Ortakoey. He died from tuberculosis at the age of thirty-eight.

Opposite, above

David Cox

LANCASTER: PEACE AND WAR

Signed on label attached to backboard *Lancaster/David Cox*, watercolour over pencil heightened with bodycolour and scratching out, 19⅛in by 29⅜in (48.5cm by 74.5cm)

London £44,000 ($73,480). 16.XI.89

Cox first explored the theme of peaceful scenery contrasted with the spectre of war in a view of Lympne Castle, now in the Lady Lever Art Gallery, Port Sunlight. Here, he transfers the scene to the grander setting of Lancaster Castle. He also painted a version in oils, in 1846.

Below

Samuel Palmer

NEAR UNDERRIVER, SEVENOAKS, KENT

Watercolour over pencil heightened with bodycolour on buff paper, *circa* 1843, 10½in by 14⅜in (26.5cm by 36.5cm)

London £70,400 ($117,568). 16.XI.89

Nineteenth-century European paintings and sculpture

Above
Jean-Louis-André-Théodore Géricault
PORTRAIT DE LAURE BRO, NEE DE COMERES
17¾in by 21⅝in (45cm by 55cm)
Monaco FF35,520,000 (£3,700,000:$5,775,610). 3.XII.89

Opposite, above
Rosa Bonheur
THE HORSE FAIR
Watercolour, signed and dated *1867*, 23in by 49in (58.4cm by 124.5cm)
New York $231,000 (£137,000). 8.VI.90
From the collection of St Hubert's Giralda

Below
Carl Emmanuel Conrad
A STREET SCENE IN FRONT OF THE PALAIS REDERN IN BERLIN
Signed and dated *1831*, 15¾in by 22¼in (40cm by 56.5cm)
Munich DM71,500 (£25,627:$40,169). 29.XI.89

Gustave Courbet
VUE D'ORNANS ET SON CLOCHER
Signed, 19½in by 24in (49.5cm by 61cm)
London £836,000 ($1,513,160). 19.VI.90
From the collection of the British Rail Pension Fund

Opposite
Jean-Baptiste-Camille Corot
VENUS AU BAIN
Signed, *circa* 1873–74, 45⅝in by 35⅜in (116cm by 90cm)
London £1,650,000 ($2,986,500). 19.VI.90
From the collection of the British Rail Pension Fund

This is one of three major classical nude compositions painted by Corot, the others being
La Toilette and *Diane au Bain*.

Jean-Léon Gérôme
BATHSHEBA
Signed, 1889, 24in by 39in (61cm by 99.1cm)
New York $2,200,000 (£1,309,524). 28.II.90

Bathsheba was painted at Bougival in Gérôme's summer studio. The concealed roof-terrace allowed him to pose his model in the open air and obtain remarkable light effects and delicate flesh tints. The painting depicts the beautiful wife of Uriah the Hittite, bathing on a roof below King David's palace, while David watches from the balcony above. The figure of Bathsheba was adapted by Gérôme in a bronze entitled *La Toilette* (1896).

Opposite
Giovanni Boldini
PORTRAIT OF THE ARTIST LAWRENCE ALEXANDER ('PETER') HARRISON
Signed and dated *1902*, 49⅝in by 39¾in (126cm by 101cm)
New York $852,500 (£507,440). 28.II.90
From the collection of Sir Valentine Abdy, Bt

Federico Zandomeneghi
LA MODISTA
Signed, 38¾in by 14⅛in (98.5cm by 36cm)
Milan L565,000,000 ($275,610:$431,298). 4.XII.89

Opposite
James-Jacques-Joseph Tissot
THE PRINCESS OF BROGLIE
Pastel on linen, signed, *circa* 1895, 66⅛in by 38⅛in (168cm by 96.8cm)
New York $1,100,000 (£683,230). 24.X.89
From the collection of Joey and Toby Tanenbaum

Helene Schjerfbeck
BALSKORNA ('THE DANCING SHOE')
Signed with initials, *circa* 1939–40, 24⅜in by 26¾in (62cm by 68cm)
London £1,100,000 ($1,881,000). 27.III.90

Born in 1862, Helene Schjerfbeck studied in Finland before moving to France in 1880. After
her return to Finland, away from mainstream contemporary European painting, she
developed a style characterized by powerful, simplified forms and strong, limited colouring.
This painting is the culmination of a popular series begun in 1882, from which Schjerfbeck
was encouraged to produce a lithograph, first published in 1938. This version was
commissioned by Gösta Stenman, Schjerfbeck's leading patron.

Joaquin Sorolla y Bastida
PLAYA DE VALENCIA ('SOL DE TARDE')
Signed and dated *1908*, 40¾in by 58¼in (103.5cm by 148cm)
London £1,815,000 ($3,285,150). 19.VI.90

Albert-Ernest Carrier-Belleuse
A white marble bust of a young woman, signed, *circa* 1870, height 24¾in (63cm)
London £16,500 ($30,030). 22.VI.90

Opposite
Giovanni Maria Benzoni
THE FLIGHT FROM POMPEII
Marble, signed, inscribed and dated *F.Roma 1868*, height 70in (177.8cm)
New York $330,000 (£195,266). 23.V.90

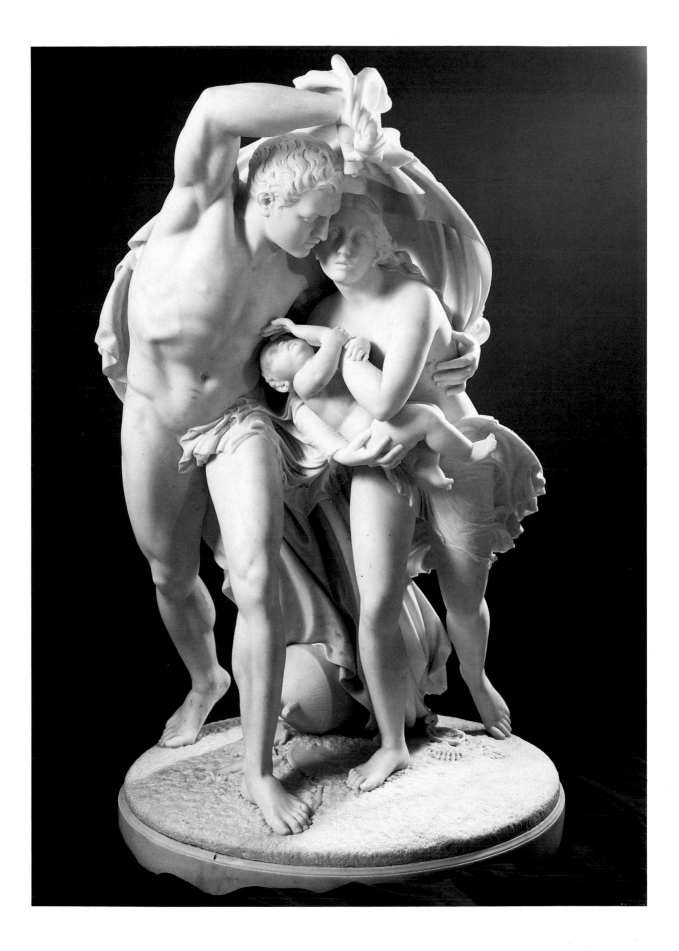

Jean-Jacques Pradier
A silvered and gilt-bronze figure of Sappho, signed, dated *1848* and stamped *V.P.* below a crown, height 17¾in (45cm)
London £39,600 ($72,072). 22.VI.90

Opposite
Jean-Antonin Mercié
A parcel-gilt bronze group entitled *Gloria Victis!*, signed, inscribed *F. Barbedienne Paris* and inset with the Collas seal, *circa* 1875, height 66in (167.6cm)
London £52,800 ($92,400). 30.III.90

Victorian paintings

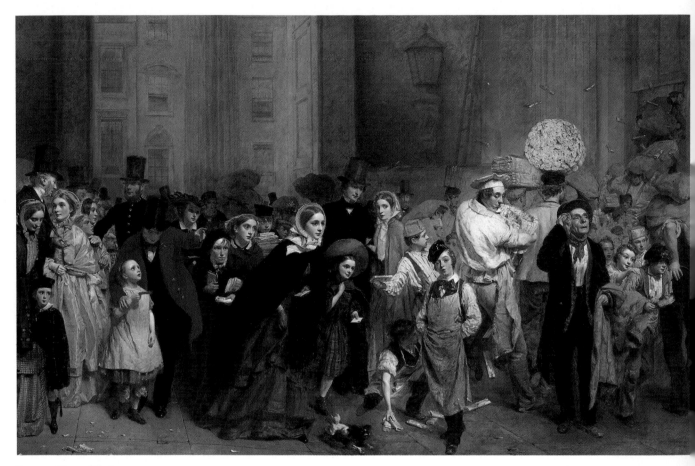

George Elgar Hicks
THE GENERAL POST OFFICE (ONE MINUTE TO SIX)
Signed and dated *1860*, 35in by 53⅛in (89cm by 135cm)
London £231,000 ($418,110). 19.VI.90
From the collection of the British Rail Pension Fund

Opposite
Sir Joseph Noel Paton, RSA
IN MEMORIAM
Oil on panel, signed with monogram and dated *1858*; signed and inscribed *Dunfermline* and *No.1* on a
label on the reverse, 48¾in by 38in (123cm by 96.5cm)
London £143,000 ($237,380). 21.XI.89

In Memoriam commemorated the Cawnpore Massacre of 1857, in particular the butchery of
British women and children by sepoy troops. When first exhibited at the Royal Academy in
1858, the painting showed a group of sepoys entering at the rear. However, the picture was
apparently considered too 'harrowing' and possibly at the suggestion of Queen Victoria, the
sepoys were replaced by rescuing Highlanders. The following dedication accompanied an
engraving of *In Memoriam*, by William Henry Simmons, published in 1862: 'Designed to
commemorate the Christian Heroism of the British Ladies in India during the Mutiny of
1857, and their Ultimate Deliverance by British Prowess'.

Frederic, Lord Leighton, PRA, RWS
SISTERS
30in by 15in (76cm by 38cm)
London £528,000 ($955,680). 19.VI.90

Frederic, Lord Leighton, PRA, RWS
DANTE IN EXILE
60in by 100in (152.5cm by 254cm)
London £1,100,000 ($1,991,000). 19.VI.90
From the collection of the British Rail Pension Fund

In the spring of 1855, Frederic Leighton, then twenty-four, sent his enormous canvas of *Cimabue's Madonna* (Royal Collection, on loan to the National Gallery, London) from his studio in Rome, to be shown at the Royal Academy. Ruskin hailed it as 'a very important and very beautiful picture', and it was bought by Queen Victoria, at Prince Albert's instigation, for 600 guineas. Leighton was concerned about whether he could sustain such success, and indeed subsequent biblical works fell far short, with *Samson and Delilah* being rejected by the British Institution in 1859. He turned to simpler motifs, and in 1862 he showed *Sisters* at the Royal Academy, which was particularly well received, not least by his rival, John Everett Millais. *Dante in Exile*, exhibited in 1864, consolidated the artist's now rising reputation, and the *Art Journal* described it as 'one of the most remarkable pictures of the year'. Leighton's exposition of the subject is masterly. Dante is 'exiled' within the composition, and his stiff stance and plain garb contrast with the finery and exaggerated poses of the courtiers. The delightful, flower-girt child at his knee emphasises his sobriety, and his great age, still further. The scene is realised in Leighton's typically sensuous handling of creamy paint, a characteristic also displayed to great effect in *Sisters*, where the elder is clad in what the *Athenaeum* described as 'soft, lustrous, maize-hued silk'. *Dante in Exile* earned Leighton election to Associate of the Royal Academy in 1864. Fourteen years later, he was elected President and is widely considered, with the exception of Reynolds, to have been the greatest ever.

Sir John Everett Millais, Bt., PRA
A HUGUENOT
Oil on board, signed with monogram, 9½in by 7⅛in (24cm by 18cm)
London £225,500 ($408,155). 19.VI.90
From the collection of the British Rail Pension Fund

Opposite
Sir Lawrence Alma-Tadema, OM, RA
LOVE'S JEWELLED FETTER
Oil on panel, signed and inscribed *Op CCCXXVIII*, 1895, 25in by 17½in (63.5cm by 44.5cm)
London £286,000 ($517,660). 19.VI.90

PROPTER·MISERIAM·INOPUM·ET·GEMITUM·PAUPERIS·NUNC·EXSURGAM·DICIT·DOMINUS·

TRANSEAMUS·USQUE·BETHLEHEM·ET·VIDEAMUS·VERBUM·QUOD·FACTUM·EST·QUOD·FECIT·DOMINUS·

Opposite, above
Sir Edward Coley Burne-Jones, ARA
NATIVITY
1888, 81⅛in by 124in (206cm by 315cm)
London £770,000 ($1,278,200). 21.XI.89

Below
Sir Edward Coley Burne-Jones, Bt., ARA
THE KING AND THE SHEPHERD
1888, 81⅛in by 124in (206cm by 315cm)
London £682,000 ($1,132,120). 21.XI.89

The pictures were commissioned in 1888 for
the church of St John the Apostle, Torquay.
One was paid for by a Miss Price, in memory
of a Miss Phelps, and the other donated by Mr
and Mrs Alfred Barton. They were intended
to flank the altar in spaces that had, in the
church's original design by G.E. Street, been
intended for mosaics. Both paintings were
presented to the church in December 1888.
Proceeds from the sale of these works have
provided funds for two replicas to be made,
and have paid for urgent repairs to the
church's other mosaics, roof and stained glass.

Sir Edward Coley Burne-Jones, ARA
KING COPHETUA AND THE BEGGAR MAID
Gouache and gum arabic, signed with initials twice
and dated *1883* and *1885*, 28½in by 14⅜in
(72.5cm by 36.5cm)
London £242,000 ($438,020). 19.VI.90

This is a smaller version of the oil painting of
the same title exhibited at the Grosvenor
Gallery in 1884 and now in the Tate Gallery,
London. The story of King Cophetua and the
Beggar Maid appears in Elizabethan ballads
and was drawn upon by Tennyson for his
poem *The Beggar Maid*, published in 1857. It
tells of King Cophetua, a prince of Africa,
who after a lengthy search finds his ideal in
the gentle and beautiful beggar-girl,
Penelophon.

Modern British paintings and sculpture

Sir William Orpen, RA, RHA
EARLY MORNING
Signed, 1922, 35½in by 33½in (90cm by 85cm)
London £319,000 ($555,060). 2.V.90

Charles Ginner, ARA
RAINY DAY, FLASK WALK
Signed, 1930, 36in by 24in
(91.5cm by 61cm)
London £74,800
($125,664). 8.XI.89

Sir Stanley Spencer, RA
THE CRUCIFIXION
85in by 85in (216cm by 216cm)
London £1,320,000 ($2,296,800). 2.V.90
From the collection of the Letchmore Trust

The Crucifixion by Sir Stanley Spencer

In 1956, Stanley Spencer was commissioned to paint his second crucifixion, the first having been completed in 1921. His patron was Jack Martineau, then Master of the Brewers Company, who wanted a work to hang in the newly-extended chapel of their school at Aldenham. The Martineaus had been close friends of Spencer's since 1943, when Jack's wife Catherine had asked if he would draw her son Richard. Spencer later painted Jack's portrait, in the winter of 1955–56, and Richard remembers one of many visits to the studio with his father, when he found a long, thin sketch for a crucifixion, stuffed into a drawer. Richard proposed Spencer for Aldenham, and Maurice Collis, Spencer's biographer, records that the work gave the artist great satisfaction – not least, perhaps, because he had recently lost an important commission to paint a Last Judgement for Llandaff Cathedral.

As with so much of Spencer's religious work, the setting is the village of Cookham. Indeed, the village high street has shaped the crucifixion's extraordinary composition. An oblong was not suited to Aldenham's chapel, and so Spencer wedged the T-shaped cross diagonally into a square frame, 'like a crashed airliner', as he put it, in a letter to *The Times*. The shape was suggested by the 'basin' formed by the perspective of village rooftops. Mirroring the semi-circular skyline, Spencer's Calvary is a dome of rubble left behind by workmen laying the village's drains. From our vantage-point behind Christ's head, we see His profile, the lusty enthusiasm of His crucifiers (wearing, it should be noted, traditional red Brewers' caps), and a group of villagers, straining out of their top-floor windows.

The houses are so accurately drawn that individual homes can be clearly identified and with them, it seems, their inhabitants. The timid onlookers could, apparently, represent a local Roman Catholic family, the Gribbins, who recognised themselves when the painting's sale was publicised, simultaneously throwing new light on its meaning. Patrick Gribbin recognised the right-hand thief as a school bully-cum-playground scapegoat, the child of deaf-mute parents, while the Magdelene, prostrate at the foot of the cross, resembles a foreign wartime evacuee who was unpopular in the village. The Gribbins were also somewhat isolated by their faith, and their father was made to suffer by local Freemasons and brewers, because of his well-known hatred of closed societies, and his tee-totalism. Spencer's brewer-crucifiers and the other carefully-cast roles in the scene, are perhaps a comment on the villagers' insularity and persecution, conscious or otherwise, of outsiders.

Spencer enjoyed a critical stir, whatever. Objections were raised to the brewers' cheerful leers, and the artist told pupils at Aldenham, 'I have given the men who are nailing Christ to the cross – and making sure they do a good job of it – Brewer's caps, because it is your governors, and you, who are still nailing Christ to the cross.'

Harrington Mann
MARDI GRAS
Signed and dated *1913*; dated *Tuesday 24th April 1913* on the reverse,
70in by 94in (178cm by 239cm)
Glasgow £63,800 ($113,564). 6.II.90

Opposite
Francis Campbell Boileau Cadell
INTERIOR (THE EAGLE MIRROR)
Signed; signed and inscribed with the title on the reverse, 40in by 30in (102cm by 76cm)
Glasgow £176,000 ($313,280). 6.II.90

Peter Lanyon
COAST WIND
Oil on board, signed and dated *57*; signed, titled and dated *57* on the reverse,
72in by 48in (183cm by 122cm)
London £104,500 ($188,100). 24.V.90

Dame Elisabeth Frink, DBE, RA
HORSE
Bronze, from an edition of three castings, length 101in (257cm)
London £110,000 ($198,000). 24.V.90

The sculpture was commissioned in 1980 by the Earl of March, for Goodwood racecourse, where one cast still stands.

Renoir and Impressionism

Nicholas Wadley

At the third Impressionist exhibition in 1877, Renoir's painting *Au Moulin de la Galette* was hailed by the artist's supporters as 'a page of history,' 'a corner of nineteenth-century Paris that will endure,' 'an afternoon in Montmartre captured for posterity.' Posterity has endorsed these views. The two large paintings that Renoir made of dancing at the Moulin de la Galette created an image of contemporary Paris at leisure that has been singled out repeatedly ever since as among his three or four greatest achievements. It follows quite naturally that these paintings have become landmarks of high Impressionism – that period from the late 1860s to the late 1870s when the very different and spectacular talents of Monet, Renoir, Degas, Pissarro, Cézanne and others were harnessed to a more or less common purpose.

It was a period that started with Monet and Renoir painting side-by-side at La Grenouillère and went on to include Monet's Argenteuil paintings and the Gare Saint-Lazare series: Degas' most polished images of Parisian life, the relaxed and assured landscapes of Pissarro at Pontoise and Sisley at Port-Marly, as well as arguably the most innovative work of Caillebotte and Morisot. For Renoir himself, other major and quintessentially Impressionist works included *Lise*, 1867, *La Loge*, 1874, *Nude in Sunlight*, 1875, *The Swing*, 1876, and finally the great *Luncheon of the Boating Party* of 1881.

The common purposes that brought these artists to exhibit together were all associated with what art critic Edmond Duranty described as a tearing down of the walls that separated the artist's studio from everyday life outside. Although his manifesto-like essay *The New Painting* (1876) was conceived and written with Degas very much in mind. Duranty pinpoints the radical character of Impressionist subject matter at large. It was not merely the literal question of painting in the open air and sunlight, but also the broader issue of making an art whose credibility depended on truth to the reality of daily life in the modern world. The strikingly new aspect of Impressionist subject matter lay in its urban-centredness. The vast majority of paintings of the 1860s and 1870s were scenes of Paris and its suburbs – Parisian people, Parisian streets, railway stations, racecourses, the *bois*, cafés, and theatres. When the countryside is painted, it is a countryside within easy reach of Paris by train, and many of the motifs painted by Morisot, Pissarro or Sisley resemble moments of landscape seen from a train. These semi-rural areas along the Seine were being built up with weekend retreats for Parisians and furnished with boating marinas, regattas, fishing locations and restaurants with gardens for dancing. It is the accessible landscape of the urban man's 'day in the country'.

Pierre-Auguste Renoir
AU MOULIN DE LA GALETTE
Signed and dated *76*,
31in by 44½in (78.7cm by
113cm)
New York $78,100,000
(£46,213,017). 17.V.90
From the collection of
Mr and Mrs John Hay
Whitney

Perhaps because they were inventing new genres and because there were few conventional precedents for treating these motifs, it was easier for the Impressionists to paint these subjects as they *saw* them rather than as they *knew* them. Early Impressionist paintings are essentially visual; they reveal most of what they have to tell us about their subject matter at the first encounter. Many of the scenes are normal, commonplace, even banal. For the most part, there are no narratives to be read, nor hidden symbolic meanings to be decoded.

This guileless simplicity evoked much hostile (but understandable) criticism at the time from the critics and a public accustomed to reading meanings below a loaded surface. The unornamented representation of ordinary life and appearances prompted suspicions of anarchic intent in some, puzzlement followed by mockery in others. 'But it's only a painting of the middle of a tree!' says a gallery-goer in a contemporary caricature.

Most other contemporary criticism of Impressionist paintings – also generated by the shock of the unfamiliar in art – concerned their incompleteness. It was a comment applicable more to some than others (less to Degas and Caillebotte, for instance, than to Monet or Renoir) but nevertheless applied universally. 'These are only suggestions', a critic observed in front of a Degas ballet picture. 'But are they enough to make a painting?' The freshness of execution that contributes so much to the senses of immediacy, movement and changing light (so unlike the even light of the studio) appeared as a lack of finish, and often as the inability to complete a painting. Although Renoir's famous story about Monet walking into the Gare Saint-Lazare, stopping the trains and knocking off half-a-dozen or so canvases in one session is exaggerated in the interests of a good anecdote, it is nonetheless true that the paintings were painted largely *in situ* and relatively fast. Monet spoke more than once of the importance of the first twenty minutes of a painting, while the 'naïve impression' of the motif remained fresh, and before the transient light conditions had changed it into something else.

Renoir's painting of the period shares all these qualities of contemporaneity and immediacy. The garden of the Moulin de la Galette was a popular Sunday afternoon venue in Montmartre. The typical quality of the scene was paramount to Renoir. He went out of his way to work on the spot as far as possible and with models who were all *habitués*, in the interests of naturalness. The painting's evocation of relaxed and spontaneous enjoyment is heightened by the loose brushwork and vibrant colours of the paint. But this apparent informality belies the serious nature of the project. The painting reminds us of Degas more than any other Impressionist in the complexity of its multi-figure composition – the Degas who stressed that 'one must contrive to give the impression of nature by false means, but it must appear true'. As in his later *Luncheon of the Boating Party*, Renoir set out at the Moulin de la Galette to compose a large-scale document of the life of his time. For all its apparently casual expression of life, movement, noise and light, such an ambitious document is by its nature an artfully calculated contrivance.

In other ways, too, the painting reveals qualities of Renoir's early maturity as a painter that distinguish him from his contemporaries. It tells us much about the way he looked at the world. Renoir's is not the sort of eye that looks intently and searchingly, wanting to grasp the physical entity of things, like Cézanne's. It is not the sort of eye that looks acutely at 'the exact colour and shape' of each fragment of visual experience and snatches it, like Monet's. Rather, it is an eye that flits across

A pastel study for *Au Moulin de la Galette* (Reproduced courtesy of the National Museum, Belgrade).

surfaces, touching with butterfly lightness on one after another, moving from incident to incident, expression to expression. Figures and settings remain almost immaterial, made of featherweight touches of colour which take the place of drawing in any conventional sense, evoking the manner he admired so much in Manet and in French eighteenth-century art.

Set beside the coolness of Monet's objectivity, Renoir's Impressionism is essentially romantic. From his own time onwards, partisan writers have distinguished between Renoir the romantic painter of people and Monet the objective painter of things. In 1903 De Wyzewa described Monet, Sisley and others as 'admirable artists who were in some sense the prose writers of impressionism; M. Renoir is its poet'. Thirty years later, Robert Rey wrote that 'Monet is content with sights captured from life in their full vigour and with the surprise of the unexpected, while Renoir is concerned with poetic perception'.

Renoir's Impressionism was a hedonistic and unashamedly chauvinist celebration of gaiety and of the most agreeable face of Parisian life. Compared to other Impressionists, Renoir was outspokenly apolitical. Public dissent and political subversion were not the proper concerns of the artist as far as Renoir was concerned; he considered them a dissipation of his energies and a disruption in his imaginative life. He appears to have been more disposed than most to ride the tide of changing events with equanimity, describing himself without apology as a 'cork floating on circumstance'.

Renoir wanted to be free to work as an accepted artist; he enjoyed, even espoused popularity. Of all the Impressionists, he was the most willing to leave the contentious area of independent exhibitions in order to have his paintings accepted and recognized at the Salon, when others – particularly Pissarro – saw this as the betrayal of a cause. Although he later justified his acceptance of public honours largely in terms of professional pragmatism, as Manet had done before him, establishment recognition

Above, left
Detail of the dancing
couple in *Au Moulin de la
Galette.*

Right
Study for the dancing
couple in *Au Moulin de la
Galette.*

was not only reassuringly welcome to Renoir, but also a desirable and perfectly ethical normalization of his life as an artist. The almost accidental mantle of a revolutionary did not lie easily on his shoulders. His eager and enormously successful participation in the Impressionist movement sprang from the coincidence of all the most radical ideas and practices of Impressionism with his own special interests and his prodigious natural facility as a painter. When the impetus that had sustained the collective identity of early Impressionism began to fade by the end of the 1870s, it precipitated a crisis in Renoir's self-confidence.

If it were not for the technical virtuosity and brilliant invention of Renoir's 1860s and 1870s paintings, all of this might suggest that his self-image of 'cork' is all too true, that he was a gifted entrepreneur in the right place at the right time. If it were not for the constancy of his attitudes towards acceptance, recognition and standards, he could be perceived as an artist who changed camps when the going got tough. But the events of the Post-Impressionist 1880s and 1890s have a great deal to tell about the deeper, lasting values and ambitions that informed his paintings of the Moulin de la Galette.

That highpoint of 1870s Impressionism was 'high' in the sense that it was the most intuitive and untroubled realization of early Impressionist principles. New ideas, new subjects, new practices were tackled at face value. Everything seemed to flow. In the next decade, almost all of the major painters associated with the group shifted their ground for one reason or another, re-evaluating the risks inherent in the radical style of the 1870s. Pissarro became worried about the incoherence of the painted surface; light fell on the array of his relatively unsystematic brushstrokes in such a way that his image was sometimes difficult to read. Monet and Cézanne both talked of their growing mistrust of things that came too easily, recognizing that painting based on looking at nature was an increasingly complicated and confusing affair, that demanded great mental stamina and a highly disciplined eye. There is a comparable shift in Degas – in his modelling in plaster and wax as well as in paintings, pastels, prints and drawings – from the succinct clarity of his images of the 1860s and 1870s towards a far more complicated range of invention and artifice. In the 1880s too, Gauguin and Van Gogh successively reconsidered the strengths and the limitations of their respective experience of early Impressionism.

For Renoir, the early 1880s crisis was extreme. He appears to have felt momentarily that the years of effortless, innocent response to senses and emotions had left him ill-equipped. In part, it was a crisis of middle age. Nearing his mid-forties, he was no longer innocent as an artist, nor enjoying the irresponsible freedom of youth as a man. As Degas remarked, 'It's easy enough to have talent at twenty-five, the problem is to have it at fifty.'

The artists to whom Renoir turned first for redirection – including Ingres and Raphael – might suggest a *volte-face*, a renunciation. But when he finally established the private pantheon that was to sustain his mature and late years as a painter, its key members were very much the same as those that might have been predicted in the 1860s: from older art, the Venetians, Velásquez, Fragonard, Watteau; from his immediate predecessors, Delacroix and Corot, and from his contemporaries, Monet and Cézanne. Cézanne is the only major addition. Perhaps too restless and troubled a genius for Renoir to have appreciated earlier, Cézanne by the 1890s had become a friend, a neighbour in Provence, and a mentor. So the late work of Renoir was founded on essentially the same hierarchy of gods as the untroubled, sensual *œuvre* of the 1870s. A late painting may be called *Judgement of Paris* rather than *Dance at Bougival*, but the fundamental cultural and sensual values behind them are more closely related than the titles suggest.

In his old age, it was almost as a matter of instinct that he drew the attention of many of his visitors to the values of eighteenth-century French art. Time and again, he held up as models Watteau, Fragonard, Boucher and Chardin, the makers of an art that was of its time, and more importantly, of an art that was charming, affirmative and full of joy. The things Renoir resented most in official art were pretension and pomposity. 'Because Fragonard put laughter in his work,' he told Albert André, 'it quickly became the accepted thing to call him a minor painter. It's the solemn, full-dress art – whether it's painting, music or literature – that will always impress.' For Renoir, French eighteenth-century painting was the shining exemplar of a great art that did not take itself too seriously.

In retrospect, it is quite clear that Renoir did not shift his loyalties in the early 1880s. He ceased to exhibit with the Impressionists not because he had changed so much but because the group had started to embrace other types of radical painting – painting with Symbolist and political tendencies for instance – which were anathema to his own values. Paintings like those of the Moulin de la Galette express the dream of Renoir's life-work in its most innocent, intuitive state. Their euphoria is not only that of 1870s Paris, but also of an art in its precocious infancy, achieving its first major statements. The spirit of those paintings, their laughing celebration of life and their relaxed sensual exuberance, is sustained in his work to the last.

Pierre-Auguste Renoir
JEUNE FILLE AU CHAT
Signed, *circa* 1881–82, 38¾in by 32¼in (98.4cm by 81.9cm)
New York $18,150,000 (£10,739,644). 17.V.90

Edouard Manet
LA PROMENADE
Circa 1880, 36¾in by 27¾in (92.4cm by 70.5cm)
New York $14,850,000 (£9,398,734). 15.XI.89
From a collection formed by Alan Bond

Odilon Redon
VASE DE FLEURS
Pastel on paper, *circa* 1905, 31½in by 25½in (80cm by 64.8cm)
New York $2,310,000 (£1,462,025). 15.XI.89

Edgar Degas
PREPARATION POUR LA CLASSE
Pastel on laid paper, signed, *circa* 1882–85, 25½in by 19⅝in (64.8cm by 49.8cm)
New York $4,950,000 (£2,928,994). 17.V.90
From the collection of the Art Institute of Chicago

Claude Monet
LE BASSIN AUX NYMPHEAS
Stamped with the atelier-mark on the reverse, *circa* 1917–19, 39⅜in by 78¾in (100cm by 200cm)
London £5,720,000 ($8,923,200). 28.XI.89

Monet's first series of water-lily paintings dates from between 1896 and 1910. This painting is from his second phase, post-1916, after a lull following the death of his wife in 1912 and his son, Jean, in 1914. The *Nymphéas* were a vast decorative scheme on which he worked tirelessly despite failing colour vision and the difficulties of painting at the pondside, perched on a stool. During this period Monet began bringing to fruition his ideas for 'grand decorations', as he called them, large rooms completely surrounded with panels of *Nymphéas* paintings. Monet himself has written:

For a moment the temptation came to me to use this water-lily theme for the decoration of a drawing room: carried along the walls, enveloping all the partitions with its unity, it would have produced the illusion of an endless whole, of a wave with no horizon and no shore; nerves exhausted by work would have relaxed there, following the restful example of those stagnant waters, and to anyone who would have lived in it that room would have offered a refuge of peaceful meditation in the middle of a flowering aquarium.

Opposite
Paul Gauguin
ENTRE LES LYS
Signed and dated *89*, 36¼in by 28¾in (92.1cm by 73cm)
New York $11,000,000 (£6,962,025). 15.XI.89
From the collection of the Rudolf Staechelin Family Foundation

The collection of John T. Dorrance, Jr

Over a thirty-year period, John T. Dorrance, Jr assembled a vast collection which ranged across a number of different fields, from European and American paintings, European ceramics, Chinese export porcelain, Chinese jades and works of art, to fine English and French furniture. The son of the founder of the Campbell Soup Company, and the company's chairman for twenty-two years, Mr Dorrance was well known as a patron of the arts in Philadelphia and at his death in 1989 was President of the Board of the Philadelphia Museum of Art.

Mr Dorrance's estate outside Philadelphia was the setting for the collection. Its gardens were populated with charmingly life-like sculpture – figures of women in peasant costume, hunting dogs, cats curled up in the sun. Inside the house, beautiful works of art greeted the eye at every turn. The hall was hung with Monets; paintings by Picasso, Renoir, Van Gogh and Sisley dominated the drawing room; Chinese jades were displayed in the library. Throughout were elegant pieces of French and English furniture, their surfaces covered with ceramics and works of art in silver.

At the centre of the Dorrance Collection was a group of Impressionist, Post-Impressionist and Modern paintings that together surveyed the art of the period from the late 1860s to the 1920s. Beginning with the delightful still-life of *Zinnias* by Fantin-Latour, the collection encompassed examples dating from the freshest period of Impressionism to early works by Picasso and Matisse (Fig. 1). The work of Claude Monet was particularly well-represented, ranging from a serene river scene painted at Argenteuil in 1877 to a fine example from the 'Haystacks' series (Fig. 2), which occupied the artist at Giverny nearly fifteen years later.

Beyond the Impressionist and modern paintings were works by European old masters and nineteenth-century artists and a fine group of American paintings. Arguably the most important were a view of Il Redentore, in Venice, by Canaletto (Fig. 4) and a small but evocative New York street scene by Childe Hassam (Fig. 3) executed in 1890 shortly after his return from Paris.

Complementing the paintings was a handsome selection of European and English furniture, silver, ceramics and Chinese works of art, reflecting a high level of connoisseurship and a concern for fine design and exquisite craftsmanship. The majority of the furniture was the work of *ébénistes* from the reigns of Louis XV and XVI. Of particular interest was the Riesener bureau plat (Fig. 5), which is stylistically related to the group of roll-top desks by this maker. With its simple mahogany veneers outlined by gilt-bronze mounts, the bureau plat reflects the restrained style that Riesener developed in the 1780s.

The collection was dispersed in a three-day auction in New York last autumn, bringing a total of $131 million, the highest ever achieved for a single-owner sale.

Fig. 2
Claude Monet
MEULES, EFFET DE NEIGE, LE MATIN
Signed and dated *91*, 25⅝in by 39¼in (65cm by 99.7cm)
New York $8,525,000 (£5,361,635). 18.X.89
From the collection of John T. Dorrance, Jr

Fig. 3
Childe Hassam
HORSE-DRAWN CABS AT EVENING
Watercolour and gouache on paper, signed and inscribed *N.Y.*, *circa* 1890,
13½in by 17¼in (34.2cm by 43.8cm)
New York $990,000 (£622,642). 18.X.89
From the collection of John T. Dorrance, Jr

Fig. 4
Giovanni Antonio Canale, called Il Canaletto
VIEW OF THE CHURCH OF IL REDENTORE, VENICE
18½in by 29½in (47cm by 75cm)
New York $1,595,000 (£960,843). 11.I.90
From the collection of John T. Dorrance, Jr

Fig. 5
A Louis XVI ormolu-mounted mahogany bureau plat, stamped *J.H.Riesener*, *JME*, last quarter
eighteenth century, width 4ft 7in (140cm)
New York $440,000 (£278,481). 21.X.89
From the collection of John T. Dorrance, Jr

Eugène Boudin
VENISE. VUE PRISE DE SAN GIORGIO
Signed, inscribed *Venise* and dated *95*, 20⅛in by 28¾in (51.1cm by 73cm)
New York $1,540,000 (£974,684). 27.X.89
From the collection of the late Count and Countess Guy du Boisrouvray

Rembrandt Bugatti
COUPLE DE PANTHERES MARCHANT
Bronze, signed, dated *1904* and stamped with the foundry mark *A.A. Hébrard cire perdue*,
length 40½in (103cm)
London £242,000 ($399,300). 4.IV.90

Cast in an edition of three, the present sculpture was one of thirty-nine works by Bugatti
from the collection of Alain Delon. Bugatti dedicated his short, but intensely dramatic, life to
the portrayal of animals, and from his arrival in Paris in 1903 until his war-time suicide, aged
thirty-two, in 1916, he travelled constantly in order to sculpt from life. His various hosts'
domestic pets provided some subjects, but the zoos in Paris and Antwerp were his greatest
inspiration. After hours and days of intense observation, he modelled his works quickly and
boldly in plasticine. The art critic Louis Vauxcelles has praised his confidence, his 'vivacious
texture', and his 'respect for truth and life'.

Vincent van Gogh
CARRIERE PRES DE SAINT-REMY
1889, 20½in by 25¼in (52.1cm by 64.1cm)
New York $11,550,000 (£7,310,127). 15.XI.89

Begun in Saint-Rémy in July 1889, this painting was completed by early October. It depicts
either the quarry at Salade or that at Noé, with Mont Gaussier in the background. A letter
to Theo, written on 12th October 1889, refers to the work: 'This week I have also done the
"Entrance to a Quarry", which is like something Japanese; you remember there are Japanese
drawings of rocks with grass growing on them here and there and little trees . . .'. Today this
view of Mont Gaussier is obscured by trees.

Henri Rousseau, called le Douanier
VUE DE LA BIEVRE-SUR-GENTILLY
Signed, 15in by 18⅛in (38cm by 46cm)
London £880,000 ($1,452,000). 3.IV.90

Rousseau continued to execute small-scale landscapes alongside his major figure paintings and jungle works, throughout his career. Often depicting the countryside around Paris, they were not painted out of doors, but based on rough compositional sketches. The pictures were planned out and manipulated in the studio to achieve perfect clarity and definition.

Fig. 1
Pablo Picasso
AU LAPIN AGILE
1905, 39in by 39½in (99cm by 100.3cm)
New York $40,700,000 (£25,759,493). 15.XI.90
From the collection of Mrs Vincent de Roulet

Picasso's *Au Lapin Agile*

John L. Tancock

In the spring of 1904, Picasso returned to Paris from Barcelona, moving into the dilapidated building at 13, rue Ravignan that was to achieve universal fame as the *Bateau Lavoir*. Immersed in the nightlife of Montmartre, he turned to the theatres, circuses and cafés for subjects, creating the images of acrobats and performers which characterized his Rose Period.

These themes had been of particular interest to French artists since the eighteenth century and perhaps even earlier. Callot, Gillot, Watteau and Gabriel de Saint-Aubin devoted many works to theatrical subjects, as did Daumier, Degas, Seurat and Toulouse-Lautrec in the nineteenth century. Of more immediate significance to Picasso, perhaps, were two paintings by Paul Cézanne, *Harlequin* and *Mardi Gras*, in which the artist's son Paul was portrayed wearing Harlequin costume. Picasso's approach, however, differed fundamentally from that of any of his predecessors. It was not the spectacle itself that appealed to him, so much as the off-stage life, imagined and idealized to be sure, of the acrobats, harlequins and strolling players who lived among the booths of the fairs which lined the boulevards in winter. Picasso's performers were generally seen either in the privacy of their own quarters or in desolate landscape settings. In *Au Lapin Agile* (Fig. 1), however, he returned to the format of figures seated in a bar, used in two of his most striking images of 1901. Both *Harlequin* and *Harlequin and his Companion* focus on figures dressed in *commedia dell'arte* costumes, deep in thought and apparently unaware of anything around them.

The title *Au Lapin Agile* is derived from the name of a celebrated tavern, said to have started life as a shooting-box built by Henri IV. In 1903, it was purchased by Aristide Bruant, who leased it to Frédéric Gerard, known as Frédé. Under his lively guidance, and the name *Lapin Agile*, the café soon became the meeting place not only for writers associated with Montmartre but also for Picasso and Fernande Olivier, Apollinaire and Marie Laurencin, Modigliani, Cocteau, Max Jacob, Suzanne Valadon and her son Utrillo, who painted many views of it in the following years.

Here, the image of Frédé strumming his guitar in the background confirms the café as the setting, but the mood of the painting is far from festive. In fact, the obvious unhappiness of the principal figures evokes a tragedy that took place several years earlier. Picasso depicts himself as a brooding harlequin standing beside, yet totally alienated from, his female companion. This woman, the notorious Germaine Pichot, was one of three models Picasso and his young artist friends, Casagemas and Pallares, met soon after their arrival in Paris. Casagemas fell deeply in love with Germaine and his despair over the impossibility of their relationship led to his suicide in February 1901.

Fig. 2
A gathering at the *Lapin Agile* in Montmartre. The café's proprietor, Frédé, is seated far right, playing his guitar. Picasso's painting *Au Lapin Agile* hangs on the back wall.

The death of his close friend had a profound influence on Picasso, and on his art. By late 1901, the bold confidence of works like *Yo Picasso* had given way to the isolation and melancholy of the works of the Blue Period. Both Casagemas and Germaine appeared in a number of paintings, with Germaine ultimately coming to represent the 'fatal woman' in Picasso's imagination. However, it is in the painting's image of himself that the depth of his sorrow is most clearly felt. As Theodore Reff has observed, 'This typically modern sense of alienation is, of course, already found in Degas' *L'Absinthe* and in the café and dance hall pictures of Toulouse-Lautrec (see opposite). Yet nowhere among the sordid or pathetic habitués of Lautrec's world, and rarely even among the introspective acrobats and clowns of Picasso's, is this suffering as intimately related to the artist himself, or as enigmatic as it is here. For its cause is apparently located not in the present but in an event that had occurred four years earlier and, above all, in his later brooding on the meaning of that event.'

Au Lapin Agile is a key work in deciphering Picasso's state of mind as the Blue Period merged into the Rose Period. In giving the painting to Frédé, who hung it in his tavern (Fig. 2), Picasso chose not to conceal his anger, suppressed though it was. Alone among the paintings of the Rose Period, it is located in a definitely contemporary setting, quite unlike the idealized interiors of the later works. Picasso distances himself, however, from the world of Frédé and Germaine by depicting himself as Harlequin, an outsider defined by his timeless costume. In its subject *Au Lapin Agile* looks back to the past, but, in its ambiguity and juxtaposition of different levels of reality, suggested principally by costume, it looks forward to the much more jarring stylistic dissimilarities of a work painted only two years later, *Les Demoiselles d'Avignon*.

**Henri de
Toulouse-Lautrec**
MISS MAY BELFORT
(MAQUETTE FOR THE
POSTER)
Gouache and pencil on
paper, 1895, inscribed
MAY BE, 32¾in by 24¼in
(83cm by 61.5cm)
New York $3,080,000
(£1,822,485). 17.V.90
From the collection of
Barbara Ginn Griesinger

Marc Chagall
ANNIVERSAIRE
Signed, 1923, 31⅞in by 39½in (81cm by 100.3cm)
New York $14,850,000 (£8,786,982). 17.V.90

Painted in 1923, and from the collection of the Solomon R. Guggenheim Museum, New York this is a replica of Chagall's *Anniversaire* in the Museum of Modern Art. One of the artists's best-known and best-loved images, the picture was inspired by the appearance of Bella, Chagall's fiancée, at his studio on his birthday with a bunch of flowers. He immediately told her to stand still and, as she recounts, he started to paint:

You throw yourself upon the canvas which trembles under your hand . . . You drag me into the stream of colours. Suddenly you lift me off the ground . . . You leap, stretch out at full length, and fly up to the ceiling . . . You bend down behind my ear and whisper something to me . . . And together we rise to the ceiling of the gaily decked room and fly away.

Opposite
Amedeo Modigliani
GARÇON A LA VESTE BLEUE
Signed, 1918, 36¼in by 24in (92.1cm by 61cm)
New York $11,550,000 (£6,834,320). 17.V.90
From the collection of the Solomon R. Guggenheim Museum, New York

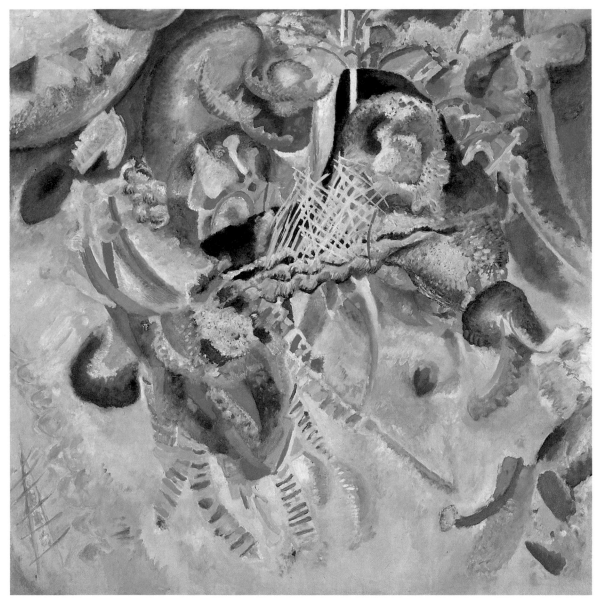

Wassily Kandinsky
FUGUE
1914, 51in by 51in (129.5cm by 129.5cm)
New York $20,900,000 (£12,366,863). 17.V.90
From the collection of the Solomon R. Guggenheim Museum, New York

The picture marks Kandinsky's final transition to abstraction. Lush colour all but conceals identifiable motifs seen in earlier paintings, and in January 1914, just two months before working on *Fugue*, Kandinsky wrote, 'I dissolved objects to a greater or lesser extent in the same picture, so that they might not all be recognised at once, and so that . . . emotional overtones might thus be experienced gradually by the spectator, one after another.'

Paul Klee
THE SINGER L. AS FIORDILIGI
Oil and watercolour on
chalk-coated ground,
signed, titled and dated
1923/39, 20⅛in by 13¼in
(51cm by 33.5cm)
London £2,640,000
($4,118,400). 28.XI.89

Pablo Picasso
TETE DE FEMME (FERNANDE)
Bronze, height 16½in
(41.9cm)
New York $2,750,000
(£1,740,506). 15.XI.89
From the collection of
Walter P. Chrysler, Jr

Opposite
Juan Gris
LE VIOLON
Papier collé, charcoal and
gouache on canvas, signed,
inscribed *A Romain Thomas,
Affection et reconnaissance*,
and dated *30–10–14*, 32¼in
by 24⅜in (82cm by 62cm)
Madrid Ptas 401,408,000
(£2,300,992:$3,674,215).
22.III.90

Piet Mondrian
FAÇADE IN TAN AND GREY
Signed and dated *1913*; signed and titled *Composition XII* on the strecher, 25¼in by 37in
(64.1cm by 94cm)
New York $9,625,000 (£6,091,772). 15.XI.89
From the collection of the late Edgar J. Kaufmann, Jr

In 1913, Mondrian began painting the façades of buildings visible from his Parisian studio
window in the rue du Départ. The highly abstract nature of these works was much
commented upon at the 'Salon des Indépendants' of that year. Architectonic paintings such as
these became a confident assertion of his position among the leaders of the Cubist avant-garde.

Opposite
Giorgio de Chirico
EVANGELICAL STILL LIFE
Signed and dated *1916*, 31¾in by 28⅛in (80.6cm by 71.4cm)
New York $5,280,000 (£3,341,772). 15.XI.89
From the collection of the Museum of Modern Art, New York

Opposite
Pablo Picasso
MERE ET ENFANT
Signed, 1921, 38¼in by 28in
(97.2cm by 71.1cm)
New York $18,700,000
(£11,835,443). 15.XI.89
From the collection of the
Alex Hillman Family
Foundation

Pierre Bonnard
NU EN HAUTEUR OU FEMME
NUE DEBOUT
Signed, 1906, 55⅛in by
31½in (140cm by 80cm)
London £2,200,000
($3,432,000). 28.XI.89
From the collection of the
J. Paul Getty Museum,
Malibu, California

Joan Miró
L'OISEAU AU PLUMAGE DEPLOYE VOLE VERS L'ARBRE ARGENTE
Signed; signed, titled and dated *12/11/53* on the reverse, 35¼in by 45¾in (89.5cm by 116.2cm)
New York $9,350,000 (£5,917,722). 15.XI.89
From the collection of the late Edgar J. Kaufmann, Jr

Opposite
Pablo Picasso
LE MIROIR
Signed; dated on the stretcher *12 Mars XXXII*, 51½in by 38⅛in (130.8cm by 96.8cm)
New York $26,400,000 (£16,708,860). 15.XI.89

Gustav Klimt
THE THREE PHASES OF WOMANHOOD
Charcoal, stamped with the *Nachlass* mark, *circa* 1905,
71⅞in by 35⅜in (182.5cm by 90cm)
London £484,000 ($900,240). 27.VI.90

Only recently discovered, this drawing does not
seem to be a preparatory sketch for the painting of
the same name, also executed in 1905. Rather, it is a
fully worked variation on the same theme. In the
drawing, the child is held to the right of the two
female figures, whereas in the painting, it is held
between them. The drawing is unusual in that unlike
other preparatory studies for large scale works such
as *Medezin* and *Jurisprudenz*, the central figures here
correspond exactly to their final size in the painting,
suggesting that Klimt was indeed working on a
variation of an already established composition.

Opposite
Egon Schiele
PORTRAIT OF THE ACTRESS MARGA BOERNER
Gouache and black crayon, signed and dated *1917*,
19in by 12in (48.2cm by 30.5cm)
London £484,000 ($900,240). 27.VI.90

Schiele was commissioned to paint Marga Boerner's
portrait by Dr Rosé, Schiele's supervisor when he
was enlisted into the Austro-Hungarian army. The
artist executed three black crayon drawings to
submit to Rosé for his approval, as was usual with
his portrait commissions. Schiele then added colour
to the chosen drawing.

Fig. 1
Piet Mondrian
COMPOSITION IN BLACK AND WHITE WITH BLUE SQUARE
Signed with initials and dated *35*; signed on the stretcher, 27⅜in by 27⅜in (69.5cm by 69.5cm)
New York $6,875,000 (£4,116,766). 16.V.90
From the collection of Lydia Winston Malbin

Futurism in context:
the collection of Lydia Winston Malbin

Elizabeth White

Energy, education and communication: these were the precepts that shaped the remarkable collection of twentieth-century art assembled by Lydia Winston Malbin. Justly admired for her role in bringing the work of the Italian Futurists out of obscurity, Mrs Winston Malbin explored virtually every avant-garde movement of this century, and the connections she found among them will remain her principal legacy. Art historian Joshua Taylor has observed that 'the Winston Malbin collection has a way of making one rethink the material, discovering new relationships and possibilities in movements and works supposedly known and historically typed.' His comment must have delighted Mrs Winston Malbin, who described her own experience of collecting as one of continuation and growth. 'Building a modern collection involves continually pushing back the frontiers of aesthetic perception,' she said in an address at Wayne State University in Michigan, where she and Marcel Duchamp both received honorary degrees.

Fig. 2
Giacomo Balla
LA SCALA DEGLI ADDII
(SALUTANDO)
Signed, *circa* 1908,
41½in by 41⅝in
(105.4cm by 105.7cm)
New York $4,400,000
(£2,634,731). 16.V.90
From the collection of
Lydia Winston Malbin

Shortly before her death in 1989, Mrs Winston Malbin was asked how she achieved such prominence in the collecting world. 'I had the right father,' she replied. He was Albert Kahn, a brilliant pioneer of modernist industrial architecture whose projects included the famous Ford plant at River Rouge, and himself a collector of nineteenth-century and Impressionist paintings. In this environment, Mrs Winston Malbin gained a sense of the pleasure of living with works of art and a respect for the challenges of modernism. Her own study of ceramics at Cranbrook Academy of Art in Michigan deepened her understanding of abstraction and of the critical balance of line, form, texture and material in the success and vitality of a piece.

Her collection began with a watercolour by John Marin, sold to her by Alfred Stieglitz, whom she approached with some trepidation in the late 1930s. He encouraged her interest, giving a context to the works and directing her towards other artists. Her early acquisitions included works by Klee, Kandinsky, Braque, Schwitters and

Mondrian (Fig. 1), and in 1946 she became the first collector to buy a painting by Jackson Pollock.

By the time Lydia Winston Malbin was introduced to Futurism in the early 1950s, she was already familiar with the major currents in twentieth-century art, and quickly grasped the significance of the movement which was to become central to her collection. In the Futurist celebration of dynamism and power, she saw a direct expression of her own belief in movement and energy as fundamental themes of this century. 'I found a total departure from realism, the sense of movement in space and time, and the idea that the viewer of the work of art is its centre, that he or she is a part of the picture,' she explained.

In approaching Futurism, and in all her collecting, Mrs Winston Malbin tried to get as close as possible to the sources of the art, travelling throughout Europe to broaden her understanding of the context in which the works had been created and, whenever possible, seeking out the artists or their heirs.

She met Severini and his family in Rome and subsequently visited his Paris studio where she made her first Futurist acquisition, *Mare = Danzatrice* (literally, 'sea = dancer') (Fig. 5). Dating from 1913, the painting is one of the earliest of the 'plastic analogies' in which Severini set up relationships between complementary images, in this case equating the rhythm of the waves and the glint of sunlight on the sea with the movements of a dancer in sequinned costume. Ultimately, Mrs Winston Malbin also purchased a study for this work, as well as many other drawings including the graceful portrait Severini made of his wife during their engagement.

Some of the most significant Futurist statements – Balla's *Injection of Futurism* and his brilliant sculpture *Boccioni's Fist* (Fig. 4), which became the symbol of the movement – were acquired from the families of the artists, including Marinetti's widow Benedetta, and Balla's daughters Luce and Elicia. Initially suspicious of her interest, they came to trust Mrs Winston Malbin, and these relationships enabled her to build a collection as multi-dimensional as the Futurist movement itself.

Early works like Balla's *Stairway of Farewells* (Fig. 2) and Russolo's *Perfume* reveal the transition between more traditional techniques and the Futurist expression of movement and the senses. Many of the drawings are studies for major Futurist works, like Boccioni's *The Drinker* and Balla's *Abstract Velocity*; others show Balla's experiments with his famous lines of force, and his designs for 'anti-neutralist' clothing.

The 1950s were a crucial decade in shaping the collection as Mrs Winston Malbin began to focus on works that complemented or extended the Futurist vocabulary. Léger's *Femme au Fauteuil* (Fig. 3), 1913, was a particularly good example. Here, the artist approached a Cubist subject, the seated woman, in a Cubist style which he redirected, in order to suggest motion. Looking at the legacy of Futurism, Mrs Winston Malbin also acquired several works by the Synchromists, a small group of American artists, led by Stranton MacDonald-Wright and Morgan Russell, who sought to convey sculptural form through colour.

One of the greatest challenges faced by Mrs Winston Malbin during this period was her effort to convince Brancusi that she 'wanted to live with his art and learn from it.' The sculptor had been unwilling to discuss selling his work for nearly twenty years, but after four or five studio visits and much negotiation, he allowed her to purchase the bronze cast of *La Negresse Blonde* (Fig. 6). Completely won over,

Fig. 3
Fernand Léger
LA FEMME AU FAUTEUIL
1913, 51¼in by 38¼in (130.2cm by 97.2cm)
New York $8,525,000 (£5,104,790). 16.V.90
From the collection of Lydia Winston Malbin

Fig. 4
Giacomo Balla
PUGNO DI BOCCIONI:
LINEE FORZE DEL
PUGNO DI BOCCIONI
Painted cardboard and
wood, signed and dated
1915, height 32½in (82.5cm)
New York $2,200,000
(£1,317,365). 16.V.90
From the collection of
Lydia Winston Malbin

he also gave her a design for the base, quickly sketched on a small piece of paper, and prints of the photographs which he had taken of the related marble, in his studio.

Until her death, Lydia Winston Malbin lived with her collection, sharing her experiences and discussing the works with scholars, students and curators. The extensive archive she assembled – detailing the acquisition and exhibition history of each work – became an invaluable resource and is now at Yale University. The installation in her New York apartment was carefully designed to suggest the connections she valued – one wall defined the Cubo-Futurist sensibility through paintings by Boccioni, Léger, Severini and Picasso; and the hard-edged geometry of Balla's *Iridescent Interpenetrations* was juxtaposed with that of Mondrian and Stella. But it was her library that best expressed the influences and interests that dominated her life. There she hung Balla's *Injection of Futurism*, with her father's T-square beside it and a group of her own ceramics below.

Gino Severini,
photographed in 1913.

Fig. 5
Gino Severini
MARE = DANZATRICE
Oil on canvas with sequins, signed; signed, titled *Danseuse aux Bords de la Mer*, inscribed with a
dedication *a Monsieur et Madame Harry Winston avec toute ma sympathie* and dated *Paris, 10 Mai 1951* on the
reverse, *circa* 1913–14, 36½in by 29in (92.7cm by 73.6cm)
New York $3,630,000 (£2,173,653). 16.V.90
From the collection of Lydia Winston Malbin

Constantin Brancusi in his studio, photographed by Edward Steichen in 1927.

Fig. 6
Constantin Brancusi
LA NEGRESSE BLONDE
Polished bronze and stone, signed, height of head 15¾in (40cm)
New York $8,800,000 (£5,269,461). 16.V.90
From the collection of Lydia Winston Malbin

Contemporary art

Jean Dubuffet
LA CALIPETTE
Signed and dated *'61*; signed, titled and dated *Août 1961* on the reverse, 35in by 45⅞in (89cm by 116.5cm)
London £2,530,000 ($4,427,500). 5.IV.90

Opposite
Jean Dubuffet
GEORGES LIMBOUR ROI MEXICAIN
45⅝in by 35in (115.9cm by 88.9cm)
New York $3,960,000 (£2,343,195). 17.V.90
From the collection of Milton A. Gordon

At the beginning of Dubuffet's career, Georges Limbour was a prominent member of his
circle, and a great admirer. As early as 1944, he had written glowingly about the artist's first
works, in *Comoedia*, and in 1954 he published a full-scale study, *Tableau bon levain à vous de cuire
la pâte: l'art brut de Jean Dubuffet*. He continued to analyze Dubuffet's art until his death in 1969.

Willem de Kooning
INTERCHANGE
Signed, 1955, 79in by 69in (200.7cm by 175.3cm)
New York $20,680,000 (£13,006,289). 8.XI.89
From the collection of the late Edgar J. Kaufmann, Jr

Bram van Velde
UNTITLED
Gouache on paper laid down on canvas, 1957, 52in by 59in (132cm by 150cm)
Amsterdam DF1977,500 (£313,301 : $511,780). 10.IV.90
From the collection of Comtesse Albina du Boisrouvray

Richard Diebenkorn
OCEAN PARK #40
Signed with initials and dated *71*; signed, titled and dated *1971* on the reverse, 93in by 80¾in (236.2cm by 205.1cm)
New York $1,760,000 (£1,053,892). 8.V.90

Mark Rothko
BLACK AREA IN REDS
Signed and dated *1958* on the reverse, 69½in by 92in (176.5cm by 233.7cm)
New York $3,630,000 (£2,283,019). 8.XI.89

Opposite
Ad Reinhardt
ABSTRACT PAINTING
1958, 108in by 40in
(274.3cm by 101.6cm)
New York $2,530,000
(£1,514,970). 8.V.90

Right
Frank Stella
TOMLINSON COURT PARK
(SECOND VERSION)
Black enamel on canvas,
1959, 84in by 109in
(213.4cm by 276.9cm)
New York $5,060,000
(£3,182,390). 8.XI.89

Below
Cy Twombly
UNTITLED
Oil and crayon on canvas,
1971, 118in by 184½in
(299.7cm by 468.6cm)
New York $5,500,000
(£3,293,413). 8.V.90

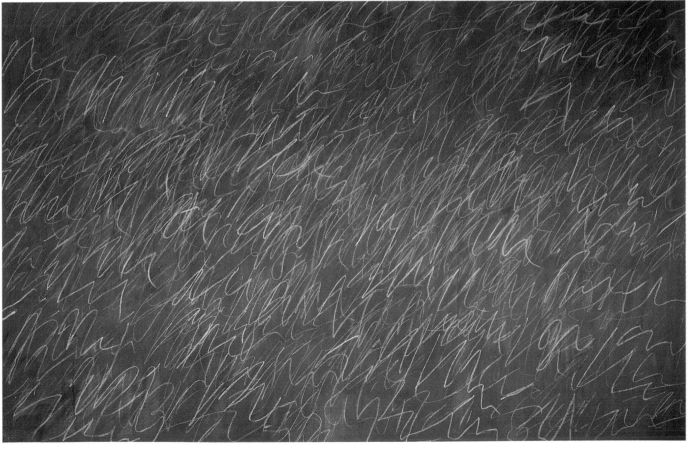

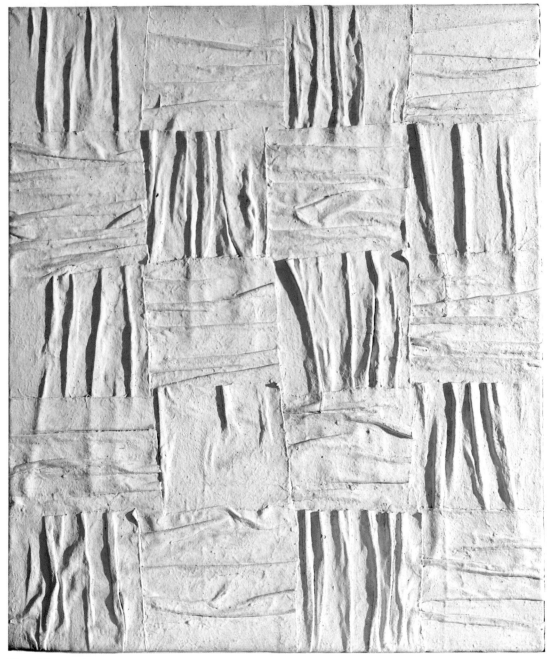

Piero Manzoni
ACHROME
Kaolin on canvas, signed and dated '59 on the reverse, 28¾in by 24⅜in (73cm by 62cm)
London £330,000 ($577,500). 5.IV.90

Jasper Johns
TWO FLAGS
Each flag composed of three panels, the left flag: oil on canvas, the right flag: encaustic on canvas,
1973, 52¼in by 69½in (132.7cm by 176.5cm)
New York $12,100,000 (£7,610,063). 8.XI.89

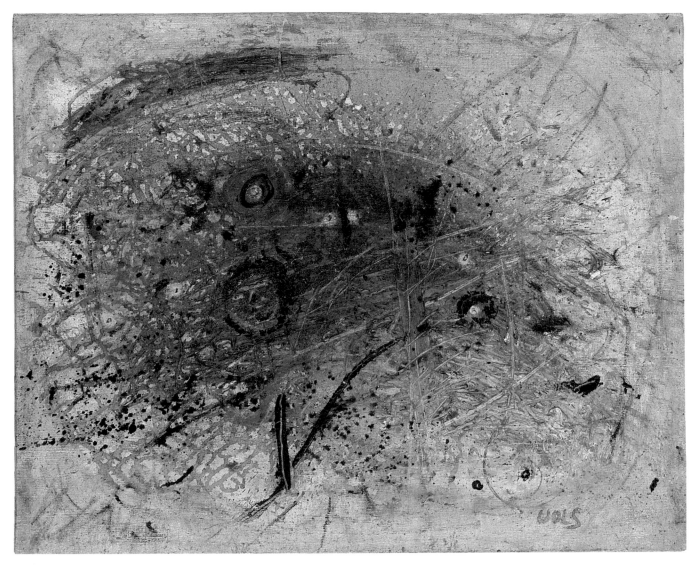

Wols
UNTITLED
Circa 1946–47, 25⅝in by 31⅞in (65cm by 81cm)
London £583,000 ($1,078,550). 28.VI.90

Opposite
Lucio Fontana
LA FINE DI DIO
Oil and glitter on canvas, signed and titled on the reverse, 70⅛in by 48⅜in (178cm by 123cm)
London £572,000 ($943,800). 30.XI.89

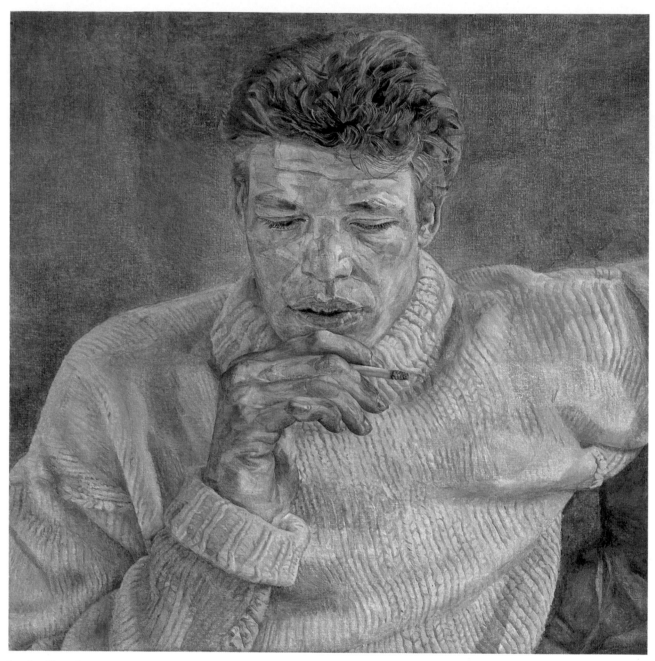

Lucian Freud
MAN SMOKING
Circa 1956–58, 22⅞in by 22⅞in (58cm by 58cm)
London £660,000 ($1,221,000). 28.VI.90

Maria-Helena Vieira da Silva
SOUTERRAIN
Oil and pencil on canvas, signed, titled and dated *1948* on the stretcher, 31⅞in by 39⅜in (81cm by 100cm)
London £495,000 ($915,750). 28.VI.90

American art

Charles M. Russell
SMOKING THEM OUT
Signed with skull, inscribed
and dated *1906 Copyrighted*,
15¼in by 21in (38.7cm
by 53.3cm)
New York $473,000
(£281,548). 24.V.90
From the collection of
Wellington S. Henderson

Below
Charles M. Russell
RETURN OF THE WAR PARTY
Signed with skull, inscribed ©
and dated *1914*, 24¼in by 36¼in
(61.6cm by 92.1cm)
New York $1,100,000
(£700,637). 30.XI.89

Leon Gaspard
THE FINISH OF THE KERMESSE
Signed and dated *1918*, 37in by 47in (94cm by 119.4cm)
New York $275,000 (£163,690). 24.V.90
From the collection of the Edmundson Art Foundation

Opposite
Charles Bird King
NESOUAQUOIT (BEAR IN THE FORK OF A TREE), A FOX CHIEF
1837, 35½in by 29½in (90.2cm by 74.9cm)
New York $385,000 (£229,167). 24.V.90

Frank W. Benson
BOATING AT VINALHAVEN
Signed, inscribed *To Henry Chaplin* and dated *1920*, 30in by 23¼in (76.2cm by 59.1cm)
New York $583,000 (£347,024). 24.V.90

Childe Hassam
GARDEN BY THE SEA, ISLES OF SHOALS
Watercolour, signed and inscribed *Iles of Shoals, circa* 1892, 14in by 10in (35.6cm by 25.4cm)
New York $495,000 (£294,643). 24.V.90

Georgia O'Keeffe
A WHITE CAMELLIA
Pastel, 1938, 21½in by 27½in (54.6cm by 69.8cm)
New York $605,000 (£360,119). 24.V.90
From the collection of Patricia Graham Young

Opposite
Georgia O'Keeffe
BLACK PETUNIA AND WHITE MORNING-GLORY II
1926, 36in by 30in (91.4cm by 76.2cm)
New York $1,045,000 (£622,024). 24.V.90
From the collection of Patricia Graham Young

Reginald Marsh
MERRY-GO-ROUND
Tempera on canvas mounted on masonite, signed and dated *1930*, 36in by 48in (91.4cm by 121.9cm)
New York $363,000 (£216,071). 24.V.90

Stuart Davis
NIGHT LIFE
Signed; signed, titled and dated *1962* on the stretcher, 24in by 32in (61cm by 81.3cm)
New York $880,000 (£560,510). 30.XI.89

Latin American, Australian and Canadian art

Matta
THE DISASTERS OF MYSTICISM
1942, 38⅛in by 51⅜in (96.8cm by 130.5cm)
New York $1,155,000 (£704,268). 2.V.90

Opposite
Joaquin Torres-García
RITMO CON OBLICUAS EN BLANCO Y NEGRO
Tempera on board, signed with initials and dated *38*, 31¾in by 19in (80.6cm by 48.2cm)
New York $286,000 (£183,333). 20.XI.89
From the collection of Royal S. Marks

Diego y Yo

Hayden Herrera

In *Diego y Yo*, as in so many of Frida Kahlo's self-portraits, the painter stares at us with imploring intensity. Her face is beautiful, or better still, nearly beautiful – Kahlo actually exaggerated her defects. But recording her features was not her primary purpose. 'I paint self-portraits,' she once said, 'because I am so often alone, because I am the person I know best.' What grips us when we look at paintings like *Diego y Yo* is the ferocious honesty of Kahlo's confrontation with herself.

Most of the self-portraits show the artist in spiritual or physical pain. Between the bus crash that almost killed her in 1925, when she was eighteen, and her death in 1954, Kahlo underwent some thirty-five operations. Her paintings express her response to this and to suffering of another kind: Kahlo was married to the Mexican muralist Diego Rivera, an incorrigible philanderer. Though she pretended to make light of his affairs (and had plenty of her own), some caused her anguish, especially his liaison in 1949 with her intimate friend, the film star María Felix.

In her self-portraits, Kahlo's frustrated desire to possess Rivera completely is a frequent theme. Almost always, her face is set in a mask of stoic impassivity. Kahlo chose to depict her pain in other ways – with images of wounds or incisions. Often, she revealed her suffering by painting tears dotting her cheeks, or with telling details such as thorn necklaces, arrows penetrating her flesh, or ribbons encircling her neck as if they were about to strangle her.

Kahlo usually wore her long hair done up with braids and flowers, in the native style that went with the full-length Mexican costumes in which she habitually dressed to hide her limp, to please her husband and to affirm her Mexican identity. In *Diego y Yo* her hair is, as usual, pulled back so tightly that it tugs at its roots. But this time it swirls out from behind and threatens to engulf her. The unfastened hair embodies Frida's all-but-unhinged emotions. Here, for the first time, the impassive mask is slipping, and she glares with rageful, tearful eyes. The artist's inner turmoil is also expressed through the distorted outline of her face, which is oddly broken at her jutting left eyebrow. Her left cheekbone and her chin seem overly large – almost as if suffering has caused her flesh to sink back upon the bone.

In *Diego y Yo*, the source of Frida's misery is revealed on her forehead in a miniature portrait of her husband. A third eye, a reference to Rivera's superior visual acuity, opens in his brow. Of the five eyes in this painting, only Frida's meet ours. Diego – who, as Frida pointed out, had wide-set eyes suitable for taking in vast multitudes and broad panoramas of the world – looks out over our heads. His gaze is fixed on an a broader, more distant horizon.

In the end María Felix refused to marry Diego, and, he returned to Frida who was 'miserable and hurt' but, as he recalled, 'Within a short space of time however, everything was well again. I got over my rejection by María. Frida was happy to have me back, and I was grateful to be married to her still.'

Opposite
Frida Kahlo
DIEGO Y YO ('DIEGO AND I')
Oil on masonite, signed, titled and dated *Mexico 1949*; inscribed on the reverse *Para Florence y Sam con el carino de Frida. Mexico, Junio de 1949.*, 11⅝in by 8⅞in (29.5cm by 22.4cm)
New York $1,430,000 (£871,951). 2.V.90
From the collection of Florence Arquin

Sir George Russell Drysdale
CHILDREN IN A BATH
Signed, 19¼in by 23¼in (49cm by 59cm)
Melbourne AUS$143,000 (£71,859:$112,598). 27.XI.89

Opposite
Paul Peel
THE YOUNG GLEANER
Signed and dated *1888*, 49in by 36¾in (124.5cm by 93.3cm)
Toronto CAN$429,000 (£217,767:$366,666). 31.V.90

Also known as *Butterflies*, this painting ranks amongst Paul Peel's most appealing works, and
dates from 1888, when he was living and studying in Paris, under the academic portrait
painter and orientalist, Benjamin Constant, whose influence is evident in the bright, light-
filled composition.

Prints

Rembrandt Harmensz. van Rijn
LANDSCAPE WITH A COTTAGE AND A HAYBARN
Etching, signed, 1641, 5in by 12¾in (12.7cm by 32.3cm)
New York $132,000 (£78,571). 16.V.90

Opposite
Wenceslaus Hollar
THE SHELLS
Two etchings from a group of thirty-two, plate size approximately 3⅞in by 5¾in (9.8cm by 14.7cm)
London £39,600 ($65,340). 30.XI.89

The rarity of these great masterpieces of etching is legendary, even in single examples (the complete series comprises thirty-eight). George Vertue, who wrote within living memory of Hollar, noted that 'Many Collectors of Hollar's works have them not; nor are they to be met with in the most numerous Collections, except two or three, where they are esteemed as great Rarities'. Exotic shells are frequently seen as components of seventeenth-century Dutch still-lifes, but are extremely rare as subjects for etching. The purpose of Hollar's works, possibly etched in Antwerp, remains obscure. Technically they may be compared in their virtuosity to his etchings of muffs, his draughtsmanship and supreme control of acid biting here suggesting hard but brittle surfaces, instead of the sensual softness of the muffs.

40/100

Tsuguharu Foujita
LES CHATS
Aquatints with engraving and *roulette* printed in colours, from a complete portfolio of ten, each signed
in pencil and numbered *40/100*, *circa* 1930, sheet sizes approximately 17¾in by 20¼in (45cm by 51.5cm)
London £198,000 ($364,320). 26.VI.90

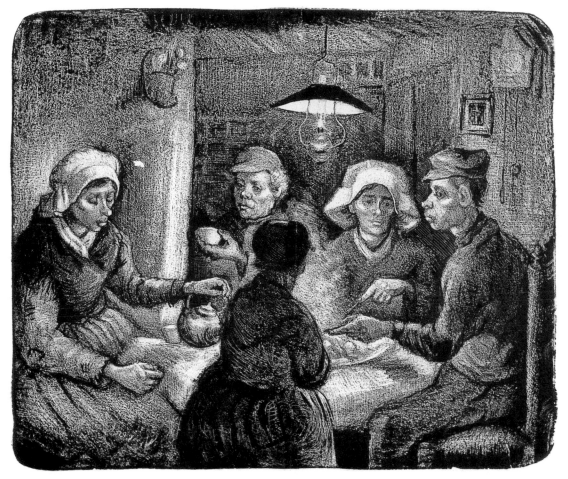

Vincent van Gogh
THE POTATO EATERS
Lithograph printed in black, 1885, 10⅜in by 12½in (26.3cm by 31.7cm)
London £93,500 ($172,040). 26.VI.90

Vincent van Gogh completed his first masterpiece, the painting of *The Potato Eaters*, at the end of April 1885, in Nuenen. It was the first painting which the artist proudly described as a *tableau*, to distinguish it from the *études* which had preceded it, and he felt he had finally achieved his ambition to become a figure painter concentrating on peasant life. Prior to commencing the finished version of the painting (now in the Rijksmuseum Vincent van Gogh, Amsterdam), Van Gogh had executed eight lithographs using a method whereby the drawing was initially composed on a special paper before being transferred to the lithographic stone for printing. Unsatisfied with the smoothness and mechanical quality of the prints thus obtained, the artist decided to draw directly on the stone itself. After printing about twenty impressions of the lithograph, Van Gogh destroyed the stone and sent an unspecified number of proofs to his brother Theo, including several for the Parisian art dealer Arsène Portier. Fourteen of these have been recorded since, including seven impressions presently in the Rijksmuseum Vincent van Gogh (four of which are signed in ink).

Edvard Munch
DAS KRANKE MÄDCHEN
Lithograph printed in colours, signed in orange crayon and numbered 5, 1896, 16½in by 22¼in
(42cm by 56.6cm)
Tokyo ¥36,300,000 (£162,271:$252,434). 13.X.89

The print exists in several colour variations which were printed in very small editions. It is
the artist's first colour lithograph, which he considered his most important print.

Opposite
Mary Cassatt
IN THE OMNIBUS
Drypoint and aquatint printed in colours, 1890–91, with the artist's monogram stamp, 14½in by 10½in
(36.8cm by 26.8cm)
New York $225,500 (£134,226). 16.V.90

24/60   Marc Chagall

Chagall's illustrations to Longus's *Daphnis and Chloé*

Ian Mackenzie

The history of this, Chagall's most important series of lithographs, goes back to a suggestion by the artist's publisher, Tériade, in 1952, that he should illustrate Longus's famous pastoral romance. Very little is known about Longus, but we can assume that he was probably a native of Lesbos, the setting for the story, and that he lived and wrote in the third century AD. Chagall, fired by Tériade's idea and eager to see Greece for himself, set off for Athens with his new bride, Vava, who he had married in July 1952.

The couple visited Delphi and stayed on Poros, where Chagall executed a number of gouaches and pastel drawings, reflecting his intense experience of the landscape, the vegetation and the sea. Two years later, they returned to Greece, visiting Poros once more, before going on to Nauplia and Olympia. On this second trip, Chagall completed nearly all the gouaches for the lithographs.

Having abandoned lithography in 1924, Chagall had returned to the medium with his *Four Tales from the Arabian Nights*, produced in New York and published in 1948. On returning to France, he continued to develop his lithographic techniques at the atelier of Mourlot Frères in the rue de Chabrol, Paris, with the assistance and advice of Charles Sorlier, who supervised the printing. Work on *Daphnis and Chloé* took place between 1957 and 1960, during which time Chagall was also commissioned to design sets and costumes for a production of Ravel's ballet of the same name, at the Paris Opéra.

Longus's original story tells how Daphnis and Chloé were abandoned in their infancy and nursed by a sheep and a cow, whose flocks they then tend throughout an idyllic childhood. Upon reaching adolescence, they fall in love, as Eros has decreed, but various misadventures ensue, before the couple are married with the blessings of their true parents, who turn out to be rich Mytileneans. Basing his prints on the earlier gouaches, Chagall makes full, uninhibited use of the fluidity and translucency of the lithographic colour, perfectly reflecting the romantic, symbolic and fantastic nature of the poem.

The complete two-volume set of the lithographs was finally published by Editions Verve in Paris, in 1961, in a total edition of 270 copies. At the same time, 60 sets of the plates were printed with large margins; these impressions were individually signed by Chagall, and many were subsequently sold separately. A complete, unfolded set of all 42 prints is therefore extremely rare. This was the first time that one such – representing what is undoubtedly some of the artist's finest work – has been sold at auction.

Marc Chagall
DAPHNIS ET CHLOE
Le piège à loup, Plate VI
from a complete set of
forty-two lithographs
printed in colours, each
signed in pencil and
numbered *24/60*, published
by Editions Verve, Paris,
1961, single sheet size
approximately 21⅜in by
14⅞in (54.1cm by 37.8cm)
London £1,815,000
($3,339,600). 26.VI.90

Jasper Johns
COLOR NUMERALS: FIGURES FROM 0 TO 9
Number 7 from the complete set of ten lithographs printed in colours, each signed in a different colour crayon, numbered *16/40* and dated 1968–69, sheet sizes approximately 38in by 31¼in (96.5cm by 79cm)
New York $577,500 (£341,716). 19.V.90

David Hockney
CARIBBEAN TEA TIME
Double-sided four-panel folding screen, offset lithograph printed in colours, with hand-colouring and
collage; silkscreen printed in colours on white lacquered wood panels on the reverse, 1987, signed in
pencil on the front and numbered *30/36*, approximately 4ft by 11ft 4in (121.7cm by 346.7cm)
Tokyo ¥51,700,000 (£198,617:$324,545). 27.IV.90

Photographs

Anna Atkins
BRITISH ALGAE
Cyanotype impression, from two volumes issued in parts from October 1843, volume I
with introductory page, title page and 191 plates, and volume II with introductory page
and 187 plates, Robert Hunt's copy, approximately 10in by 8¼in (25.5cm by 21cm)
London £90,200 ($160,556). 10.V.90

Opposite
Hippolyte Bayard
STILL LIFE COMPOSITION WITH ITEMS OF STATUARY
Albumen print from glass negative, monogrammed in the negative *HB*, *circa* 1850–54,
10⅜in by 8in (26.4cm by 20.1cm)
London £26,400 ($46,992). 10.V.90

Photographs from the collection of Graham Nash

Over the course of nearly two decades, pop musician Graham Nash, of the group Crosby, Stills & Nash, assembled one of the finest private collections of photographs in the history of the medium. A photographer himself – 'I had a camera before I had a guitar' – Graham Nash traces his interest back to his childhood in northern England where he spent hours watching his father develop prints in a makeshift darkroom. For his collection, he selected a diverse group of photographs ranging from mid-nineteenth-century prints by the pioneers of the new medium to twentieth-century images by the most prominent masters of the field, including Julia Margaret Cameron, Peter Henry Emerson, Henri Cartier-Bresson, André Kertèsz, Pierre Dubreuil, Paul Outerbridge, Walker Evans, Edward Weston and Edward Steichen (see Fig. 3 for his portrait by Heinrich Kuehn).

Graham Nash's approach was simple. He focused on images with 'the power to move', such as Diane Arbus's disturbing visions of Middle America. Her devastating image of a *Child with Toy Hand Grenade in Central Park* was his first purchase, at a time when he was active in the movement against the Vietnam War. Of this work Graham Nash has said: 'The moment is chilling; the madness of war seems to crystallize in that photograph. I have always been drawn to images that create that kind of artistic tension.'

The remarkable depth of the Nash Collection was evident in the photographs of North American Indians, a subject to which Mr Nash was drawn in the 1960s because of the insight it gave him into an entirely different time and culture. Richard Throssel's *Portrait with Indian Blanket* (Fig. 2) is one of a group of photographs of the Crow Indians taken between 1902 and 1910. Throssel, who was of Cree Indian and French-Canadian descent, became an adopted member of the Crow tribe, and his work represents a unique insider's viewpoint of Indian life.

Many of the photographs were acquired from galleries in California where Mr Nash lives. These included Outerbridge's *Self-Portrait* (Fig. 1), 1927, which depicts the artist masked and wearing a top hat. Outerbridge, known primarily as a commercial photographer, made only a few prints from each of his negatives. Only four unique variants of the *Self-Portrait* are known to exist. He laboured endlessly to compose his final image and often made preliminary sketches of compositions which he would then replicate in his photographs, a technique used with *H.-O. Box*. Both the preliminary drawing and the final platinum print were included in the Nash Collection, the only instance where such a pairing has appeared at auction.

Edward Weston, one of the giants of the medium, perplexed many of his critics with *Epilogue (Margrethe Mather)* (Fig. 4), 1919, a classic image from his Pictorialist period. In 1914 Weston and his business partner Margrethe Mather were among the

Fig. 1
Paul Outerbridge
SELF-PORTRAIT
One of four variants of this image, each thought to be unique, 1927, 15in by 11¼in (38.1cm by 28.5cm) New York $99,000 (£60,366). 25.IV.90
From the collection of Graham Nash

Fig. 2
Richard Throssel
PORTRAIT WITH INDIAN BLANKET
Hand-coloured silver print, numbered *840* in pencil in an unknown hand on the reverse, early 1900s, 8in by 6in (20.3cm by 15.2cm)
New York $12,100 (£7,378). 25.IV.90
From the collection of Graham Nash

Below
Fig. 3
Heinrich Kuehn
EDWARD STEICHEN
Waxed gum-bichromate and carbon print on tissue, *circa* 1907, 11¼in by 9in (28.6cm by 22.8cm)
New York $29,700 (£18,110). 25.IV.90
From the collection of Graham Nash

eleven founding members of the Camera Pictorialists of Los Angeles. Weston's portrait of Mather exhibits the typical conventions of this group – a stage-like setting, stylized pose, dramatic lighting, and soft-focus shadows. This photograph is important because Weston later abandoned this style and adopted the realistic, straightforward aesthetic (exemplified by the photographs of shells, peppers and nudes) for which he is so famous. As a result, these earlier images displeased him and he destroyed many of his negatives and prints from this period.

The sale of this collection does not mark the end of Graham Nash's interest in photography. Always drawn to the work of innovative artists, Mr Nash plans to focus his collecting interests on contemporary photography, especially computer-derived images.

Opposite
Fig. 4
Edward Weston
EPILOGUE (MARGRETHE MATHER)
Platinum print, signed, titled and dated by the photographer in pencil on the mount, 1919, 9⅝in by 7¼in (24.5cm by 18.4cm)
New York $82,500 (£50,305). 25.IV.90
From the collection of Graham Nash

Man Ray
THE PRIMACY OF MATTER OVER THOUGHT (PRIMAT DE LA MATIERE SUR LA PENSEE)
Solarized silver print, signed by the photographer in pencil on the reverse, 1929,
11¾in by 9in (28.9cm by 22.8cm)
New York $121,000 (£76,582). 1.XI.89

Opposite
Clarence H. White and Alfred Stieglitz
THE TORSO (MISS THOMPSON)
Waxed platinum print, signed by Clarence White on the mount, 1907,
9½in by 7¾in (24.1cm by 18.7cm)
New York $93,500 (£57,362). 26.IV.90

Printed books, autograph
Letters and music manuscripts

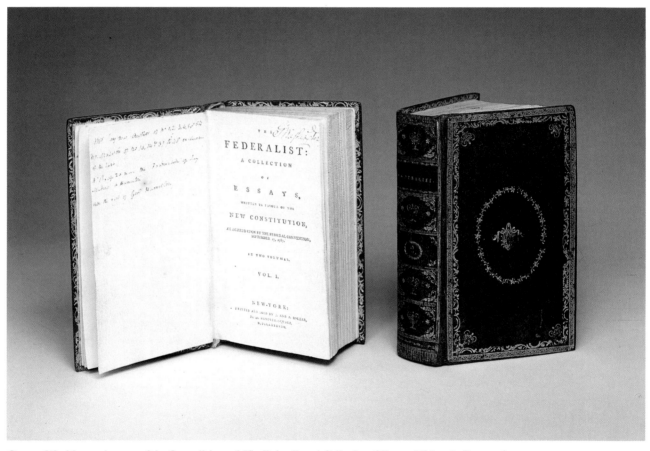

George Washington's copy of the first edition of *The Federalist: A Collection of Essays, Written in Favour of the New Constitution, as Agreed upon by the Federal Covention, September 17, 1787*, two volumes, by Alexander Hamilton, James Madison and John Jay, John and Andrew M'Lean, New York, 1788, both with George Washington's signature and bookplate
New York $1,430,000 (£851,190). 31.I.90
From the library of H. Bradley Martin

Opposite
The Declaration of Independence, one of twenty-three surviving copies, printed by John Dunlap, Philadelphia, 4th or 5th July 1776
New York $1,595,000 (£949,405). 31.I.90
From the library of H. Bradley Martin

In CONGRESS, July 4, 1776.

A DECLARATION

By the REPRESENTATIVES of the

UNITED STATES OF AMERICA,

In GENERAL CONGRESS Assembled.

WHEN in the Course of human Events, it becomes neceſſary for one People to diſſolve the Political Bands which have connected them with another, and to aſſume among the Powers of the Earth, the ſeparate and equal Station to which the Laws of Nature and of Nature's God entitle them, a decent Reſpect to the Opinions of Mankind requires that they ſhould declare the cauſes which impel them to the Separation.

We hold theſe Truths to be ſelf-evident, that all Men are created equal, that they are endowed by their Creator with certain unalienable Rights, that among theſe are Life, Liberty, and the Purſuit of Happineſs--That to ſecure theſe Rights, Governments are inſtituted among Men, deriving their juſt Powers from the Conſent of the Governed, that whenever any Form of Government becomes deſtructive of theſe Ends, it is the Right of the People to alter or to aboliſh it, and to inſtitute new Government, laying its Foundation on ſuch Principles, and organizing its Powers in ſuch Form, as to them ſhall ſeem moſt likely to effect their Safety and Happineſs. Prudence, indeed, will dictate that Governments long eſtabliſhed ſhould not be changed for light and tranſient Cauſes; and accordingly all Experience hath ſhewn, that Mankind are more diſpoſed to ſuffer, while Evils are ſufferable, than to right themſelves by aboliſhing the Forms to which they are accuſtomed. But when a long Train of Abuſes and Uſurpations, purſuing invariably the ſame Object, evinces a Deſign to reduce them under abſolute Deſpotiſm, it is their Right, it is their Duty, to throw off ſuch Government, and to provide new Guards for their future Security. Such has been the patient Sufferance of theſe Colonies; and ſuch is now the Neceſſity which conſtrains them to alter their former Syſtems of Government. The Hiſtory of the preſent King of Great-Britain is a Hiſtory of repeated Injuries and Uſurpations, all having in direct Object the Eſtabliſhment of an abſolute Tyranny over theſe States. To prove this, let Facts be ſubmitted to a candid World.

He has refuſed his Aſſent to Laws, the moſt wholeſome and neceſſary for the public Good.

He has forbidden his Governors to paſs Laws of immediate and preſſing Importance, unleſs ſuſpended in their Operation till his Aſſent ſhould be obtained; and when ſo ſuſpended, he has utterly neglected to attend to them.

He has refuſed to paſs other Laws for the Accommodation of large Diſtricts of People, unleſs thoſe People would relinquiſh the Right of Repreſentation in the Legiſlature, a Right ineſtimable to them, and formidable to Tyrants only.

He has called together Legiſlative Bodies at Places unuſual, uncomfortable, and diſtant from the Depoſitory of their public Records, for the ſole Purpoſe of fatiguing them into Compliance with his Meaſures.

He has diſſolved Repreſentative Houſes repeatedly, for oppoſing with manly Firmneſs his Invaſions on the Rights of the People.

He has refuſed for a long Time, after ſuch Diſſolutions, to cauſe others to be elected; whereby the Legiſlative Powers, incapable of Annihilation, have returned to the People at large for their exerciſe; the State remaining in the mean time expoſed to all the Dangers of Invaſion from without, and Convulſions within.

He has endeavoured to prevent the Population of theſe States; for that Purpoſe obſtructing the Laws for Naturalization of Foreigners; refuſing to paſs others to encourage their Migrations hither, and raiſing the Conditions of new Appropriations of Lands.

He has obſtructed the Adminiſtration of Juſtice, by refuſing his Aſſent to Laws for eſtabliſhing Judiciary Powers.

He has made Judges dependent on his Will alone, for the Tenure of their Offices, and the Amount and Payment of their Salaries.

He has erected a Multitude of new Offices, and ſent hither Swarms of Officers to harraſs our People, and eat out their Subſtance.

He has kept among us, in Times of Peace, Standing Armies, without the conſent of our Legiſlatures.

He has affected to render the Military independent of and ſuperior to the Civil Power.

He has combined with others to ſubject us to a Juriſdiction foreign to our Conſtitution, and unacknowledged by our Laws; giving his Aſſent to their Acts of pretended Legiſlation:

For quartering large Bodies of Armed Troops among us:

For protecting them, by a mock Trial, from Puniſhment for any Murders which they ſhould commit on the Inhabitants of theſe States:

For cutting off our Trade with all Parts of the World:

For impoſing Taxes on us without our Conſent:

For depriving us, in many Caſes, of the Benefits of Trial by Jury:

For tranſporting us beyond Seas to be tried for pretended Offences:

For aboliſhing the free Syſtem of Engliſh Laws in a neighbouring Province, eſtabliſhing therein an arbitrary Government, and enlarging its Boundaries, ſo as to render it at once an Example and fit Inſtrument for introducing the ſame abſolute Rule into theſe Colonies:

For taking away our Charters, aboliſhing our moſt valuable Laws, and altering fundamentally the Forms of our Governments:

For ſuſpending our own Legiſlatures, and declaring themſelves inveſted with Power to legiſlate for us in all Caſes whatſoever.

He has abdicated Government here, by declaring us out of his Protection and waging War againſt us.

He has plundered our Seas, ravaged our Coaſts, burnt our Towns, and deſtroyed the Lives of our People.

He is, at this Time, tranſporting large Armies of foreign Mercenaries to compleat the Works of Death, Deſolation, and Tyranny, already begun with circumſtances of Cruelty and Perfidy, ſcarcely paralleled in the moſt barbarous Ages, and totally unworthy the Head of a civilized Nation.

He has conſtrained our fellow Citizens taken Captive on the high Seas to bear Arms againſt their Country, to become the Executioners of their Friends and Brethren, or to fall themſelves by their Hands.

He has excited domeſtic Inſurrections amongſt us, and has endeavoured to bring on the Inhabitants of our Frontiers, the mercileſs Indian-Savages, whoſe known Rule of Warfare, is an undiſtinguiſhed Deſtruction, of all Ages, Sexes and Conditions.

In every ſtage of theſe Oppreſſions we have Petitioned for Redreſs in the moſt humble Terms: Our repeated Petitions have been anſwered only by repeated Injury. A Prince, whoſe Character is thus marked by every act which may define a Tyrant, is unfit to be the Ruler of a free People.

Nor have we been wanting in Attentions to our Britiſh Brethren. We have warned them from Time to Time of Attempts by their Legiſlature to extend an unwarrantable Juriſdiction over us. We have reminded them of the Circumſtances of our Emigration and Settlement here. We have appealed to their native Juſtice and Magnanimity, and we have conjured them by the Ties of our common Kindred to diſavow theſe Uſurpations, which, would inevitably interrupt our Connections and Correſpondence. They too have been deaf to the Voice of Juſtice and of Conſanguinity. We muſt, therefore, acquieſce in the Neceſſity, which denounces our Separation, and hold them, as we hold the reſt of Mankind, Enemies in War, in Peace, Friends.

We, therefore, the Repreſentatives of the UNITED STATES OF AMERICA, in GENERAL CONGRESS, Aſſembled, appealing to the Supreme Judge of the World for the Rectitude of our Intentions, do, in the Name, and by Authority of the good People of theſe Colonies, ſolemnly Publiſh and Declare, That theſe United Colonies are, and of Right ought to be, FREE AND INDEPENDENT STATES; that they are abſolved from all Allegiance to the Britiſh Crown, and that all political Connection between them and the State of Great-Britain, is and ought to be totally diſſolved; and that as FREE AND INDEPENDENT STATES, they have full Power to levy War, conclude Peace, contract Alliances, eſtabliſh Commerce, and to do all other Acts and Things which INDEPENDENT STATES may of right do. And for the ſupport of this Declaration, with a firm Reliance on the Protection of divine Providence, we mutually pledge to each other our Lives, our Fortunes, and our ſacred Honor.

Signed by ORDER and in BEHALF of the CONGRESS,

JOHN HANCOCK, PRESIDENT.

ATTEST.
CHARLES THOMSON, SECRETARY.

PHILADELPHIA: PRINTED BY JOHN DUNLAP.

Left

Henri de Toulouse-Lautrec

A coloured lithograph of Mademoiselle Lender, from *Pan*, edited by Julius Meier-Graefe and Otto J. Bierbaum, a complete set of twenty-one parts bound in six volumes, comprising 102 etchings, lithographs and woodcuts, Berlin, 1895–1900

London £37,400 ($61,710). 29.XI.89

Below, left

Jean de La Fontaine

Les Amours de Psyché et de Cupidon, including the poem *Adonis*, with the eight original drawings by Moreau, printed on vellum, the red straight-grained morocco gilt with the monogram of Prince Eugène de Beauharnais, by Jean-Claude Bozerian, Didot le Jeune, Paris, 1795

London £154,000 ($267,960). 26.IV.90

Right

Robert Adam

Ruins of the Palace of the Emperor Diocletian at Spalatro in Dalmatia, first edition, morocco gilt binding with the royal arms of the dedicatee, George III, probably intended for presentation to the Earl of Bute, designed by Robert Adam, printed for the author, London, 1764

New York $176,000 (£102,924). 14.VI.90

From the library of H. Bradley Martin

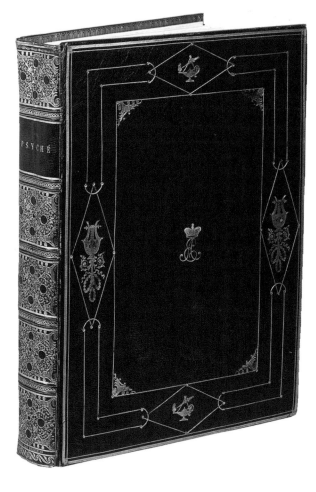

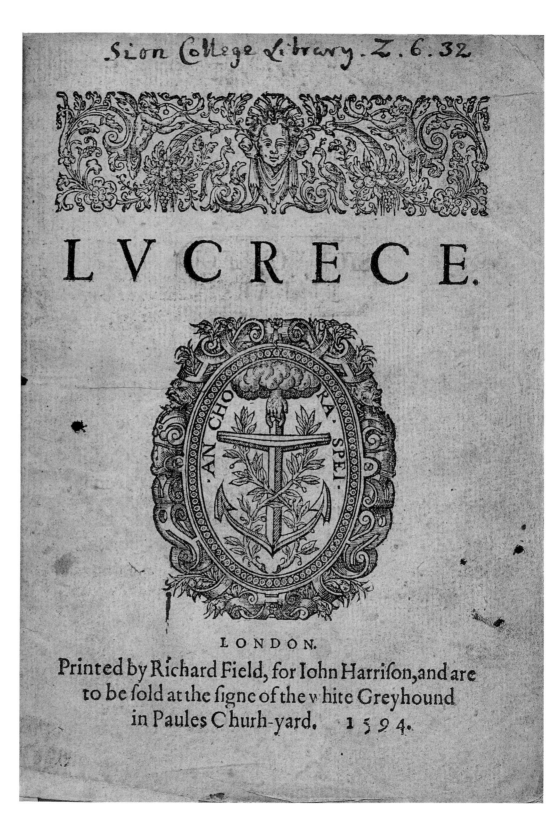

William Shakespeare
Lucrece, first edition,
Richard Field for John
Harrison, London, 1594
New York $561,000
(£342,073). 1.V.90
From the library of
H. Bradley Martin

Lucrece is Shakespeare's
third published work,
preceded only by *Venus
and Adonis*, 1593, of
which the only known
copy is in the Bodleian
Library, and by *Titus
Andronicus*, published
earlier in 1594, of which
the only copy known
is in the Folger
Shakespeare Library.

Fig. 1
William Shakespeare
Comedies, Histories, and Tragedies, a complete set of the four Folios; the First, London, 1623; the Second, London, 1632; the Third, London, 1664; the Fourth, London, 1685; bound in fine crimson levant and morocco gilt
New York $2,090,000 (£1,322,785). 9.XI.89
From the collection of The Garden Ltd

The power to move us:
the collection of The Garden Ltd

Jay Dillon

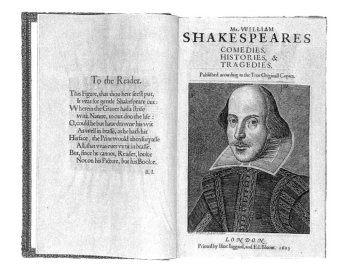

No other sale in memory had contained so many books that touched so many hearts so easily. It was truly remarkable that such a wonderful library should have been assembled in only fifteen years, and the sale in November 1989, when the books and manuscripts were passed to their new owners, was a memorable event. Conceived and collected by Haven O'More, and funded by Michael Davis, both of Cambridge, Massachusetts, the collection of The Garden Ltd had as its goal nothing less than to illustrate the whole history of ideas by gathering together the world's greatest and most influential books, in their first and finest forms. Haven O'More himself, in his preface to the catalogue *On the Mystery of the Book*, called these the 'great or supreme works of the mind'.

The sale comprised 309 lots ranging from a Japanese manuscript *sutra* dated AD 730, to Albert Camus' corrected proofs of *The Plague*, and from a magnificent classical text printed on vellum in 1471 and illuminated by the Putti Master, to another illustrated by Braque, in a lovely mosaic binding by Renée Haas in 1964.

The library was designed from the outset as a collection of 'high spots', and so the sale became almost a litany of superlative books – a papyrus scroll from the Egyptian Book of the Dead; the complete book of Daniel from the Gutenberg Bible; Darwin's *On the Origin of Species*; the diaries of Vaslav Nijinsky, still largely unpublished – and superlative prices. The library's greatest glory was its collection of literature. The first edition of the *Divine Comedy* (1472), the foundation of Italian literature and the greatest of all Italian books, was sold to a Dutch library for $198,000. This was the first copy to be sold at auction in America for forty years and its price was constrained only by the want of thirteen leaves. In early German literature, the first edition of the medieval epic *Parzival* (1477) fetched $209,000 going to the same Dutch library, and the first edition of Luther's Bible went to a New York collector and bookseller

EL INGENIOSO
HIDALGO DON QVI-
XOTE DE LA MANCHA,

Compueſto por Miguel de Ceruantes
Saauedra.

DIRIGIDO AL DVQVE DE BEIAR,
Marques de Gibraleon, Conde de Benalcaçar, y Baña-
res, Vizconde de la Puebla de Alcozer, Señor de
las villas de Capilla, Curiel, y
Burguillos.

Año,   1605.

CON PRIVILEGIO,
EN *MADRID*, Por Iuan de la Cueſta.

Vendeſe en caſa de Franciſco de Robles, librero del Rey nſo ſeñor.

for $352,000. But the greatest surprise was the Spanish literature, including the exceedingly rare first edition of *Don Quixote* (1605–15), from the library of John Pierpont Morgan (Fig. 2), which was hotly contested by booksellers and private collectors alike, finally going to Quaritch of London, for $1.65 million.

The English literature, too, was of the first quality, and included the third and earliest obtainable edition of Surrey's *Songes and Sonettes* (1557), known as Tottell's *Miscellany*, often cited as 'the beginning of modern English verse'; *The Booke of Common Prayer* (1549), a fine copy of the first edition in a contemporary London binding; and the first printing of the King James Bible (1611) in a contemporary red morocco binding. It was no surprise that Shakespeare shone brightest of all. The 1619 quarto edition of *A Midsommer Nights Dreame*, a relic of the first attempt to produce a collected issue of Shakespeare's plays, brought $110,000. And an exceptionally fine and complete set of the four Folios (Fig. 1) – 'incomparably the most important work in the English language' and together the greatest books ever printed in English – was sold to a New York collector (bidding against a Japanese collector) for $2.09 million. The famous Lamport Hall copy of Milton's *Paradise Lost* (1667), preserved in its original calf binding, was acquired by a private collector for $256,000, and one of the greatest English literary manuscripts still in private hands – John Locke's autograph manuscript first draft of *An Essay Concerning Human Understanding* (1671–1700) – went to the same collector for $907,500 (Fig. 4). An exceptionally fine copy of Johnson's *Dictionary* (1755), untrimmed in the original marbled boards, went to a London bookseller for $66,000. One of only three known copies of the first complete issue of Blake's *Songs of Innocence and of Experience* excited some of the strongest competition, being sold at $1.32 million.

American literature was represented notably by the first edition of *Moby Dick* (still called *The Whale*, and published in London) and the first edition of *Leaves of Grass*, in its original green cloth binding. Modern literature was represented by Yeats's first book, a slim pamphlet called *Mosada*, and the corrected typescript of the opening episode of *Finnegans Wake*. The lasting power of these great works of art was matched only by the masterpieces of science in the collection. These ranged from the esoteric – for example, a Ramon Lull manuscript from the early fifteenth century – to the most celebrated triumphs of scientific insight and investigation. These included the first edition of the first printed book on biology, Aristotle's treatise *De animalibus*, printed in 1476; the 1478 edition of Ptolemy's *Geography*; the first edition of Euclid; the first printed announcement of Copernicus's heliocentric theory (Fig. 3); an extraordinary association copy of Gilbert's classic *De magnete*, and Newton's *Principia*. Closely related to these, and yet in a class of its own, was the extraordinary presentation copy of Thomas Jefferson's *Notes on the State of Virginia* (1785), inscribed by Jefferson at length to Georges-Louis Leclerc, Comte de Buffon.

In the catalogue, the main body of the collection was arranged in roughly chronological order, in order to emphasize some of the historical relationships at work among these 'great or supreme works of the mind.' These were followed by the private-press books, which included one of the finest copies known of the Kelmscott Chaucer, printed on paper and lavishly bound for T. J. Cobden-Sanderson; the Ashendene *Dante*; the Doves Bible and the Cranach Press *Hamlet* all printed on vellum. The catalogue itself is a monument, hailed by *The Spectator* as 'one of the most interesting books published this year'.

The collection of The Garden Ltd realized $16.22 million over two days – a record total that is likely to stand for many years.

Fig. 2
Miguel de Cervantes Saavedra
El ingenioso hidalgo don Quixote de la Mancha, first edition, two volumes, Juan de la Cuesta for Francisco de Robles, Madrid, 1605–15, 7¼in by 5in (18.5cm by 12.8cm)
New York $1,650,000 (£1,044,304). 9.XI.89
From the collection of The Garden Ltd

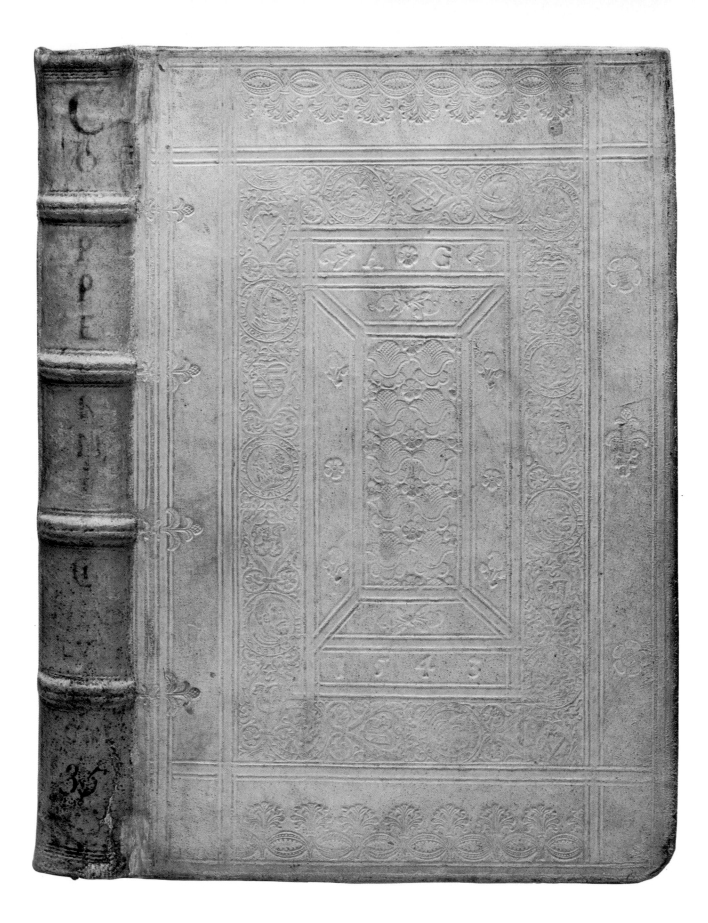

¶ Cristianus ad solitariū quendam de ymagine mundi · Honorio ꝫ

Eptiformi spiritu in trina fi-
de illustrato ac septemis ri-
uis trifarie philosophie in-
undato · post septimonam
huius vite · septem beatitu-
dīnibꝫ laureari · & in octa-
ua trinitatem in vnitate cō-
templari · Quia cū ignoran-
tibꝫ ignorantie tenebris inuoluor · idcirco me stam
lugubremꝗ uitam ut cecꝰ ducere uideor · Quare ·
quia te immēsa sapieutia circumfulsum cognosco ·
Cum alỹs multis deposco · quatinꝰ aliquam scinti-
llam tue flamminee scientie cum tibi nō minuatur ·
nobis impartiaris & positionē orbis quasi i tabella
nobis desczibas · Miserum ēm uidet · ꝗꝓ nos res
factas ꝗtidie spectare · cum iumentis insipientibꝫ
quid sint penitꝰ ignorare

¶ · Prologus de ymagine mundi · Honoriꝰ ꝫ

Apientie alūno abdita diligenter
scrutanti · i scientie ꝓfundo utri-
usꝗ homīs salute nō vigere & pꝰ
in sỹon dñi in ꝗ omnes thesauri
sapiētie & scientie sunt abscōditi
oculo ad oculum videre · Cū igit
lectiom studiosius incubas ac totius scripture me-
dullam sitibūdus exigas poscis a me amicissime · ut
quemadmodum vulgo dicitur · ꝗp ouis a capra pe-

The George Abrams Collection

The catalogue of the George Abrams Collection of books of the fifteenth and sixteenth centuries was widely acclaimed as one of the finest that Sotheby's has ever produced, and remains as a splendid record of this library. It is unique in that it was printed in a typeface designed specifically for it by the collector George Abrams himself – a calligrapher and graphic designer by profession. 'Abrams Venetian' is a particularly legible and graceful typeface modelled on those of the earliest European presses, many very fine examples of whose work were included in this sale. The accompanying italic type, modelled on typefaces used by the sixteenth-century Italian typographer Lodovico Arrighi, is unusually beautiful. William Morris was perhaps the first to appreciate the simplicity of these earliest books and the highly successful solutions they provided to design problems still encountered by the modern typographer.

It is therefore fitting that the highlight of this sale should have been a book which had been (in a different copy) William Morris's first significant acquisition – Boccaccio's *De claris mulieribus* (Fig. 1), printed at Ulm in 1473 – one of the finest illustrated German books of the fifteenth century. Of this book Morris wrote that it was 'perhaps the first . . . that gave me a clear insight into the essential qualities of the medieval design of the period'. The Abrams copy of this work represents the only complete copy of the first issue of this book known to exist with a variant colophon. It was bound together with what was probably the first book to be printed by the great Nuremberg printer, Anton Koberger, and with a Bolognese manuscript of Cicero, *De officiis* (*circa* 1464). It is also a particularly fine, unpressed copy with deep type impressions and margins wider even than those of the William Morris copy, now in the Pierpont Morgan Library.

Owing to their particularly fine state of preservation, many other books in the collection provide important bibliographical information. Several copies escaped subsequent pressing, sometimes even preserving the blind impress of bearer type, which in one case casts light on the order of composition of the type pages. Many fifteenth-century books were undated by the printer and dated rubrications can be invaluable to help us ascertain the date of printing. Undated editions of two works by pseudo-Albertus Magnus, *Mariale* and *De laudibus mariae*, printed and issued together by Johann Mentelin at Strassburg, were traditionally dated before 1474 on the basis of copies of these works in Paris and Munich with rubrication or purchase dates of 1474. The Abrams copy, however, bears a rubrication date of 1473 (see Fig. 3), thereby advancing the date of this edition by a year to not after 1473. Even when the book is dated by the printer, inscriptions by the rubricator or early owners can give us helpful insights into the trade and distribution of books in the fifteenth century. For example, a copy of the Constitutions of Clement V, printed in Mainz in 1471,

·J·e·A·3·

·Petrp apiyenstein e liber ste··
La 9. ecclie sti Stephani. Azgont·
Et emit ingemicolaus a dnm
gevma affectictario i augentina
que oreth den pa

was in the possession of Johann Kaltenmarkter in Vienna in 1473. Kaltenmarkter, a leading figure in the Faculty of Law at the University of Vienna in the late fifteenth and early sixteenth centuries, wrote extensive biographical notes on the endleaves of this book and also recorded the date of purchase together with the prices of the book, the binding and the illumination.

Even without explicit inscriptions, there is much evidence of the distribution of books to be gained from the study of bindings and illumination. Several books in the George Abrams Collection were in contemporary bindings that indicate a widespread trade. A copy of Balbus's *Catholicon*, printed in Strassburg not later than 1475 was bound in a contemporary Viennese binding of calf; a Venetian imprint, *Rosarium decretorum* by Baysio (1481; Fig. 4), was bound in calf by a contemporary anonymous Cologne workshop; the second volume of another Venetian imprint, Appianus's *Historia romana* (1477), was bound in contemporary calf which has been localised specifically to St Georgenberg (for manuscript see Fig. 5). Illumination can be equally informative: a Venetian edition of Ovid's works of 1474 was illuminated and rubricated in the Flemish style, very similar to the manuscripts collected by Raphael de Mercatellis, abbot of St Bavo, Ghent. The Pierpont Morgan Library copy of this work was decorated in the same shop as the Abrams copy. This would indicate that a portion of the Venetian edition was marketed in Flanders.

Several of the books in the collection are particularly finely illuminated, perhaps the best being the copy of Cicero's *Tusculanae quaestiones*, printed by the great Venetian printer Nicolaus Jenson in 1472, with five initials (for one, see Fig. 2) illuminated with great delicacy by the famous anonymous artist the Maestro de Putti, who worked during the 1460s and 1470s and specialized in illuminating Venetian incunables for leading patrician families of the city.

Finally, George Abrams owned several very fine illustrated books such as the splendid copy of Nider's *Die vierundzwanzig goldenen Harfen*, printed in Augsburg in 1478 and bound in a contemporary Augsburg binding, with two magnificent large woodcuts of the *Coronation of the Virgin* (Fig. 6) and *King David playing the Harp*, both brightly coloured by a contemporary hand. Other fine illustrated books included an unpressed copy of Hroswitha's *Opera*, printed in Nuremberg in 1501 and containing two unsigned woodcuts by Albrecht Dürer, and a copy of the 1501 Nuremberg edition of Aesop's *Fables* illustrated with 335 lively woodcuts, from the library of Augustus Frederick, Duke of Sussex, the son of George III.

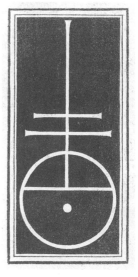

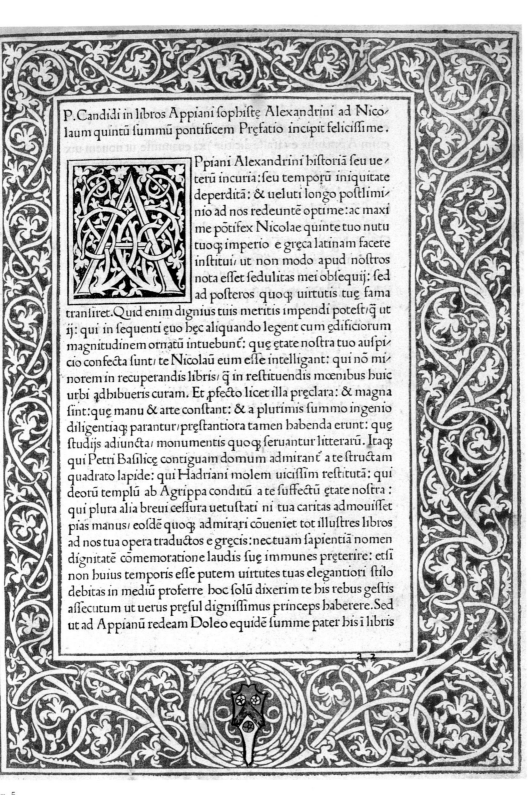

Opposite
Fig. 6
Johannes Nider
Die vierundzwanzig goldenen Harfen, fourth edition, second with illustrations, contemporary Augsburg leather binding, Johann Bämler, Augsburg, 25th September 1478
London £79,200 ($132,264). 16.XI.89
From the George Abrams Collection

Fig. 5
Appianus
Historia romana; De bellis civilibus, first complete edition, 2 volumes, contemporary calf binding, Bernhard Maler, Erhard Ratdolt and Peter Löslein, Venice, 1477
London £22,000 ($36,740). 16.XI.89
From the George Abrams Collection

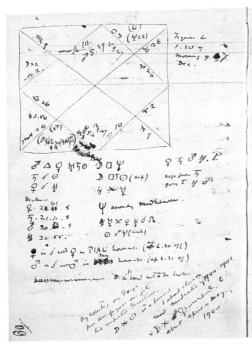

Marcel Proust
Du côté de chez Swann, first edition, signed, inscribed to
Anatole France on the half-title, N.R.F., Paris, 1914
Monte Carlo FF444,000 (£42,286:$68,308). 17.X.89
From the library of H. Bradley Martin

T. E. Lawrence
Seven Pillars of Wisdom, an autograph manuscript with
revisions by Lawrence for the subscribers' edition of 1926
London £39,600 ($67,320). 14.XII.89
From the collection of the late D. G. Hogarth

William Butler Yeats
An autograph manuscript
journal recording Yeats's
dream life and his visions
(some induced by mescaline)
and describing his spiritual
marriage to Maud Gonne,
two volumes, signed,
11th July 1898 to 31st
March 1902
London £59,400 ($115,236).
19.VII.90

Sir Arthur Conan Doyle
The Valley of Fear, an autograph manuscript of the Sherlock Holmes story, 1913–14
New York $286,000 (£167,251). 15.VI.90
From the collection of Dr James Bliss Austin

The Valley of Fear stands as one of Doyle's longer tales completed in his later years. It first
appeared in *The Strand Magazine* from September 1914 to May 1915. The same sale featured
a copy of the first appearance of Holmes in Doyle's *A Study in Scarlet* ($57,200:£33,450) in the
1887 *Beeton's Christmas Annual*.

Robert Schumann
An autograph manuscript of the piano concerto in A minor, Op. 54, the full score of the complete work, with autograph title-page, the first and last movements signed and dated *Dresden den 29sten Juli 1845 R. Schumann* and *Dresden den 12ten Juli 184[5] R. Schumann*, the 'Intermezzo' and 'Finale' also dated *['Intermezzo'] d. 14 Juli [18]45', ['Finale'] d. 21 Juni [18]45*; working manuscript, with numerous alterations, revisions, deletions, erasures and corrections by the composer in brown ink, pencil and brown crayon, 192 pages
London £880,000 ($1,460,800). 22.XI.89

Robert Schumann: the autograph manuscript of the piano concerto in A minor Op.54

Stephen Roe

Schumann's piano concerto is undoubtedly one of the greatest examples of the form after Beethoven, and holds a secure and much-loved place in the repertoire of many of the world's finest pianists. Although Schumann attempted to write piano concertos at several stages of his life, and indeed completed two other concertante works for piano and orchestra, the A minor work alone is dignified with the title 'Concerto'. The autograph manuscript is the only known early source for the concerto – no preliminary sketches appear to have survived – and as such is of the utmost importance in our understanding of one of Schumann's most profoundly beautiful compositions.

Schumann began work on the first movement in 1841. At this time he clearly only envisaged a one-movement *Phantasie* corresponding more or less to the first movement of the concerto. In 1845 he was persuaded by his publisher to add two further movements – an 'Intermezzo' and final 'Rondo' – to complete the work that we know today. The manuscript shows the reworking of the first movement, documenting the change in Schumann's ideas from the original *Phantasie* to concerto first movement, in the addition of an orchestral ritornello and in making alterations to the scoring, the piano writing and minor structural details. The 'Rondo' was composed next and the 'Intermezzo' last. Schumann evidently had great difficulty in linking these second and third movements, to judge from the number of reworkings of the transition passage between these sections. It is instructive to note that Schumann evidently at one time deleted much of this wonderful transition, one of the most magical passages in the work.

Although the manuscript is predominantly in Schumann's hand, much of the piano part of the first movement was written out by a copyist. Schumann did, however, heavily alter and annotate the copyist's transcription. Close study of the manuscript revealed another hand, that of Clara Schumann, the composer's wife, his chief inspiration and the first performer of the work. She had evidently assisted her husband in the virtually mechanical task of writing out repeated material in all three movements. Very occasionally she had corrected a passage or added a missing clef here and there. The similarity of the handwritings of husband and wife had misled previous scholars into believing that the manuscript was almost entirely in Schumann's hand, and the presence of Clara's notation can be claimed as an interesting and intriguing discovery.

PLATE CCXXVI

Hooping Crane. GRUS AMERICANA. *Adult Male.*

Turkey and the library of Henry Myron Blackmer II

David Park

The Greeks have been devoted book collectors for generations, and for the origin of their relationship to London one has to look no further than Joannes Gennadius (1844–1932) and the library in Athens that bears his name. Gennadius spent sixty years in England, much of the time as an accredited diplomat, and formed a collection of Greek printing and other books embracing every aspect of Hellenic interest. Despite a sale of duplicates at Sotheby's in 1891, and a more serious sale in 1895 when financial pressures mounted, his library remains unrivalled in its field and one of the treasures of modern Athens. One of the Gennadius Library's loyal supporters was Harry Blackmer, an American who made his home in Athens for thirty years. For him book collecting became an abiding passion, and as an outsider his collecting was not restricted by any of the regional considerations that tend to affect collections formed in the Eastern Mediterranean. Most people, and perhaps the collector himself, regarded his library as one relating to Greece against a wider backdrop of the Ottoman Empire. Given the size of the collection even the subsidiary themes qualified as collections in their own right.

Pre-eminent among these was that relating to Constantinople and modern Turkey. The Blackmer Collection provided a rare opportunity to see something of the potential for the growing number of Turkish collectors, especially bearing in mind that for Blackmer it was a secondary theme. The earliest group of watercolours in Blackmer's collection was a series of Turkish costumes with German captions (Fig. 1), paralleled by another in the Gennadius Library, dated to around 1573.

There was a vast European literature on the Ottomans, thanks not least to the fact that the fall of Byzantine Constantinople in 1453 almost coincided with the first printed book (1455). For the next century-and-a-half, the Sultans threatened Christendom with armies that penetrated as far as Vienna, swallowing up medieval Christian kingdoms and principalities in their path. At sea, the Ottoman navy conquered the Aegean, threw the Knights of St John out of Rhodes, captured Cyprus and later Crete, and beseiged Malta on more than one occasion. In addition, pirates from ports at least nominally under the Sultan's suzerainty ravaged shipping from beyond Gibraltar to Aleppo, Christian captives being sold into slavery.

From this sprang a tremendous literature of hate, a little appreciation, reports of victories and disasters, and 'background' books catering for the fascination that went hand-in-hand with the dread. Turkishness found its way into Elizabethan and Jacobean literature, not least Shakespeare, and Marlowe's play *Tamburlaine*, recounting the story of Sultan Bayezid I. Perhaps most interesting of all are the accounts of

Fig. 1
A series of eight watercolour drawings depicting costumes of Constantinople, some heightened with white and gold, captioned in German, Constantinople, late sixteenth century
London £28,050 ($46,563). 11.X.89
From the library of Henry M. Blackmer II

merchants and diplomats who actually lived within the Empire and had first-hand knowledge of Ottoman customs and court life. Printing in Turkish did not commence until the eighteenth century, and even then was rather limited in its scope. There is a rich Turkish literature, particularly in poetry, but the Ottomans were not ones to encourage individuals to pen (let alone publish) independent observations of a social or political nature. Therefore the accounts as seen through Christian eyes, notwithstanding prejudices and misunderstandings, are a vital resource in reconstructing a view of Turkey's history.

The part played by the English in producing this record was a modest one until well into the reign of Elizabeth I. In the second half of the sixteenth century England obtained the commodities of the Orient from Antwerp, which was linked to the seaborne trade of the Portuguese to India and the Far East, via the Cape of Good Hope. Trouble brewing in the Netherlands from the 1560s onwards cast doubts over the wisdom of relying on Antwerp, however, and kindled an interest in trade with the Ottoman Empire, the last stop before Europe overland from the East.

The growth of this interest in Turkey could be traced through the Blackmer Library, from the end of the sixteenth century with the foundation of the English Levant Company. The Queen supported the attempts of London merchants to secure *capitulations* (rights to trade and freedom of passage) for English merchants within the Sultan's realms. Such *capitulations*, a system inherited by the Ottomans from Byzantine Constantinople, were already possessed by the French and Venetians, whose ambassadors (the Venetian always being titled the *Bailo*) sought to keep the newcomers out. Nevertheless in 1581, Elizabeth for her part granted an exclusive right to a group of London merchants to trade with Turkey for seven years. This was the first of several such grants and, later, charters, and marks the beginning of the Levant company. One William Harborne was sent to Constantinople where, with the requisite degree of flamboyance and self-confidence, he secured the rights required, aided by a skilful deployment of gifts. As the Company's chief appointee in Constantinople he was also the English ambassador, and this close connection between the Company and the Crown remained until the winding up of the former in 1824. The Company had to adjust to the custom of paying sweeteners (locally styled *avianas*) for the business to prosper, notwithstanding the theoretical protections and freedoms set out in the *capitulations*. The pashas saw European merchants (*giaours*) as fair game and required payments for business transacted through their provinces. At sea there was piracy to contend with, but English complaints in this regard were complicated by the presence of English *corsairs* whose reputation was quite as bad as any from harbours under the control of the Porte. Despite these obstacles, trade triumphed, with leather one of the major imports to England.

Harborne and the men who followed him were products of the 'enterprise culture' that began during the reign of Elizabeth I. Ambassadors were quite as keen on the creation of wealth through trade as the merchants themselves. Many were members of companies, or were involved in colonization schemes, and the Crown itself always had some sort of stake in new commercial ventures. A whole class of new men was driven by that first-generation will to succeed. They were determined, tough, colourful, flamboyant characters, perfect for a posting like Constantinople, where a man was judged on his costumes, jewels and personal style.

Appropriately, the earliest account of Turkey by an Englishman in the Blackmer Collection was attributed to an ambassador, Giles Fletcher. Giles was not an envoy

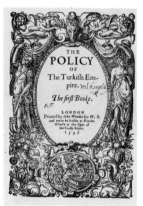

Fig. 2
Giles Fletcher
The Policy of the Turkish Empire, The first Booke, first edition, John Windet for W.Stansby, London, 1597
London £12,100 ($20,086). 11.X.89
From the library of Henry M. Blackmer II

Fig. 3
Anthony Nixon
The Three English Brothers, John Hodgets, London, 1607
London £6,600 ($10,956). 11.X.89
From the library of Henry M. Blackmer II

to the Porte, but to Russia, where he served from 1588 to 1589. His *Policy of the Turkish Empire* (1597; Fig. 2), is marked by its lack of prejudice, which is surprising since he viewed Turkey from a nation, who, following the fall of Constantinople, regarded herself as the saviour of Christian Orthodoxy and the avowed enemy of the Ottomans. The Blackmer Library also contained an account by Richard Knolles (*circa* 1550–1610) who never visited Turkey, but who produced the classic description of the Empire in his *Generall historie of the Turks*, first published in 1603. The reputation of his prose was great enough to be commended by Samuel Johnson years later.

The first account in the Blackmer Collection of an actual visit to Turkey was *The Three English Brothers* (1607; Fig. 3), which recounts the adventures in the Middle East of Sir Anthony, Robert and Sir Thomas Sherley, a trio whose picaresque careers demonstrated that being a bit of a rogue was no handicap in those days. Indeed, the latter of the three was one of those English pirates who so embarrassed the Levant Company in its efforts to obtain redress from the Porte. A bungled attempt to plunder the Aegean island of Milo found him captured by its inhabitants, from where he was taken as a prisoner to Constantinople. His problems were multiplied by the Porte's knowledge that his brother Robert had served with distinction in the Imperial armies fighting the Turks, while Sir Anthony had been sent to Persia by the Earl of Essex and had persuaded the Shah Abbas to agree to an alliance with European states against Turkey. Sir Thomas was lucky to be released after three years as the result of a letter sent from James I to the Grand Signor, delivered by the then ambassador Henry Lello.

The first Scot in print on the subject of Turkey was William Lithgow. His account of Greece, Crete, Chios, and Turkey proper, is enlivened with details of coffee-drinking, Turkish baths and the pigeon post from Aleppo to Baghdad. That he, like all the other successful Britons in this earliest phase of contact, was almost as exotic as the Turks themselves, is shown in the woodcut illustrating his *Totall Discourse* (Fig. 4), where he is depicted in stylish Ottoman garb.

The struggle between Parliament and Charles I had a knock-on effect for the English at Constantinople. The ambassador from 1638 was Sir Sackville Crowe, an ardent Royalist whose estates in England were seized by Parliament. His revenge on the English at Constantinople and Smyrna is detailed in an anonymous pamphlet *Subtility and Cruelty: or a true relation of the horrible and unparalleled abuses . . . by Sir Sacville Crow* (1646), when he proceeded to confiscate all the English property he could lay hands on. The King was persuaded to recall him and confirmed Sir Thomas Bendysh as his replacement. By the time Bendysh reached Constantinople he found Crowe, still in the city, had already discredited him with the Turks. Officials at the Porte, seeing the opportunity, made Bendysh pay heavily before he was recognized as ambassador. Crowe was then forcibly removed to London and the Tower, where he remained until 1656. All this is described by 'W.L' in *Newes from Turkie* (1648).

After 1650, the number of works by Englishmen in the library seems to increase. In 1650 James Howell added an appendix for travellers in Turkey and the Levant, to his *Instructions and directions for forren travell*, and three years later Robert Withers gave a description of the Seraglio.

At the end of the century (1687–91) Sir William Trumbull (1639–1716) was appointed to Constantinople. Two months after the sale of the Blackmer Collection, the Marquess of Downshire sold his large diplomatic correspondence to the Nation, as part of the wider Trumbull Papers archive (see pages 16–18). Travel books from

Fig. 4
William Lithgow
The Totall Discourse, of the Rare Adventures and Painefull Peregrinations of long nineteene yeares Travailes from Scotland, to the most famous Kingdomes in Europe, Asia and Affrica, second edition, contemporary calf binding, J. Okes, London, 1640
London £2,090 ($3,469). 11.X.89
From the library of Henry M. Blackmer II

the same library were offered later, including one of Sir Paul Rycaut's histories with annotations by Trumbull (Rycaut was also one of Trumbull's correspondents), as was the dedication copy of Pido de Saint-Olon's *Present State of the Empire of Morocco* (1695).

    The contrast between the first ambassadors to Turkey and those in place at the end of the eighteenth century reflects not only the changing times, but also changing fortunes. At the Porte, however, the *Recueil des différents costumes . . . de la Porte* (1775; Fig. 5), shows that the earlier splendour of its costumes was undiminished. The men who filled diplomatic posts at the outbreak of the Napoleonic Wars came from families whose position and wealth were now the result of the accretions of several generations. A preoccupation with the creation of wealth had given way to aristocratic pursuits, chief among which were the study and collecting of antiquities. Sir Robert Ainslie, ambassador from 1775 until 1794, was a numismatist, and amassed a vast collection. He also commissioned Luigi Mayer to paint a series of watercolours illustrating views and costumes throughout the Ottoman Empire. These were later engraved and published in London to great acclaim, helped no doubt by the public awareness that they illustrated Syria, Palestine and Egypt where British arms, in support of the Sultan, had had the better of Napoleon. These books were included in Blackmer's collection, while the original watercolours were also sold this year. From the same era, and reflecting continuing British interest in the Turks, this time as allies, comes Young's *Series of Portraits of the Emperors of Turkey* (1808; Fig. 6), with a magnificent series of 30 mezzotints printed in colours.

    Five years after Ainslie left Constantinople, Thomas, Earl of Elgin was appointed to the posting. His collecting was of a much more massive kind than Ainslie's coins, and by no means limited to modern Greece. His consummate good taste led him to make an audacious purchase, enviable by the fashion of the times, that will ensure he remains the best-known of all British ambassadors to the Sublime Porte.

Fig. 5
Recueil des différents costumes des principaux officiers et magistrats de la Porte, first edition, 96 plates in gouache heightened with silver and gold, some signed *Juillet* after Pitre, contemporary marbled calf gilt binding, Onfroy, Paris, 1775
London £60,500 ($100,430). 11.X.89
From the library of Henry M. Blackmer II

Fig. 6
John Young
A Series of Portraits of the Emperors of Turkey, from the foundation of the monarchy to the year 1808, first edition,
with 30 hand-finished colour plates, contemporary half morocco binding, William Bulmer & Co.,
London, 1815
London £24,200 ($40,172). 12.X.89
From the library of Henry M. Blackmer II

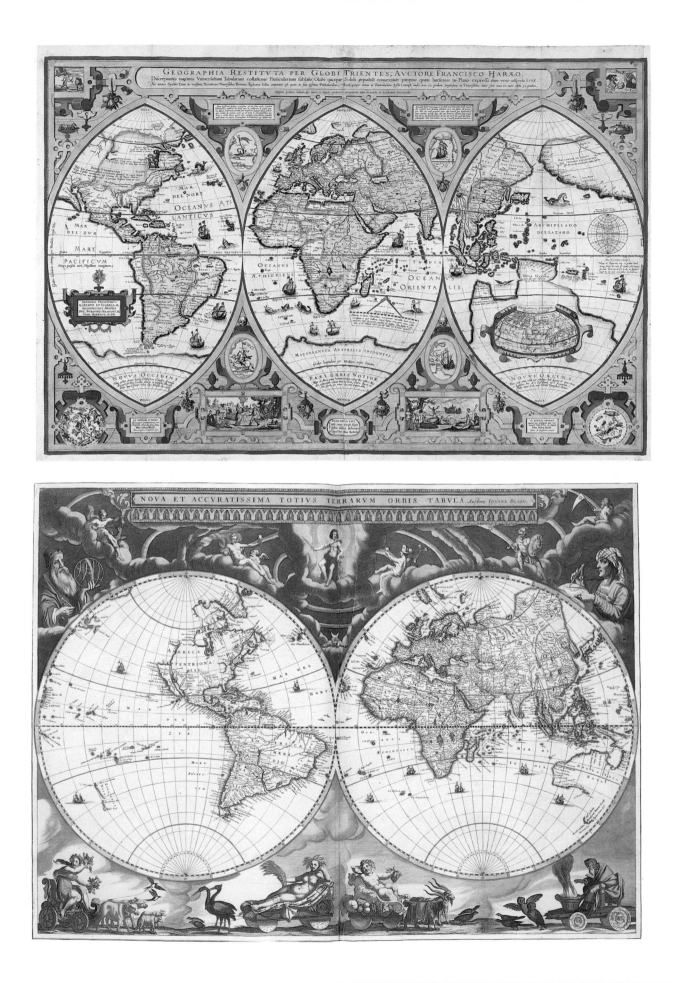

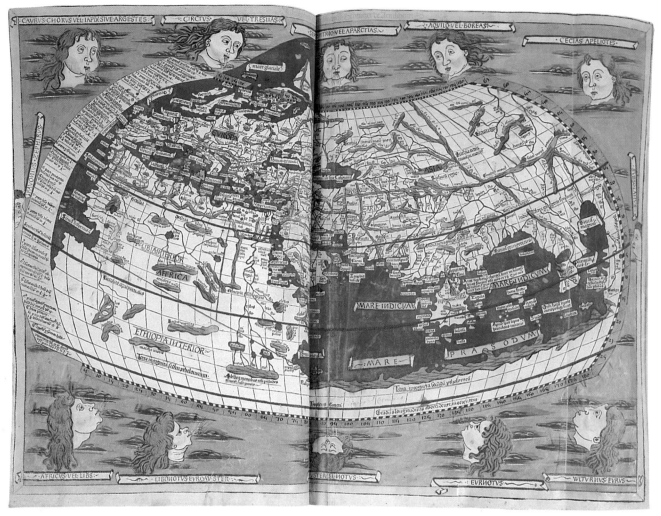

Ptolemy
Cosmographia, translated by Jacobus Angelus, cartography by Dom Nicolaus Germanus, printed on
vellum with contemporary hand-colouring, including 32 full-sheet wood-cut maps, Lienhart Holle,
Ulm, 16th July 1482
New York $1,925,000 (£1,125,731). 14.VI.90
From the library of H. Bradley Martin

Opposite, above
Frans Verhaer
Geographia restituta per globi trientes, a triptych-style world map on two sheets, engraved by Boëtius Adam
van Bolswert, with contemporary hand-colouring, Antwerp, *circa* 1614
London £26,400 ($43,824). 7.XII.89

Below
Johannes Blaeu
Cosmographia Blaviana, first complete edition, 11 volumes, Latin text, 597 engraved maps, plans, views
and plates, frontispieces heightened with gold and with contemporary hand-colouring, Amsterdam, 1662
London £110,000 ($200,200). 21.VI.90

Manuscripts

The Durbar of Nawab Muhammad Bahawal Khan of Bahawalpur, gouache on canvas, with *nasta'liq*
inscriptions naming each figure, by Muhammad Bakhsh and his son Karim Bakhsh, signed and dated
AH 1263/AD 1851, 30in by 48in (76.3cm by 122cm)
London £26,400 ($45,936). 26.IV.90
From the collection of the late Marquess of Dalhousie, Colstoun, East Lothian

Among those being received by Nawab Muhammad Bahawal Khan is a European, identified
as Captain Macpherson. The work may well have been among gifts presented by the Nawab
to Lord Dalhousie during his governorship of the Punjab.

Two from a compendium of six imperial edicts relating to the land granted by Süleyman the Magnificent to his Chief White Eunuch, Ibrahim Agha, each headed by an illuminated tughra, issued at Constantinople and Edirne, *circa* AH 944–48/AD 1537–41, 27 leaves, contemporary red morocco and gilt binding, 10½in by 6⅞in (26.7cm by 17.5cm)
London £63,800 ($105,908). 13.X.89

Opposite
Qur'an, Arabic manuscript on paper, signed by Hamdullah, better known as Ibn al-Shaykh, contemporary red morocco and gilt binding, Ottoman, *circa* 1515, 8¼in by 5½in (21cm by 14cm)
London £297,000 ($516,780). 26.IV.90

سورة فاتحة الكتاب

بِسْمِ اللهِ الرَّحْمٰنِ الرَّحِيمِ
الْحَمْدُ لِلّٰهِ رَبِّ الْعَالَمِينَ الرَّحْمٰنِ الرَّحِيمِ
مَالِكِ يَوْمِ الدِّينِ اِيَّاكَ نَعْبُدُ وَاِيَّاكَ
نَسْتَعِينُ اِهْدِنَا الصِّرَاطَ الْمُسْتَقِيمَ
صِرَاطَ الَّذِينَ اَنْعَمْتَ عَلَيْهِمْ غَيْرِ
الْمَغْضُوبِ عَلَيْهِمْ وَلَا الضَّالِّينَ

وَهِيَ سَبْعُ آيَاتٍ مَكِّيَّةٌ

الظلف لتمّ به حاجة المشي والبلاغ فسبحان من أعطى كلّ شيء ما يحتاج اليه دون الزيادة والنقصان
ولذلك كان بعض ما يتعلق بأصناف الدوابّ إن شاء الله تعالى وهو الموفق للصواب

فــرس

من أواحش الحيوانات بعد الإنسان صنعة وأشدّ الدوابّ عقلاً وذكاءً وأحلاً
محموده وأخلاق مرضيّة من ذلك حسن صورته وتناسب أجزائه وأعضائه وصفاء لونه وسرعة عدوه
وحسن طاعته لفارسه كيف شاء أفاده له ومن الخيل ما يقال له خوكان وهو الفرس الذي يلعب على ظهر
الكرة فلا يحتاج الراكب أن يصرفه فإنّه لا يزال بعينيه إلى الكرة كلما دارت الكرة تعدو خلفها

من الخيل ما يمرّ به صاحبه فلا يملك عنه من ركوبه ومن الخيل ما المحمود الطلق حتى يهتدى راكبها
السبق ... محمد بن النبي الكلبي أن الصافنات المعروضة على سليمان عليه السلام كانت ألف فرس وردها
ظهرت الله فلما أعرض عليه وقت صلاة العصر حتى توارت بالحجاب وهي الأفراس أعرض عليها فقد عقله
سهم من الأرض وكانوا أصابه فلما أرادوا الرجوع قال ولا بأن الله أبدلنا أيضاً ناسعة أجود من الأول فلما
إليها فأعطاهم عطاءً ونال من تلك الخيل قال إذا أردتم من لكم غلاماً واحطوا فإنّكم لا تورثوا نار الأوقد
أن يطعم فنادوا بالفرس وكان للأمير عليه ما لكي أن وصلوا الكلام وعوا ذلك الفرس ذاك
الكاتب فذكر هذا أن خيول العرب من نتاجه أسماها خمسة أخرى نسبة يشدلي القيم ذات أسناد

An illustrated copy of al-Qazwīnī's *The Wonders of Creation*

Stefano Carboni and Anna Contadini

Fig. 2
Two Hares, from *ʿAjāʾib al-makhlūqāt wa gharaʾib al-mawjudat*, folio 72 *recto*.

The appearance on the market of a hitherto unrecorded illustrated manuscript must always be welcomed, especially when the codex belongs to a period of Islamic miniature painting – the thirteenth and fourteenth centuries – which is certainly not the most prolific in terms of extant works.

This is indeed the case with the *ʿAjāʾib al-makhlūqāt* sold last April, whose importance both for the history of Mamluk miniature painting, and for the history of Arabic literature, is outstanding. A general analysis of the paintings, the calligraphic style, and the quality of paper and ink, leaves little doubt that the manuscript was copied and illustrated in a Mamluk atelier during the first half of the fourteenth century.

The codex is fragmentary and contains about one third of the text originally composed by its author, Zakariyā ibn Muḥammad ibn Maḥmūd al-Qazwīnī, in about 1270 at Wasit, near Baghdad. Al-Qazwīnī was a *qadi* (judge) under Mongol rule here, and the book is dedicated to ʿAṭā Malik al-Juwaynī who was governor of the region at the time. Its full title, *ʿAjāʾib al-makhlūqāt wa gharaʾib al-mawjudat* can be translated as *The Wonders of Creation and the Oddities of Existence*. The work is a 'cosmography', a literary genre which became popular in the thirteenth century, and which attempts to sum up the scientific knowledge of the period. According to the extant Arabic sources, al-Qazwīnī most probably was the first writer to collect a résumé of previous literature on the book's subjects, and incorporate it in an encyclopaedic work, organizing the description of plants and animals in alphabetical order. His cosmography summarizes literature on astronomy, geography, botany, mineralogy and zoology by dividing the known universe into the Spheres of Heavenly

Fig. 1
The Horse, from *ʿAjāʾib al-makhlūqāt wa gharaʾib al-mawjudat* (*The Wonders of Creation and the Oddities of Existence*), folio 73 *verso*, an illuminated Arabic manuscript on paper in *naskhi* script, with 59 illustrations, by Zakariyā ibn Muhammad al-Qazwīnī, early Mamluk period, 12⅝in by 9in (32cm by 23cm)
London £495,000 ($861,300). 26.IV.90

Bodies (with the Planets, the Fixed Stars and the Angels); the Sphere of Water (with the Islands of the Seas and the strange peoples and animals living there), and the Sphere of Earth, including the vegetable and animal kingdoms, and minerals.

Extant thirteenth- and fourteenth-century copies of the *'Ajā'ib al-makhlūqāt* are exceedingly rare, and illustrated versions even more so. Indeed, only one complete codex with paintings is known (Munich, Staatsbibliothek, cod. ar. 464). The importance of this Munich manuscript is increased by the fact that it was copied and illustrated in 1280, during the author's lifetime and may have been inspired either directly or indirectly by al-Qazwīnī himself. The manuscript must be considered as the model for all later copies, both textually and pictorially, giving the correct number and position of the miniatures within the text.

The *'Ajā'ib al-makhlūqāt*, to judge from the surviving manuscripts, seems to inaugurate the tradition of illustrating geographical and cosmographical works. It does so most lavishly, with the Munich Qazwīnī containing as many as 468 paintings. This number became the norm, and was sometimes even exceeded by later illustrated copies. The text became extremely popular from the sixteenth century up to the nineteenth, and appeared in both Persian and Ottoman Turkish translations.

The present manuscript establishes a trio of incomplete codices which were produced during the first half of the fourteenth century and which closely follow the Munich

Qazwīnī in size (20cm to 23cm in width by 29cm to 32cm in height); in the number of folios of the hypothetical reconstructed manuscripts (around 215–20); in the number of lines of text to the page (twenty-five to twenty-seven), and in the large quantity of illustrations.

The earliest of the three is probably a manuscript purchased by the British Library in 1983 (ms. Or. 14140) produced in North Jazira or South Anatolia between 1300 and 1315. The surviving 135 folios, about two thirds of the original, measure 20cm by 31cm, with twenty-five lines to the page. With 359 surviving miniatures, this manuscript was clearly even more lavishly illustrated than the complete copy preserved in Munich.

The second manuscript (Gotha, Forschungsbibliothek, ms. A 1506) is perhaps the most recent: it seems to have been copied and illustrated in a Persian atelier between 1330 and 1340. The town of Shiraz, in Southern Persia, has been suggested as its place of origin, however the codex has not yet been properly studied. It has 108 surviving folios, about half of the original, including 264 illustrations mainly of trees and plants; the pages measure 21cm by 29cm, with twenty-seven lines to the folio.

The present Qazwīnī probably dates somewhere between the two previous manuscripts but it belongs to an entirely different school of painting, far removed from the Persian Il-khanid world where the text was originally written, and the first codices copied and illustrated. It also has the smallest number of extant pages (only 76, about one third of the once complete codex), and many of these contain plain text, leaving 59 paintings, plus two diagrams. Moreover, the pages have been bound in a totally haphazard sequence, and a proper reconstruction of the textual order is needed. Its measurements, approximately 23cm by 32cm, with twenty-five lines to the page, relate it to the other two manuscripts and confirm its affiliation to the Munich Qazwīnī.

The present manuscript is remarkable for the way in which it incorporates various decorative features, such as classical scrolls, vine leaves and pomegranates providing backgrounds to some of the animal paintings (folios 72v, 74v, 75v and 76r: see Fig. 3). Classically-derived elements are present in some of the earliest examples of Islamic art, such as the mosaic of the Dome of the Rock in Jerusalem, or the stucco decorations at Samarra, as well as in early Dioscorides miniature paintings. Close examination of the Qazwīnī paintings also reveals a certain Mongol influence, evident in the lotus flower (folios 71r and 72r: see Fig. 2), adapted here in characteristic

Below, left
Fig. 4
A detail showing the cheetah from the Baptistère de Saint Louis, *circa* 1290–1310 (Reproduced courtesy of the Musée du Louvre, Paris).

Right
Fig. 5
The Cheetah and the Lizard, from *Kitāb al-hayawān,* folio 9 *recto* (Reproduced courtesy of the Biblioteca Ambrosiana, Milan, Ms. D 140 inf. S p. 67).

Fig. 6
The Hodinat al-af'an
(literally, 'viper-nesting bird'), from *ʿAjāʾib al-makhlūqāt wa gharaʾib al-mawjudat*, folio 67 *recto*.

Mamluk style, and which is also found in the Vienna and Oxford *Maqāmāt* manuscripts (Nationalbibliothek, A.F. 9, dated 1334, and Bodleian Library, Marsh 458, dated 1337). One further very original motif establishes the eastern flavour of the manuscript, namely, the floral additions to the landscapes and plants, made in the same red ink as the titles in the text. The idea that this was an initiative of the calligrapher at the last stage of supervision of the manuscript is appealing, but it is not possible to prove at the moment. Whichever artist was responsible for these extemporary additions, it is remarkable that they were carried out using ink instead of pigment, with a free brush-stroke and without contours – materials and techniques normally associated with far eastern art, and unusual in Arab painting. The additions were surely not an attempt to improve the paintings, which were already accurately and magnificently drawn, but were probably intended simply to add a further element of originality to the manuscript.

In order to suggest, however tentatively, an artistic environment for the Qazwīnī manuscript, we have to search for parallels. This is a difficult task, but at first glance, at least, the work can easily be associated with the *Kitāb al-hayawān* (Book on the Animals) in the Ambrosiana Library in Milan (Ms. 140 inf. S.P. 67), an illustrated manuscript in al-Jahiz's bestiary tradition. The two codices, although different enough to exclude the possibility of a common painter, share several features. The absence of frames for the miniatures, the large size of the animals (in the Qazwīnī from a minimum of 13cm by 6cm to a maximum of 19cm by 11cm), their posture and the curious stasis of their forms even when depicted running, are all characteristics shared by the two manuscripts. In this context, another distinctive element of the Qazwīnī manuscript becomes obvious, so far only common to bestiaries: the animals represented are imposing and monumental in appearance and size, and this is further enhanced by the fact that they are illustrated without any additional narrative elements. The Qazwīnī manuscript and the Milan Bestiary also share some similar compositional details, such as the gold collar with circular plates – folios 69r, 70v, 72r, 76r (Fig. 3) and 76v, for the Qazwīnī and examples at folios 9r (Fig. 5) and 22v, for the Bestiary – and in a few cases the gold anklets. The fur of the two cheetahs (Figs 3 and 5) is very similarly treated, and the palettes used are also alike.

If the Milan Bestiary is the most obvious parallel in miniature painting, the Qazwīnī manuscript has similarities with other Islamic works of art, as seen before in the case of the round scrolls and the lotus flowers. More strikingly we may notice the similarity in composition between the animals in the Qazwīnī manuscript and the friezes found in metalwork of the Mamluk period, depicting running animals on scrolling backgrounds. They share the same posture, the same slender and elongated bodies, the same long, curled tail, the same underlining of the belly by means of double curved lines forming a kind of lunette (which in the present manuscript is filled with gold), and more particularly the collar tied around the neck of the horse terminating in a tuft (Fig. 1). This type of frieze is also to be found on the Baptistère de Saint Louis (Paris, Louvre, L.P. 16; Fig. 4), attributed to Egypt and dateable to between 1290 and 1310 (but recently dated to 1260–77), and on other Mamluk metalwork such as the base of a candlestick in Baltimore (Walters Art Gallery, 54.459) produced around 1290, and a ewer in Cairo (Museum of Islamic Art, 15089) dateable to around 1300.

Considering these characteristics, the manuscript can be assigned with certainty to the Mamluk school of painting. The Milan *Kitāb al-hayawān* is unfortunately not dated, but has always been assigned, on the basis of comparison with other dated Mamluk manuscripts, to the second quarter of the fourteenth century. The attribution to Syria or Egypt has been suggested without sufficient grounds to support either hypothesis, and similarly it is not possible, at present, to suggest a provenance for the Qazwīnī. In this context it is useful to remember that not one of the illustrated Mamluk manuscripts from the fourteenth century indicates its provenance, and only in very few cases has a Syrian origin been accepted: for the *Maqāmāt* in the British Library (Or. 9718), dateable to not later than 1310, and four other manuscripts recently discussed as being of Syrian origin, all from between 1334 and 1354. No Syrian or Egyptian provenance can be established for either the present Qazwīnī or the Milan Bestiary. Although the decorative elements, such as the scrolls with vine leaves, have a parallel in classical Byzantine art, they are not sufficient to exclude an Egyptian provenance as they are common also to Coptic and Fatimid art.

In conclusion, it is fascinating to notice that the distribution and popularity of the *Wonders of Creation* had spread in only a few decades after its author's death. This is true not only within the boundaries of the Il-khanid empire but also for the traditional enemy of the Mongols, the Mamluks. Can it be assumed, then, that lavishly illustrated copies of the ʿAjāʾib al-makhlūqāt were considered so valuable that they travelled together with *Qur'ans* as prized diplomatic gifts to the Mamluk sultans? Or, was it simply the initiative of private owners who took illustrated copies of the book outside the Mongol empire? Although the former hypothesis seems more appealing, it is, once again, not possible to confirm without further research.

The Nativity of Christ and *The Annunciation to the Shepherds*, a miniature from the Du Boisrouvray Psalter, an illuminated manuscript on vellum, with Calendar, Canticles, Litany and Prayers, in Latin, 212 leaves, Amiens, *circa* 1260, 6¾in by 4¾in (17.3cm by 12.2cm)
London £748,000 ($1,241,680).
5.XII.89

From the collection of the late Count Guy du Boisrouvray, retained by the family from the du Boisrouvray bequest of illuminated manuscripts to the Bibliothèque Nationale in 1961.

Opposite
The Genealogy of the Counts of Pereira, an illuminated manuscript on vellum, in Portuguese, six leaves, 42 portrait miniatures, including those of Ferdinand the Catholic and Emperor Charles V, Evora, Portugal, dated *1534*, 17¾in by 12⅞in (45.1cm by 32.8cm)
London £242,000 ($401,720).
5.XII.89

Saint Dominic, a detail showing a miniature by Nicolo di Giacomo da Bologna from a leaf of a manuscript Matricola on vellum, in Latin, Bologna, *circa* 1386, 13¾in by 9⅝in (35cm by 24.5cm) London £68,200 ($117,304). 19.VI.90 From the collection of the late Eric Korner

Opposite
The Three Maries at the Sepulchre, and *The Resurrection of Christ*, two historiated initials from a leaf of a manuscript noted Breviary on vellum, Salzburg, mid twelfth century, 11½in by 8⅛in (29.3cm by 20.7cm) London £143,000 ($245,960). 19.VI.90 From the collection of the late Eric Korner

AEVIA. AEVIA. AEVIA.

Laudate dnm oms gentes. IN EVO

ESPERE

AVTE.

SABBATI

quircescit

IN PRIMA SABBA

ti uenit maria

magdalena et altera maria uidere sepulchrum aeuia.

Ds qui hanc sacratissima nocte gla-
dinice resurrectionis illustras · con-
serua innoua familie tue pgenie spm
adoptionis que dedisti. utmente et cor-
pe renati. pura t exhibeant seruitute. F.

Conuerte nos. Ad completorium.
Cu inuocare · F Inre dne Vsq:
odisti · F Qui habitat · F Ecce ne · ymn.
Te lucis ante terminum. Cap. Si cresurrex-
istis cu xpo. q sursu s querite · u xpc e
in dextera di sedens · v Custodi nos dne. HEV.
A Aeuia Quem queris mulier ae uia uiuentem
cum mortuis a utra aeuia. F Hunc dimnrf.
v In pace inid ipsum. Dorm: Credoinnm · pc es. Inre
surrecnone tua. xpc aeuia. Celi enrra I. a. OR.
Os q hanc sacratissima necte. In uir.
EVIA AEVIA AE VIA. F Venite
Ego sum qui sum et consilium meum non
est cum inpus sed inlege domini uoluntas mea est
aeuia. F Beatus uir. a Postulau patrem meum

ae uia dedit michi gentes ae uia inheredmatem ae
Quare frem. a Ego dormiui et somnum cepi
exurrexi quoniam dominus suscepit me ae ui
aeuia. F Dne quid mult. v Resurrex dns. S

IN ILLO TEMPORE. Secm. Mar.

Maria magdalene · et maria ia
cobi. et salome emerunt a
mata: ut uenientes ungerent ih

ITEM
Omelia
Gregor
pape.

MULTI

VOBIS

lectioi

fres kr

pdiu

tu loqui osueuera. s qa lascescent
stomacho ea q dictauero legere i
n possu qscda urm min ubem aud
tes intueor: Vnde nc ammetipso
igere contra morem uolo. ut int sac
missaru sollempnia. lectiones sc
euglii n dictando s colloqndo ed
sere sicq: excipiant ut loquim: q
collocutionis uox corda torpenti
plusqua sermo lectionis excitat. e
quada manu ut euigilet pulsat. E
adhoc opus me sufficere n posse ui
s tam uires qs impicia denegat. c
tas ministrat. scio naq; q dixit. a
ostiu: et ego adimplebo illud. O p
q bonu nobis inuoluntate sit. na

uota uotorum sentiat obtinuisse

suffragia. per dnm ;

INCIPIT ORDO

BAPT ⫶ MISSA

QVAE PRO SCRVTINIO CAE

LIBRATVR ⫶

DA qs dne electis nris digne atque sa
pienter ad confessionem tuę laudis
accedere. ut dignitati pristinę quā
originali trans gressione perdide
rant per tuam gratiam reformen
tur. p dnm; **SVPER OBLATA**
Miseratio tua ds ad hec per cipienda

Hebrew Bible, comprising the Pentateuch, Greater and Minor Prophets, and Hagiographa, with the
Masora Magna and Minora, a manuscript on vellum, 396 leaves, Iraq or Syria, perhaps Babylon,
ninth or tenth century, 13⅞in by 11¾in (35.2cm by 30cm)
London £2,035,000 ($3,378,100). 5.XII.89
From the collection of the British Rail Pension Fund

The above is one of the five primary manuscripts of the Hebrew Bible.

Opposite
The Pontifical of Salomo I, a manuscript on vellum, in Latin, 116 leaves, Reichenau Abbey, Lake
Constance, second quarter ninth century, 6¼in by 3⅜in (15.8cm by 8.7cm)
London £638,000 ($1,097,360). 19.VI.90

Judaica

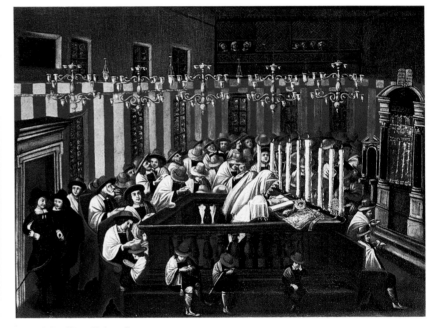

North Italian School
ITALIAN JEWS PRAYING IN THE SYNAGOGUE ON ROSH HASHANA
Early eighteenth century, 28in by 37¾in (71.1cm by 95.9cm)
New York $41,250 (£25,621).18.XII.89

Left
A carved wood Esther scroll case, by Yecheskel Joshua Maisels, Dolina, Western
Ukraine, 1913, height 30¾in (78cm)
Tel Aviv $70,400 (£40,229).19.IV.90

Opposite
Seder Haggadah shel Pessach ('Passover Haggadah'), first folio, inscribed with an
extract from the Talmud *Because of the righteous women, the Jews were redeemed from
Egypt*, from an illuminated manuscript on vellum in Hebrew, signed and dated
1746, with colophon in German, by Aaron Ben Wolf Herlingen of Gewitsch in
Moravia, Vienna, 10¼in by 6¾in (26cm by 17.2cm)
Tel Aviv $275,000 (£158,046).18.IV.90

סדר
הגדה של
פסח
באותיות׃
אמשטרדם ❖
נעשה פה עיר וויען ׃ על הוצאות בהקטן
מהרן כהדר כמיהן זלב זל ינגיטוש׃
ויעשבן אהרן ׃
לפק׃

בזכות נשים צדקניות נגאלו ישראל ממצרים ׃

Aaron Wolff Kayserlicher und Königlicher Bibliothec-
Schreiber, Wienn 1746.

Islamic art

A Sicilian bronze ewer, tenth–eleventh century, with *kufic* inscription *al-mulk lillah* ('The sovereignty is
for God'), height 8⅝in (22cm)
London £57,200 ($99,528). 25.IV.90

Opposite, below
A Fars silver-inlaid brass bowl, late thirteenth century, diameter 10¾in (27.5cm)
London £7,150 ($12,441). 25.IV.90

Left to right
A Persian bronze tripod stand, late twelfth–early thirteenth century, height 6¾in (17cm)
London £7,700 ($13,398). 25.IV.90
A Persian bronze tripod stand, late twelfth–early thirteenth century, height 7⅛in (18cm)
London £16,500 ($28,710). 25.IV.90

Opposite
A panel of six Iznik tiles,
circa 1560, each tile 9½in by
9½in (24cm by 24cm)
London £41,800 (72,732).
25.IV.90

An Iznik pottery jug with
English gilt-copper
mounts, *circa* 1580–90,
height including cover
8in (20.4cm)
London £19,800
($34,452). 25.IV.90

The rosewater sprinkler –
Beykoz or Bohemia?

Professor John Carswell

The recent sale of a large number of rosewater sprinklers from an English private collection prompted some research into how to identify Turkish glass from the Beykoz factories, from Bohemian glass of almost identical design.

There is a long history of the export of Venetian glass to the East – one surviving order from the Grand Vizier Mohammed Pasha, dated 1569, requests the Venetian Ambassador at Constantinople to supply 900 glass lamps for a mosque – and the oldest record of the export of Bohemian glass to Turkey dates from 1700. It was also exported indirectly to the Ottoman empire through merchants in Italy, who were stationed at Genoa, Livorno, Trieste and Naples. Throughout the eighteenth century, glass continued to be exported to Turkey, either through the merchants, or purchased directly by Turks and Jews from the glass-makers themselves, to the annoyance of the merchants.

The production of glass in Turkey itself was well-established by the sixteenth century, and the Turkish traveller Evliya Celebi (1611–84) discourses on the glass-makers at length, saying that they made plain glass, stained glass and crystal. Some of the varieties of glass made, particularly tulip vases, can be discerned in miniature paintings of guild processions in eighteenth-century Istanbul.

However, it is with rosewater sprinklers that the most instructive comparison between Bohemian and Beykoz production can be made. The Beykoz sprinklers are usually of opaque glass, in opaline, white, blue, green or other colours, often decorated with sprigs of flowers. The floral sprays are arranged symmetrically in lattice-like panels, and the globular body is of swollen form with a thin ring base. The Bohemian sprinklers, on the other hand, are often of vividly coloured clear glass, with a sturdy foot, sometimes of square design. They are frequently decorated with baroque patterns akin to those on contemporary Bohemian cut-glass. The multi-coloured enamel is often enlivened with little coloured-glass dots. All the sprinklers, Bohemian or Beykoz, are ground inside the neck to take a glass screw stopper, drilled with a narrow hole.

What were the sprinklers used for? Rosewater was a popular flavouring and scent throughout the Islamic world and rosewater sprinklers are still commonly used in Turkey, Syria, Egypt, Iraq, Iran and India, often made of silver as well as glass. Although a gracious addition to everyday life, rosewater also has a more subtle role; recent research has shown that essence of rose enhances the potency of female pheromones. What the poets knew – that roses are a welcome gift to any woman – apparently has some scientific basis!

A group of clear glass Turkish (Beykoz) and opaque Bohemian enamelled-glass rosewater sprinklers, nineteenth century, heights approximately $7\frac{1}{4}$ in to $11\frac{1}{2}$ in (18.4cm to 29.2cm), from a collection of 60 London £31,845 ($55,410). 25.IV.90

Japanese art

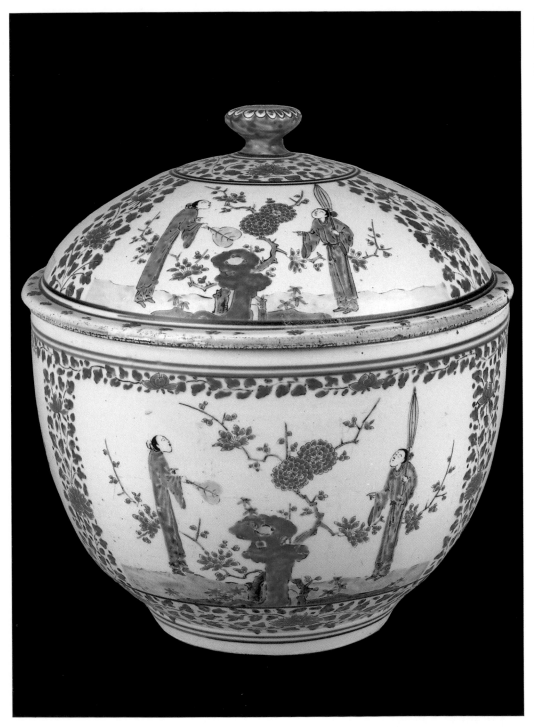

A Kakiemon bowl and cover, late seventeenth century, height 14⅝in (37.2cm)
London £440,000 ($734,800). 16.XI.89

Opposite
A pair of cloisonné enamel vases by Namikawa Sosuke, signed with a silver wire seal, Meiji period, heights 18⅛in (46cm)
London £82,500 ($141,075). 20.III.90

An earthenware vase, Yabu Meizan mark, Meiji period, height 11⅝in (29.5cm)
New York $44,000 (£25,731). 19.VI.90

Opposite
Toshusai Sharaku
A half-length portrait of the actor Bando Hikosaburo as the character of Sagisaka Sanai, in a scene
from the play *Koi Nyobo Somewake Tazuna*, 'Beloved Wife at the Coloured Reins', performed at the
Kawarazaki-za Theatre in Edo, in 1794, signed, with censor's seal *kiwame* and publisher's mark *Tsutaya
Juzaburo*, 15⅛in by 9⅞in (38.4cm by 25.1cm)
London £231,000 ($392,700). 20.XII.89

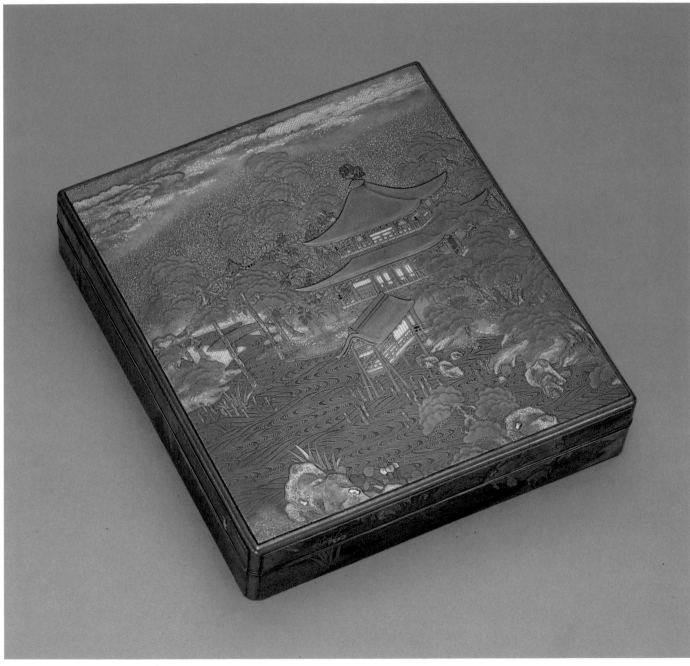

A lacquer *suzuribako*, Meiji period, 10½in by 9½in (26.7cm by 24cm)
New York $104,500 (£62,202). 2.II.90

An ivory *netsuke* of a boar and young by Masanao, signed, late eighteenth century, 2⅛in (5.4cm)
London £93,500 ($167,365). 17.V.90

A wood *netsuke* of a baku, late eighteenth century, 2⅛in (5.4cm)
London £48,400 ($81,312). 15.XI.89

A wood *netsuke* of three monkeys quarrelling by Toyomasa of Tamba, signed, nineteenth century, 1⅞in (4.8cm)
London £41,800 ($70,224). 15.XI.89

An ivory *netsuke* of a Buddhist celestial being by Rensai, signed, nineteenth century, length 1¾in (4.5cm)
London £19,800 ($33,264). 15.XI.89

An ivory *netsuke* of a grazing horse by Tomotada, signed, late eighteenth century, 3¼in (8.3cm)
London £154,000 ($275,660). 17.V.90

Chinese art

Two views of an imperial *famille-rose* cup, mark and period of Yongzheng, diameter 3⅛in (8.1cm)
Hong Kong HK$16,500,000 (£1,334,951:$2,112,676). 14.XI.89

Opposite
An imperial *famille-rose* vase, mark and period of Yongzheng, height 16½in (42cm)
Hong Kong HK$12,100,000 (£978,964:$1,549,296). 14.XI.89

A Ming blue-and-white fluted washer, early fifteenth century, diameter $7\frac{1}{8}$in (18.2cm)
Hong Kong HK$11,220,000 (£907,767: $1,436,620). 14.XI.89

Opposite
A copper-red decorated double-gourd vase, mark and period of Qianlong, height $11\frac{5}{8}$in (29.6cm)
Hong Kong HK$3,190,000 (£242,789:$409,552). 15.V.90

A sancai glazed pottery figure of a caparisoned Fereghan horse, Tang Dynasty, height 26¾in (68cm)
London £3,740,000 ($6,133,600). 12.XII.89
From the collection of the British Rail Pension Fund

Opposite
A bronze covered ritual wine vessel (*fangyi*), Shang Dynasty, twelfth–eleventh century BC,
height 9⅜in (23.7cm)
London £715,000 ($1,172,600). 12.XII.90
From the collection of the British Rail Pension Fund

A gilt-bronze figure of Buddha, Ming Dynasty, height 37in (94cm)
Hong Kong HK$4,950,000 (£376,741:$635,512). 15.V.90

Opposite
A marble Buddhist votive stele, Northern Qi Dynasty, height 52⅜in (133cm)
London £935,000 ($1,533,400). 12.XII.89
From the collection of the British Rail Pension Fund

Left
A rhinoceros horn carving of the goddess *Guanyin*,
sixteenth–seventeenth century, height 5½in (14cm)
New York $104,500 (£66,139). 6.XII.89

Opposite
A pair of jadeite figures of *Meiren*, nineteenth century,
Qianlong marks in two seals on the backs, heights 17in
(43.2cm)
Hong Kong HK$17,050,000 (£1,379,450:$2,183,099).
16.XI.89

Below
A pair of jadeite bangles, late Qing Dynasty,
diameters approximately 2⅛in (5.5cm)
Hong Kong HK$12,320,000 (£996,764:$1,577,465).
15.XI.89

Tang Yin

MOONLIT STREAM

Handscroll, ink on paper, signed, inscribed with a dedication to Yuequan, with four seals of the artist,
Wu Qu, Tang Bo Hu, Tang Zi Wei Tu Shu, and *Liu Ru Ju Shi*, the colophon by Zhu Yunming, dated
Zhengde yi hai, 1515, third month, 12in by 44in (30.5cm by 111.8cm)
New York $561,000 (£330,000). 30.V.90

Wu Bin

TEN VIEWS OF A FANTASTIC ROCK

Handscroll, ink on paper, signed, each view of the rock inscribed by Mi Wanzhong the owner of the
rock, the last view dated *Wanli geng xu*, 1610, mid autumn, 21⅞in by 372⅜in (55.5cm by 945.8cm)
New York $1,210,000 (£765,823). 6.XII.89

Zhang Daqian
LANDSCAPE WITH WATERFALL AND PINE
Ink and colour on silk, signed *Yuanweng*, inscribed and dated *geng xu*, 1970, with three seals of the artist
Da Qian Wei Yin Da Nian, *Wu Ting Hu* and *Ba De Yuan Chang Nian*, 56in by 69⅝in (142.2cm by 176.8cm)
Hong Kong HK$2,970,000 (£240,291:$380,282). 15.XI.89

The art of Cameroon

Tamara Northern

The art of Cameroon – more specifically, the prestige arts of the Cameroon Grassfields kingdoms – ranks highly among the several major traditions of African wood sculpture and has engendered a special allegiance among connoisseurs of African art. It has gained recognition as a major art tradition not only for the prolific output of its many gifted and inventive artists, working under the tutelage of royal and wealthy patrons, but also for its profound expression of the major and enduring themes of the human experience.

In its diverse manifestations of imagery and style, the corpus of Cameroon art addresses the fundamental issues of human existence. Its figural and mask sculptures mark the ultimate threshold experiences of birth, death and supernatural intervention. They commemorate the vital attributes of virility, physical vigor, mental strength, fertility and nurture. They celebrate fidelity and loyalty and the harmonious balance of a social world in which governance is assured by orderly royal succession and by the maintenance of lineages through which a farming society is sustained. Conceived and given form within the particular cultural matrix of Cameroon society, this art nonetheless bespeaks and thus evokes timeless and universal themes that transcend cultural boundaries.

Its aesthetic qualities are indeed commensurate with the profundity of its themes. In statuary, masks, stools, drums, vessels and personal accoutrements, it is the bold, vigorous, and often dramatic conception of the forms articulating these themes that infuses the work with the extraordinary expressive and evocative power that is the hallmark of Cameroon art. Irrespective of the differences of regional and specific atelier styles, this mode of expression is always forceful and elemental, dynamic and compelling in its power to affect.

The works in the Franklin Collection bear ample testimony to this. The masks representing human and animal heads are of a monumental scale with large, distinct features; they often have towering superstructures reinforcing the main image. Worn upon the head of the costumed dancer, they effect a transformation into a vision of grandeur that is superhuman. The masks' male and female faces epitomize the ethos of male authority and female compliance, while the animal representations connote the empowering ability of intercourse with the supernatural, enabling mighty kings to turn into mighty animals and claim their power to enhance their own. The so-called Batcham mask (Fig. 3), more likely originating from the Bamileke Kingdom of Bandjoun, reaches the apogee of bold yet coherent distortion of the human face and stands unsurpassed for its dramatic conceptionalization not only in Cameroon art but in all of African art. Its ingenious artist, working in a localized

Fig. 1
A Bangwa memorial figure of a royal titled wife, height 32½in (82.6cm)
New York $3,410,000 (£2,079,268). 21.IV.90
From the Harry A. Franklin Collection

tradition that spawned only a small number of these works, further exaggerated the typically prominent facial features of male human masks – hairdress, eyes, cheeks, toothed mouth – and set them within alternating vertical and horizontal planes, thereby creating an expression of tension. The frozen, blank stare of the mask's eyes and the aggressive bulge of its schematized teeth heighten the intensity of the composition and bestow upon the image a supernatural quality, one that is symptomatic of the awesome power inherent in this mask.

The Franklin Collection includes outstanding examples of free-standing figural sculpture, among them several titled memorial figures, a most important genre of Cameroon art. The paired figures of a Queen and King (Figs 1 and 2) from one of the (western) Bangwa kingdoms, exemplify the formal and expressive characteristics of the best of classical African sculpture.

Both were collected among the Bangwa between 1897 and 1899 by Gustav Conrau, a German merchant-explorer and colonial agent and the first white man to reach the Bangwa kingdoms. Uniquely representing a royal woman in her dual role as priestess of the earth cult and titled wife or princess, the Queen is shown dancing and singing the song of the earth as she would at the funeral celebration for a deceased king. She bears the valued attributes of full sexual and social maturity and is shown with the basketry rattle of the leader of the dance of the earth, and with the accoutrements of royal status – collars of glass beads, a necklace of carved leopard teeth pendants, beaded loin string, and ivory armlets and anklets. The King is adorned with similar regalia.

The Queen is conceived as a composition of swelling and receding volumes that pirouette around a central axis, creating a dynamic silhouette of contained motion. The King shares the same stylistic elements and is a worthy partner whose animated vigor and regal demeanor symbolize the ease of one who rules with confidence and moral authority. Together they radiate the vitality of the prime of life and resonate with the values that signify fruition and success.

By comparison, the seated maternity figure (Fig. 4), while also of regal bearing, provides an example of the more typical manner of direct frontal representation in Cameroon art. The nursing woman sits squarely and securely in calm repose, tenderly cradling her infant's head. This sculpture evokes an aura of the generous fulfilment of motherhood, of affection and nurture. It is a timeless and universal image that is touching in its appeal and by its serenity reaffirms those essential human experiences.

In its native setting, Cameroon art comes alive as a focus of public spectacles with the vibrant colours of bright costumes, brilliant sunlight, and red dust swirling up from under the feet of dancers urged on by driving rhythms. In the seclusion of palace interiors and the quiet, dark shelters of secret societies or under the enveloping cover of night, when flickering firelight creates grotesque shadows that move about furtively, this art becomes an empowering conduit for supernatural intercession in human affairs. In either context, such works assert their commanding presence by the commonly understood symbolism of their imagery and by the compelling evocative power of their aesthetic canon. They are a source of prestige and pride for royals, nobles and commoners alike and constitute the sacred treasure of the Cameroon Grassfields kingdoms.

Fig. 2
A Bangwa royal memorial male ancestor figure, height 35in (88.9cm) New York $330,000 (£201,220). 21.IV.90 From the Harry A. Franklin Collection

Opposite
Fig. 3
A Central Bamileke mask,
height 35in (88.9cm)
New York $319,000
(£194,512). 21.IV.90
From the Harry A.
Franklin Collection

Fig. 4
A Bamileke royal
maternity figure,
height 29⅛in (74cm)
New York $33,000
(£20,122) 21.IV.90
From the Harry A.
Franklin Collection

Opposite
A Songe male community
magical figure, height
42⅞in (109cm)
London £170,500
($318,835). 2.VII.90
From the collection of
Nancy and Richard Bloch

A Baule face mask,
height 10in (25.4cm)
New York $209,000
(£127,439). 21.IV.90
From the Harry A.
Franklin Collection

Opposite
A Ngbaka harp,
height 34¼in (87cm)
London £104,500
($195,415). 2.VII.90
From the collection of
Nancy and Richard Bloch

An Easter Island male
figure, height 13in (33cm)
London £165,000
($278,850). 26.III.90

An early classic Navajo man's wearing blanket, First Phase, 6ft 1in by 4ft 9in (185.4cm by 144.8cm)
New York $522,500 (£332,803). 28.XI.89
From the collection of the late Edwin Janss, Jr

Opposite
A Teotihuacan III stone funerary mask, Classic, *circa* AD 450–650, height 7½in (19cm)
New York $214,500 (£130,793). 2.V.90

An international style gold anthropomorphic pendant, Parita, Azuero Peninsula, *circa* AD 500–1000,
height 4¼in (10.8cm)
New York $71,500 (£45,253). 27.X.89
From the collection of the late Count and Countess Guy du Boisrouvray

A Frenchman who studied mining at the prestigious Ecole Centrale, and spent eight years
prospecting for gold in French Equatorial Africa, the late Count Guy du Boisrouvray
assembled a spectacular collection of pre-Columbian gold. Distinguished both by its size and
superb quality, the du Boisrouvray Collection represented the full range of styles and
techniques employed by the ancient American goldsmiths from all of the four major gold-
working regions of Peru, Colombia, Panama and Costa Rica. Count du Boisrouvray acquired
his pieces from André Emmerich, the most eminent scholar and dealer in the field, during a
unique period in the 1960s when an unusual amount of pre-Columbian gold emerged on the
market. The Count's personal taste was revealed in his extensive trove of ornamental
figurines of animals and deities, which were worn as emblems of social status and believed to
possess magical powers. The 79 lots of the du Boisrouvray Collection comprised some of the
finest pre-Columbian gold ever to appear at auction.

A Middle Mochica gold duck effigy, Ayabaca region, *circa* AD 200–500, length 7in (17.8cm)
New York $93,500 (£59,177). 27.X.89
From the collection of the late Count and Countess Guy du Boisrouvray

Asian art

A Sino-Tibetan copper-gilt group depicting Vajrabhairava in *yab-yum* with his *sakti*, *circa* eighteenth century AD, height 9½in (24cm)
London £19,800 ($34,452).24.IV.90

Opposite
A Pala black stone stele of Vishnu, Eastern India, twelfth century AD, height 51¼in (130.2cm)
New York $34,100 (£21,312).21.III.90

Antiquities

An Egyptian turquoise-glazed faience hippopotamus, Middle Kingdom, Twelfth–Thirteenth Dynasty,
1850–1700 BC, excavated in 1907 at Abydos, Tomb 416, length 4¼in (10.8cm)
London £528,000 ($1,013,760).10.VII.90
From the collection of the late Madame Marion Schuster

Opposite
A Greek bronze helmet, *circa* early sixth century BC, height 9½in (24.1cm)
New York $96,250 (£61,306).29.XI.89
Formerly in the Albert Gallatin Collection

Opposite
A detail from an Egyptian limestone architrave relief, Old Kingdom, early Sixth Dynasty, *circa* 2345–2300 BC, carved with five representations of the priest of Ptah and overseer of the House of Impy, called Ptah-shepsus, overall size 17¾in by 56¾in (45.1cm by 144.1cm) New York $198,000 (£115,116).20.VI.90 From the Breitbart Collection

An Egyptian mud plaster, gesso plaster and paint fragment, from the 'Tomb of the Two Sculptors', Theban Tomb 181, Theban Necropolis, New Kingdom, Eighteenth Dynasty, *circa* 1350 BC, 16¼in by 9in (41.3cm by 22.9cm) London £187,000 ($359,040).10.VII.90 From the collection of the late Madame Marion Schuster

An Egyptian anhydrite cosmetic vessel in the form of a trussed duck, Middle Kingdom, Twelfth–Seventeenth Dynasty, 1835–1540 BC, length 4½in (11.5cm) London £154,000 ($257,180).11.XII.89

A Cycladic pottery double
kandila, Early Bronze Age I,
circa 3000–2800 BC,
length 7½in (19cm)
London £88,000
($168,960). 9.VII.90
From the Erlenmeyer
Collection

A Cycladic pottery
cylindrical pyxis and cover,
Pelos group, Early Bronze
Age 1, *circa* 3000–2800 BC,
height 4⅝in (11.8cm)
London £66,000
($126,720). 9.VII.90
From the Erlenmeyer
Collection

A late Minoan pottery bridge-spouted jar, *circa* 1400 BC, height $7\frac{7}{8}$in (20cm)
London £77,000 ($147,840). 9.VII.90
From the Erlenmeyer Collection

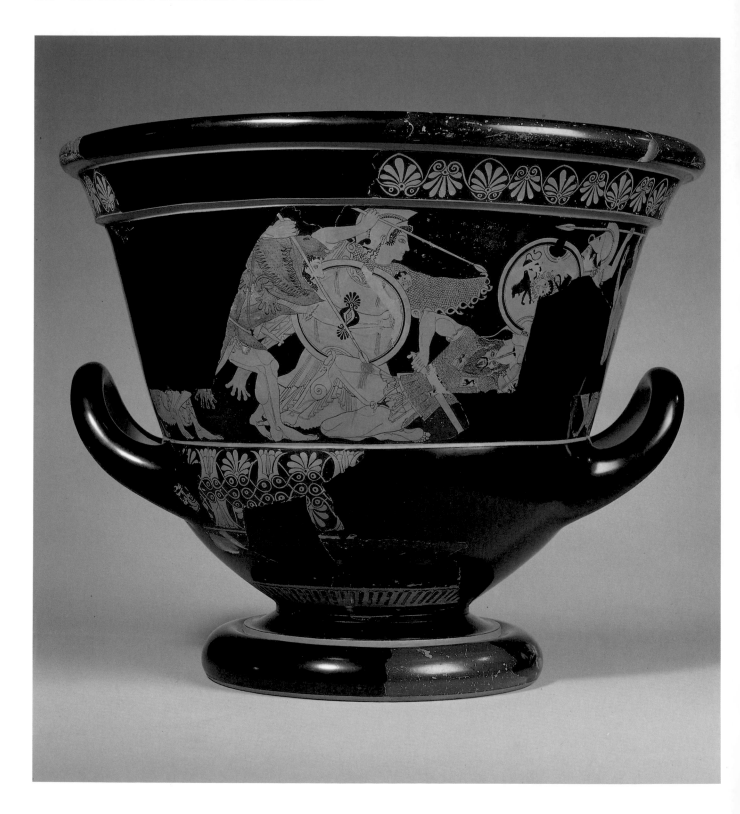

An Etruscan bronze figure of a horse, possibly by Vulci, *circa* late sixth – early fifth century BC,
height 4⅛in (10.5cm)
New York $517,000 (£337,908).19.VI.90
From the William Herbert Hunt Collection

Opposite
A fragmentary Attic red-figure Calyx krater, signed by Euphronios, *circa* 510 BC, painted with the
death of Kyknos in battle with Herakles, an episode from *The Shield of Herakles*, height 17¾in (45.1cm)
New York $1,760,000 (£1,150,327).19.VI.90
From the Nelson Bunker Hunt Collection

Western Asia Minor, electrum stater, *circa* 575 BC
New York $308,000 (£179,070). 19.VI.90
From the Nelson Bunker Hunt Collection

This unique coin is a magnificent example of the very earliest coinage which was issued in
western Anatolia from around the end of the seventh century BC. The metal is electrum, a
natural alloy of gold and silver; it was not until the time of King Croesus in the middle of the
sixth century that coins of pure gold and silver were introduced. Coins of this early period are
difficult if not impossible to attribute to specific cities and the griffin motif could just as well
be a personal badge of a prominent individual, perhaps a merchant or a banker.

Agrigentum, decadrachm, *circa* 410 BC
New York $572,000 (£332,558). 19.VI.90
From the Nelson Bunker Hunt Collection

The decadrachm was the largest Greek silver denomination and those of Agrigentum in
Sicily are the rarest, the Hunt specimen being one of only eight known. Although unsigned,
the dies are attributed to the artists Myron and Polyainos, active at Agrigentum in its most
brilliant artistic phase shortly before its destruction by the Carthaginians in 406 BC. It is
recorded that one of its citizens, a certain Exainetos, won a chariot race at the Olympic
Games in 412 BC, an event which was followed by great celebrations in the city, and it is
thought that decadrachms were struck to commemorate the victory, the design of Helios
driving his chariot through the skies being particularly appropriate.

Roman, Hadrian (AD 117–38), sestertius, AD 135
New York $214,500 (£124,709). 19.VI.90
From the Nelson Bunker Hunt Collection

This coin represents the pinnacle of Roman Imperial portraiture during the reign of Hadrian, and the artist has been identified as the Alphaeus Master. Hadrian was a great admirer of Greek classical art and his coin portrait, of medallic proportions, reflects the idealized hellenistic style which he sought. Only five specimens of this great rarity are known, of which this is perhaps the finest. Struck in anticipation of Hadrian's vicennalia, the reverse depicts a standing figure of Pax, symbolic of the virtues of the Emperor.

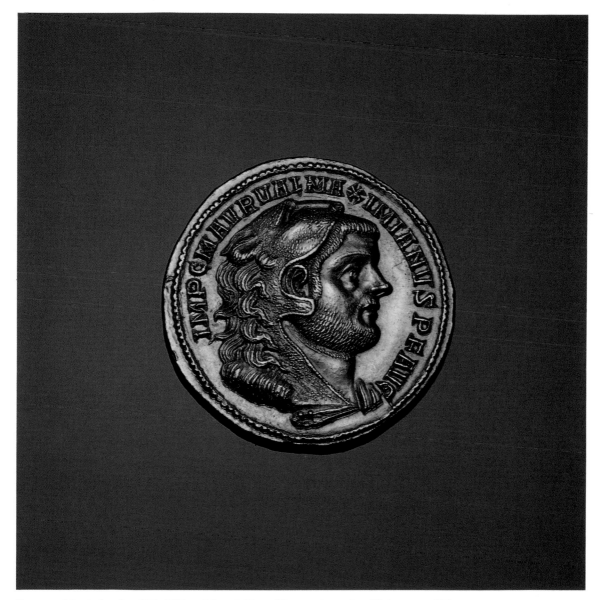

Roman, Maximian (AD 285–305), gold medallion of five aurei struck at Ticinum, AD 293
New York $297,000 (£172,674). 19.VI.90
From the Nelson Bunker Hunt Collection

This unique medal was originally discovered at O Szoni in Hungary in 1885. The portrait of the Emperor shows him wearing the lion-skin headdress, one of the attributes of Hercules, and the medal was struck to commemorate his pacification of the Rhine frontier from German invaders. Gold medallions struck to the weight of multiple aurei were issued only occasionally and are considered as donatives or gifts to high ranking individuals from the Emperor himself. Maximian was co-Emperor with Diocletian and the reverse of the medal further records their joint consulship in AD 293 as well as the fact that it was struck in Ticinum (modern Pavia) in northern Italy.

Italy, Guglielmo II Palaeologus of Casale (1494–1518), doppio ducato
London £14,850 ($25,097). 23.III.90

Opposite
Japan, Manen period (1860–62), gold oban with machine-made crenellations and original ink brush-markings surviving
London £18,700 ($31,977). 6.X.89

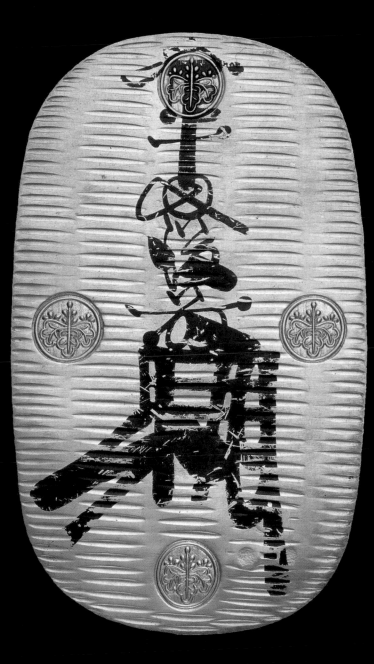

Adrien de Vries and Rudolfean court sculpture

Lars O. Larsson

When Adrien de Vries died in 1626 in Prague, the great age of Central European bronze sculpture came to an end. His most important competitor, Hubert Gerhard, mainly active in Munich and Augsburg, had already died in 1622. The reason why these exceptional artists had no notable successors can be found in the political situation of Europe at the time. The Thirty Years War had broken out in 1618, and against that background, it seems understandable that the garden sculptures of the grand palace built by General Albrecht von Waldstein at the *Kleinseite* of Prague, should have been de Vries's last major commission. The sculptures were the last major artistic project to get underway in Bohemia and, for that matter, in all Central Europe, before the same war through which von Waldstein had risen to power and prosperity rendered any further, similar schemes impossible. The great war brought a sudden end to the splendour of imperial Prague. In 1648 the town was seized and looted by Swedish troops; most of the imperial *Kunstkammer* and all the bronze garden sculpture of the Waldstein palace were carried off as trophies. This is why only a few works by Adrien de Vries can still be seen in Prague, and why by far the greater part of his oeuvre is to be found in Stockholm today.

Adrien de Vries was born in The Hague around 1545. He died at about 80 years of age – a long life for his time. The most convincing corroboration of this is a portrait medal (Vienna, Kunsthistorisches Museum) which, according to its inscription, shows Adrien de Vries at 81. Perhaps surprisingly, de Vries seems to have remained remarkably active right up to his death. Among the works of his last ten to fifteen years are a large tomb monument for Count Ernst von Schaumburg-Lippe, in Stadthagen, near Hanover; a large fountain with sixteen figures, some of them life-size, for Frederiksborg Castle in Denmark (now in Stockholm); and the garden sculptures for the Waldstein palace in Prague (now also in Stockholm). This poses several questions. Is it possible that a man in his seventies could have laboured to produce works on this scale? How much can we attribute to the hands of his work-shop assistants? Perhaps we are wrong about his presumed date of birth, after all? Definite answers are difficult to provide.

We do not know where Adrien de Vries was trained, but in 1581 he appears in a Florentine document as working with Giambologna, a position he held up to the end of the 1580s. How long he worked under Giambologna is unclear, but the great bravura sculptor of the late Renaissance was de Vries's most formative influence.

The first documented work by Adrien de Vries is the large group of *Mercury and Psyche*, now in the Louvre. It was executed for Emperor Rudolf II in Prague, in 1593, as can be seen from three copper plates of the sculpture by the Netherlandish engraver Jan Mueller (see Fig. 2a and b for two). The engravings depict the ensemble from different angles, indicating how it should be viewed. Sixteenth-century sculptors were obsessed with creating works that could be viewed from any angle – and none more so than Giambologna. Benvenuto Cellini, the contemporary Florentine sculptor and one-time goldsmith, expounded this ideal in his treatise on sculpture, and de Vries takes up the theme in a series of impressive compositions.

The *Mercury and Psyche* group also demonstrates how Adrien de Vries developed the art of Giambologna. The composition can be seen as a combination of two of the Florentine's most famous works, the *Flying Mercury* (Florence, Bargello) and the *Rape of a Sabine*, the model for which can be seen in the Accademia in Florence. From the *Flying Mercury*, de Vries took both the idea of a 'flying' sculpture defying gravity, and the youthful type of the messenger of the gods himself. By combining this with Giambologna's *figura serpentinata* or spiral composition, and by realizing the whole larger than life, de Vries surpasses his former employer with a masterly *tour de force*.

How and when Adrien de Vries arrived in Prague is also not known; he was presumably summoned by the Emperor on Giambologna's recommendation. Giambologna frequently procured artists for the imperial courts of Vienna and Prague and in the late 1580s Rudolf II had just tried, without success, to lure Giambologna himself to Prague.

In 1596, de Vries was commissioned to build two fountains for the town of Augsburg, then enjoying a period of great prosperity and power. The large fountains were part of an extensive scheme of urban beautification and rejuvenation which had its most magnificent expression in the new town hall by Elias Holl. Augsburg was proud of its Roman origins, and of its status as a *freie Reichstadt*, acknowledging no external political authority other than the Emperor himself. This civic pride was manifest in the iconographical programme of the first large fountain erected in front of the town hall, the fountain of Augustus finished by Hubert Gerhard in 1594. Both of de Vries's works, executed some years later, also relate to Augsburg's Roman past and to humanist ideals in general. The smaller of the fountains, finished first, is crowned by an over life-size figure of Mercury, in this instance probably a symbol of trade. And with the considerably larger Hercules fountain (Fig. 3a), decorated with ten bronze figures (see detail, Fig. 3c) and three reliefs, de Vries created one of the masterpieces of European fountain-building, developing on the Florentine sculpture-fountains of the sixteenth century. Once again, the sculptures all display the influence of Giambologna, but de Vries's figures have a much more lively appeal; they are sensual and vital in a way that Giambologna's restrictive, formal compositions are not, and they could be said to usher in the early Baroque.

The Hercules fountain was officially inaugurated in 1602, and we then find Adrien de Vries back in Prague, as *Hofstatuarius* to the court of Rudolf II. The years leading up to the death of the Emperor in 1612 mark the highest point of Rudolfean court art. De Vries, like the other court artists, worked for the Emperor himself, which meant that he worked mainly on small-scale commissions. Rudolf II, although a lover of horticulture with several fountains in his gardens, eschewed sculpture-

Fig. 2a and b
Two engravings after Adrien de Vries's *Mercury and Psyche* group, 1593, by Jan Mueller, sixteenth century, heights 22⅜in (57cm) (Reproduced courtesy of the Staatens Konstmuseer, Stockholm).

Left
Fig. 3a
A bronze fountain group of the labours of Hercules, by Adrien de Vries, Augsburg, 1602
(Reproduced courtesy of the Staatliche Kunstsammlungen, Augsburg).

Above
Fig. 3b
A detail of the fountain showing the front view of Hercules.

Below
Fig. 3c
A detail of the Hercules fountain, showing the bronze figures.

fountains of the type erected in the Medici gardens of Florence, and was not given to commissioning public monuments.

In these years de Vries created his most important works for the imperial *Kunstkammer*, including three remarkable portraits of the Emperor. The first is the large bust of 1603 (Vienna, Kunsthistorisches Museum), depicting the Emperor as *Triumphator* (Fig. 4), and for which Leone Leoni's bust of Charles V, which Rudolf II had just acquired, served as a model. The war against the Turks, in which the Emperor had scored some of his rare successes around 1600, provides the political background for this portrait. But perhaps more impressive, and more poignant, is the portrait relief of 1609 (Fig. 5). In it we find an expression of the wide discrepancy between the high political and symbolic aspirations implicit in the title of Emperor, and the profound personal low of Rudolf the man, stripped of all his powers by his brother Matthias, after military failures and increasing political weakness. This portrait was originally placed in the imperial *Kunstkammer* between two reliefs by de Vries, depicting an *Allegory of the War against the Turks* (Vienna, Kunsthistorisches Museum) and *Rudolf II as Patron of the Arts and Sciences* (Windsor Castle). Seen by a small number of contemporaries, in the relative privacy of the *Kunstkammer*, we can imagine them as a moving document for posterity, of the pathos of Rudolf's position.

The works created by the court sculptors also played a prominent part in imperial diplomacy. The magnificent bust of the young Elector of Saxony, Christian II, created by de Vries after the model of the great imperial bust of 1603, is a good example. At its base, two female figures join hands as a symbol of *Concordia*. The young Elector is being encouraged to maintain his political allegiance to the Emperor, represented on the medallion he is wearing on his chest.

There was evidently a great demand for equestrian figures by de Vries, and many, often quite large, examples survive (Fig. 6), although only two models are known to exist – one of a trotting or pacing horse, and one rearing up on its hind legs. Each of the extant bronzes is unique and, despite apparent similarities, no two horses were cast in the same mould. Unlike Giambologna, Adrien de Vries was not in the habit of re-casting his small bronzes in great numbers; there is no known example of a work by de Vries, for which a second autograph cast exists. In the case of the *Hercules, Nessus and Deianira*, which de Vries cast for Rudolf II, we should regard the example in the Louvre as the original and the other known versions as later casts, not made by the artist himself.

Rudolf II died in 1612 and his successor Matthias transferred the court to Vienna. Adrien de Vries, however, remained in Prague. He was probably reluctant to leave his foundry, and was by now advanced in years. The great commissions for Christian IV of Denmark, and for Count Ernst von Schaumburg-Lippe (Fig. 7a and b) were both executed in Prague and sent to his patrons along the Moldau and Elbe rivers.

Rudolfean court art in Prague is rightly regarded as a peak of international Mannerism, but it was far from homogenous in style. Along with the elaborate artifice of numerous mythological images and themes, we find robust realism in the many genre paintings, flower paintings and landscapes of the imperial collection. This diversity can also be found in the work of individual artists. In principle, this is also true of de Vries. The realism of his equestrian works stands in marked contrast to the elegant *maniera* of, for example, his *Mercury and Psyche* group.

Fig. 4
A bronze portrait bust of Emperor Rudolf II as *Triumphator*, by Adrien de Vries, Prague, 1603 (Reproduced courtesy of the Kunsthistorisches Museum, Vienna).

If a unity is to be found, it is in de Vries's strongly classical roots. The art of the antique was, however, allowed to play but a minor role at the Prague court. It is true that Rudolf II owned some important antique sculptures, but weighed against the quantity of his collection, they were of little consequence, and were certainly not a decisive influence on the works of the court artists. De Vries often turned to antique models, and while he never tried to impose an entirely antique character on his work, he did aspire to create works both equalling and surpassing those of the most celebrated classical artists. A very few of his sculptures are copies or 'paraphrases' of famous antique works, and one of the most remarkable is the *Dancing Faun* (Fig. 1), which appeared at auction last autumn. The work is not documented, but its style dates it to around 1610 or 1615, and it is certainly one of de Vries's masterpieces. The Greek *Dancing Faun* in the Uffizi is its classical prototype, and this corroborates the suggestion that the famous antique was already in the Medici collection in the sixteenth century, despite it's not being documented there until the mid-seventeenth century. De Vries must have seen it no later than 1595, when he travelled to Rome.

The classical *Faun* was generally attributed to Praxiteles, one of the most famous antique sculptors, and this must have been a particular incentive to de Vries to 'contest' with the work. Once we compare the two sculptures it becomes obvious that de Vries treated his model rather freely. The length of time that had passed between his first viewing of the original and the final modelling of his own version might in part account for this, but he evidently intended to create an independent variation upon it. By straightening the pose, and opening up the composition, de Vries's *Faun* gains a livelier and more elegant outline. The heaviness which seems to weigh down the movements of the antique *Faun* is dissolved in a dance-like arabesque. It is probable that Adrien de Vries studied the antique masterpiece less for the accuracy of its anatomy than for its animal expression and rhythm. These characteristics are manifest in a heightened and refined way, in his own version.

The same free and self-confident relation to antiquity can be found in the Laocoon group, which de Vries modelled for the garden of the Waldstein palace. The artist's

Fig. 5
A bronze portrait relief of Emperor Rudolf II, Prague, 1609 (Reproduced courtesy of the Board of Trustees of the Victoria and Albert Museum, London).

Fig. 6
An equestrian bronze figure by Adrien de Vries, 1607, height 37in (94cm) (Reproduced courtesy of the Staatens Konstmuseer, Stockholm).

Left
Fig. 7a
The mausoleum monument of Count Ernst
von Schaumburg-Lippe, by Adrien de Vries,
Stadthagen.

Below
Fig. 7b
A detail of the monument showing one of
the bronze figures.

intention to out-do the celebrated model in this case is even more apparent. De Vries transforms the antique group, which was conceived from one viewpoint only, and creates a conically-tapering, multi-faceted composition which, more than almost any other Mannerist sculpture, observes Cellini's dictat that it be equally beautiful from all sides. It is fascinating to observe how de Vries applies only minimal changes to the individual figures to achieve this. The comparison with the antique Laocoon also shows how little de Vries was concerned with physiognomical expression. Except for his portrait busts, he was not interested in portraying strong emotions or individual characters; his art is the art of body language, and movement is its central theme.

We are dealing, here, with something like a *querelle entre les anciens et les modernes*. Challenging the antique as he does, Adrien de Vries is a masterly and eloquent advocate of the modern. The characteristically personal, sketchy style of modelling that he developed in the long years of his activity is typical of this. This style is sometimes carried to such extremes that the sculptures appear almost unfinished. It would seem, also, to prove that de Vries worked on the essential features of his sculptures with his own hands. His supremely 'impressionistic' treatment allowed him to bring his statues' surface to life through the play of reflected light. A workshop assistant would scarcely have been able to copy the ease of his free, *sprezzatura* modelling, and in this quality, de Vries is the ideal of the international Mannerist artist.

An Upper Rhenish gilt, silvered and painted wood group of the Madonna and Child, *circa* 1480–90,
height 31in (78.7cm)
New York $242,000 (£144,048). 31.V.90
From the collection of Richard F. Sterba

A Florentine bronze statuette of David with the head of Goliath by Gianfrancesco Susini, signed with monogram on sword grip, *circa* 1630–40, height 15¼in (38.7cm)
London £286,000 ($474,760). 7.XII.89

Left
A Florentine bronze statue of Hercules supporting the globe, seventeenth century, height 35in (88.9cm)
London £148,500 ($258,390). 12.IV.90

Opposite
A Roman terracotta Bacchanalian group by Claude Michel, called 'Clodion', signed and dated *1765*, height 16¼in (41.3cm)
New York $242,000 (£144,048). 31.V.90

Below
A North Italian bronze oil-lamp in the form of an acrobat with silver eyes, *circa* 1500, probably Mantua, height 5½in (14cm)
London £187,000 ($310,420). 7.XII.89

Opposite
An English marble bust of Alexander Pope by Louis-François Roubiliac, signed and dated *1741*, overall height 24⅞in (63.2cm) London £935,000 ($1,776,500). 5.VII.90 From the collection of The Rt Hon. the Earl of Rosebery

A bronze bust of Edward Herbert, 1st Baron Herbert of Cherbury (1581/3–1648) by Hubert Le Sueur, dated *1631*, height 21¼in (54cm) London £264,000 ($459,360). 12.IV.90

The bust is now alternated between Powys Castle (National Trust) and the National Museum of Wales.

A South German or Austrian bronze-mounted steel strong box, first third eighteenth century, length
34in (86.4cm)
New York $88,000 (£53,012). 9.I.90

Opposite
A German gilt-silver-mounted rock crystal pilgrims' flask, late sixteenth century, height 11in (27.9cm)
New York $209,000 (£124,405). 31.V.90

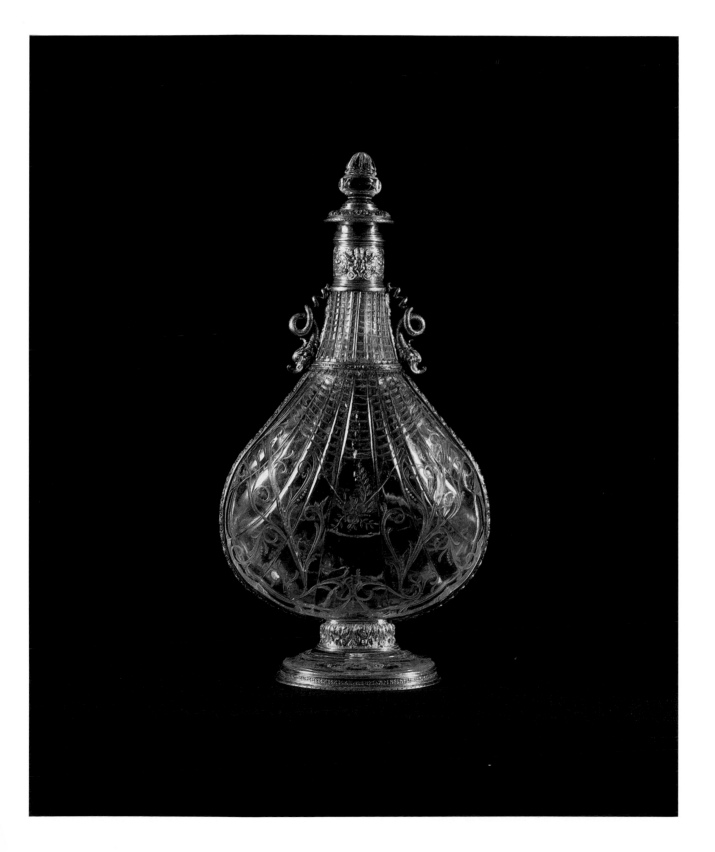

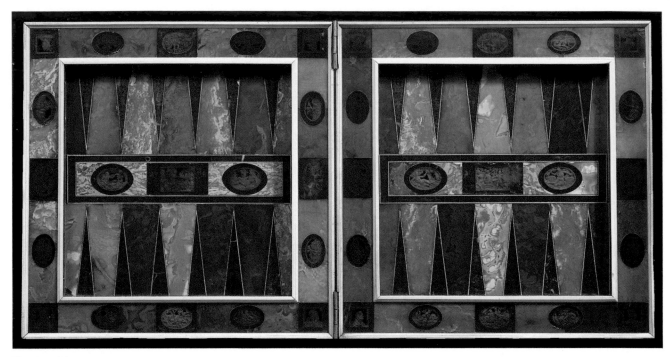

Figs 1 and 2
An amber gaming board by Georg Schreiber, Königsberg, signed and dated *1616*, showing the interior,
for backgammon and the exterior, for chess and Nine Men's Morris, 13¾in by 13¾in (35cm by 35cm),
with a complete set of amber chessmen and twelve opaque and twelve clear amber draughtsmen
London £330,000 ($574,200). 12.IV.90

An amber gaming board

Tim Ayers

Amber works of art are exceptionally rare, because the substance itself is scarce, fragile and difficult to work. The completely unrecorded amber gaming board sold last April (Figs 1 and 2) was therefore keenly competed for in the saleroom. It dates from a key period in the history of amber carving – the later Renaissance in northern Europe – but amber has in fact been prized for very much longer. The static electricity that it can collect may explain in part the fascination that it has held for man since prehistory; and the material has other unusual qualities, being light and surprisingly warm to the touch.

Amber is fossilised resin, from trees that perished millions of years ago. It is to be found in many places around the world, but the Baltic has been the primary source of raw material for European carvers since the end of the Roman empire. The beds of resin lie under both sea and land, so that pieces may be washed up on the beach or mined. Those large enough to make into works of art were highly treasured and extremely valuable.

The golden age of amber carving was from the later sixteenth to the eighteenth century. Its popularity coincided with the love of finely worked precious materials that manifested itself in the *Kunstkammer* of that period, the aristocratic connoisseur's 'cabinet of curiosities'. The supply of amber was controlled profitably by the rulers along the Baltic coast. The man who exploited it most successfully in the sixteenth century was Albrecht von Hohenzollern, Duke of Prussia from 1525. The Prussian court was located at Königsberg and remained there until 1618, when it moved to Berlin, upon the inheritance of the Duchy by the Elector of Brandenburg.

The present gaming board was signed and dated in Königsberg just two years previously, *Georgivs Scriba Borvssvs Civis et Incola Regiomonti Borvssorum Hoc Fecit 1616* ('Georg Schreiber, Prussian citizen and inhabitant of Königsberg of the Prussians made this in 1616'; see above). A precious survival from this early period in the development of Renaissance amber carving, it is an eloquent expression of the standards that Königsberg craftsmen had attained by this time.

Stenzel Schmidt is the first recorded amber carver at the Königsberg court, in the early 1560s, with an annual stipend of one hundred marks. The names of a number of other carvers are also known. In the first half of the seventeenth century Georg

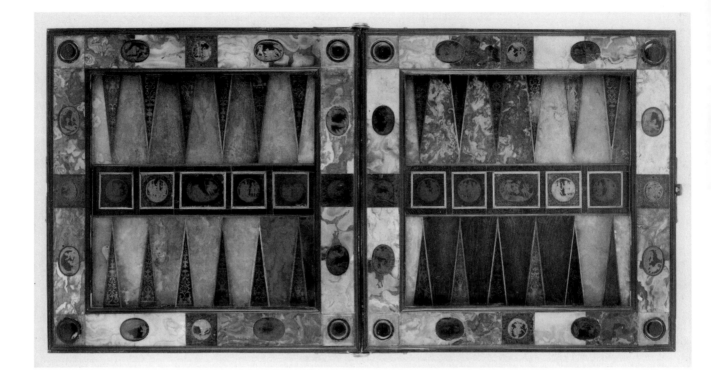

Schreiber (d.1643) was certainly a leading figure, if not the leading figure in Königsberg, and with Lorenz Schnipperling, he was a founder of the amber workers' guild there in 1641.

Two caskets and a lidded tankard are signed by him; all three are distinguished by fine low relief carving. A portable altar in the Museo degli Argenti in Florence, signed and dated 1618 and 1619, in the same wording as the gaming board, is the grandest of all the artist's known pieces, standing 47½in high (121cm). The newly discovered board is now Schreiber's earliest dated work and the only board to be signed by him.

It is remarkable for its condition – amber is a fragile material, vulnerable to light and heat. On exposure to these over time its colour can change from yellow to red, and oxidisation may cause crazing and brittleness. This board has clearly been kept with great care and it demonstrates many of the ways in which amber carvers have exploited their material. The variety of colour is used here to brilliant effect, to differentiate the fields of play and borders, from opaque white, through spectacular mottled shades, to clear amber now in every shade from yellow to red. The translucency is used to advantage, for some of these pieces are laid over cut openwork roundels of white amber, like panes of glass. They are also enamelled on the reverse, a technique similar to *verre eglomisé*, with metal foil behind: alternate squares on the chessboard depict soldiers in contemporary costume; the points of the backgammon board are decorated with scrolls, and the narrow borders contain running animals. The ovals, circles and squares of white amber show classical allegories, infants riding on sea creatures and portrait busts.

Fig. 3
An amber gaming board, probably Königsberg, dated *1606*
(Reproduced courtesy of the Württembergisches Landesmuseum, Stuttgart).

Fig. 4
An amber gaming board, probably Königsberg, early seventeenth century
(Reproduced courtesy of the Bayerisches Nationalmuseum, Munich).

Amber gaming boards were made in Königsberg from an early date, primarily as courtly presents. In 1567 Stenzel Schmidt is reported to have made two boards, decorated with heads of huntsmen, and in November 1597 Michael Fischer was paid 750 marks for an amber board. A surviving board, dated 1594, in the Hessisches Landesmuseum, Kassel, bears the arms of Landgraf Moritz von Hessen. Decorated in ways similar to the present example, it too must have been made in Königsberg. Another, dated 1606, was acquired recently by the Württembergisches Landesmuseum in Stuttgart (Fig. 3), and further comparable amber boards, or parts of them, are to be found in the Bayerisches Nationalmuseum in Munich (Fig. 4) and the Victoria and Albert Museum, London.

Schreiber's gaming board is one of the finest amber works of art to appear at auction in recent years. His signature, and the date, set the seal on this splendid survival from the period of ducal residence in Königsberg, when amber was among the grandest gifts that the Duke could bestow.

East Christian icons

John Stuart

The first person in modern times to raise the question of the aesthetic value of icon painting was Goethe.

Goethe had heard something about a flourishing of painterly tradition in fifteenth-century Suzdal, and he was anxious to discover more about it. He turned for help to the Queen of Würtemburg, the Russian-born sister of Alexander I; but she knew nothing. She did, however, pass on Goethe's query to be dealt with by the Foreign Office in St Petersburg. Officials there, who no doubt found the Queen's request unusual, followed it up by contacting the local governor of the Province of Vladimir, where the ancient town of Suzdal is situated. The governor took the matter up with the district authority of Suzdal, and in due course received a letter – from the local police – saying that, regrettably, they had not discovered any information about a tradition of icon painting in their town. The clergy of Suzdal had been consulted, and had provided the names of craft centres in the villages of Palekh, Mistera and Kholui, where attractive icons were currently being produced; could it be, they asked, that Goethe had these centres in mind?

So Goethe learnt nothing; but his enquiry astonished the Russian educated public. Icons were seen as sacred objects, and therefore the question of their aesthetic value did not arise. Moreover, educated Russians tended to be culturally orientated towards the West, and to hold their own artistic heritage in rather low esteem. This is not perhaps as surprising as it may seem. The process of cleaning and restoring icons began only in the late nineteenth century, so Goethe's contemporaries had a completely erroneous conception of what medieval icons looked like in their original state. Numerous are the references in nineteenth-century Russian literature to 'ancient black icons'. But icons were only black because their varnish had absorbed years of candle soot and grime from incense. Worse still, they were periodically refreshed by retouching with new layers of paint; and the custom of encasing icons in elaborate metal covers often obscured everything with the exception of the faces and hands. Often, all that remained of the original work of art was the silhouette.

Once they had been cleaned, however, icons began to attract the interest of avant-garde painters. Matisse, who encountered them during his visit to Russia in 1911, believed the study of icons to be of immense value to the modern movement. Vrubel was fascinated by the treatment of drapery, and by the cumulative use of colour glazes. Kandinsky and Goncharova were struck by the pure contrasting and primary colours, found in the icons of Novgorod, while Tatlin learnt something of his mastery of line from the icon painter's technique.

Fig. 1
A Byzantine icon of Saint George and Saint Dimitri of Thesaloniki, first half fifteenth century, 14⅜in by 10½in (36.5cm by 26.7cm) London £93,500 ($163,625). 5.IV.90

Opposite
Fig. 2
A Byzantine icon of the
Mother of God Hodigitria,
circa 1400, 30¼in by 23¼in
(77cm by 59cm)
London £93,500
($163,625). 5.IV.90

During the last season a number of top quality icons appeared on the market. Pride of place both chronologically and in terms of rarity must go to the examples painted during the Byzantine period – before Constantinople fell to the Ottoman Turks in 1453. One such image (Fig. 1) represents the mounted warrior saints George and Dimitri, idealised prototypes of the early Christian warrior-martyr. George of Cappodocia, a soldier in Diocletian's army, is remembered in legend for his bravery and handsome appearance, and as such was invoked by Byzantine armies. Here George is represented with another champion and military saint, Dimitri, whose cult is interwoven with the history of Thessaloniki, the second city of the Empire, where his relics are enshrined. Another very similar panel is in the Vatican museum; both icons were evidently painted in the same workshop, sometime before the fall of Constantinople.

An icon of the Virgin as Hodigitria ('the guide' or 'the one who leads the way'; Fig. 2) was probably painted around 1400, half a century before the fall of Constantinople. By tradition, the original version of this image is believed to have been painted from life by the evangelist Luke, and had been the palladium (or symbolic 'standard') of the city. The present version is imbued with a sense of extraordinary inner emotion masked by outer control, and it is this tension which accounts for the unforgettable, haunting quality of the Virgin's glance. Face painting of this kind, characteristic of the best images associated with Constantinople, testifies to a long artistic and spiritual tradition.

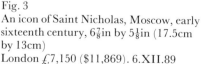

Fig. 3
An icon of Saint Nicholas, Moscow, early sixteenth century, 6⅞in by 5⅛in (17.5cm by 13cm)
London £7,150 ($11,869). 6.XII.89

Fig. 4
A double-sided processional icon painted with
the Fiery Ascent of the Prophet Elijah to
Heaven, and on the reverse with the Virgin of
the Sign, Northern Province of Novgorod or
Trans-Volga region, late sixteenth century,
height including shaft 43¾in (111cm)
London £55,000 ($96,250). 5.IV.90

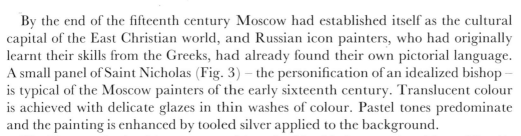

By the end of the fifteenth century Moscow had established itself as the cultural capital of the East Christian world, and Russian icon painters, who had originally learnt their skills from the Greeks, had already found their own pictorial language. A small panel of Saint Nicholas (Fig. 3) – the personification of an idealized bishop – is typical of the Moscow painters of the early sixteenth century. Translucent colour is achieved with delicate glazes in thin washes of colour. Pastel tones predominate and the painting is enhanced by tooled silver applied to the background.

The Novgorod school is represented in a double-sided processional icon (Fig. 4); its style and content reflect the great northern mercantile republic with an emphasis on strong drawing and vivid colour contrasts as opposed to quiet, lyrical tonal harmonies. The original image of the Virgin of the Sign, painted on the reverse of the present panel, was the miraculous palladium of Novgorod; the obverse depicts the Ascension of Elijah to Heaven in a chariot drawn by three blazing horses. Both images focus on the depiction of holy fire and divine light – the Virgin of the Sign being thematically related to the Old Testament story of the Burning Bush, which survives the flames intact just as Mary conceived and contained the Divine Logos while remaining a Virgin. Icon painters were preoccupied with the depiction of light, both figuratively and metaphysically, as an emanation of divine energy.

A late-fifteenth-century icon of the Dormition of the Virgin (Fig. 5) is instantly recognisable as an example of the classic Novgorod style. Here again, the boldly-constructed composition is emphasised with a strong graphic element, and vibrant contrasting planes of green and red paint. The scene shows the Virgin laid out on a bier, surrounded by the apostles. In the foreground, the impious Aphonios, his head draped with a turban-like cloth, attempts to overthrow the bier, but is forestalled by an Angel who appears with a drawn sword, and strikes off his hands. This remarkable painting achieved a world record auction price for a panel icon.

Woodworm, Stalin, rot and fire have been responsible for the destruction of countless icon treasures, but each season more undiscovered works appear, and as interest in East Christian art grows, the outdated notion that icons are synonymous with derivative and generally indifferent nineteenth-century panel painting is finally being overthrown.

Opposite
Fig. 5
An icon of the Dormition
of the Virgin, Novgorod,
circa 1480, 21½in by 16½in
(54.5cm by 42cm)
London £132,000
($231,000). 5.IV.90

A Fabergé two-colour gold
and enamel photograph
frame, St Petersburg,
late nineteenth century,
diameter 4in (10.3cm)
Geneva SF41,800
(£17,787:$29,857).
17.V.90

A Fabergé carved agate
model of a chicken, *circa*
1900, height 2¾in (7cm)
SF77,000 (£29,961:$47,531
A Fabergé carved bowenite
model of a pig, *circa* 1900,
height 2⅞in (7.4cm)
SF104,500 (£40,661:$64,506)

Both Fabergé carvings
were sold in Geneva on
16th November 1989.

A Fabergé gold and translucent enamel *bonbonnière* in the form of an Empire *fauteuil*, marked with initials of workmaster Henrik Wigström, St Petersburg, *circa* 1911, height 2⅞in (7.4cm)
New York $220,000 (£136,646). 15.XII.89

A silver-gilt and enamel
easter egg by Fyodor
Rückert, Moscow, *circa*
1900, height 3½in (8.9cm)
New York $22,000
(£12,865). 13.VI.90

A silver and enamel bowl,
Solvychegodsk, late
seventeenth century,
diameter 6in (15.2cm)
London £6,600 ($11,550).
5.IV.90

This bowl was bought by
the Hillwood Museum,
Washington, DC.

Leon Samoilovich Bakst
A TURBANED BLACK
SERVANT FROM THE BALLET
'SALOME' DANCING WITH
VEILS
Charcoal and bodycolour,
heightened with gold,
signed, 26⅜in by 17⅜in
(67cm by 44cm)
London £55,000
($91,300). 5.XII.89

Pietro de Rossi
PRINCE ALEXEI IAKOVLEVICH LOBANOV-ROSTOVSKY
Signed and dated *1828*, height 2⅛in (5.5cm)
Geneva SF28,600 (£11,128:$17,654). 16.XI.89

Jean-Etienne Liotard
JEAN-BAPTISTE MASSE, AFTER A SELF-PORTRAIT
Enamel, the backing paper inscribed in a later hand
*Jean-Baptiste Massé/Name of our Ancestor/Court Painter
to/Louis XV/Born 1688/Our Great-grandmothers/ brother*,
height 2½in (6.5cm)
Geneva SF93,500 (£36,381:$57,716). 16.XI.89

A French two-colour gold *boîte-à-miniature*, set *à cage* with six miniatures by Louis-Nicolas van
Blarenberghe, Paris, 1781, width 3⅛in (8.1cm)
Geneva SF154,000 (£65,532:$110,000). 17.V.90

A *quatre-couleurs* gold and diamond Imperial presentation snuff box, maker's mark *PAG* in monogram,
St Petersburg, *circa* 1768, width 3⅜in (8.5cm)
Geneva SF2,035,000 (£791,829:$1,256,173). 16.XI.89

The box was presented by Catherine the Great and her heir Grand Duke Paul to Thomas
and Nathaniel Dimsdale, English doctors, in 1768. Thomas Dimsdale, celebrated for
his practice of inoculation against smallpox, had been summoned in hasty secrecy to
St Petersburg by Catherine when a severe epidemic swept Russia. On arrival, he was
disconcerted to discover that Catherine wished him to inoculate both Paul and herself, not
just to protect their lives but as an example to her suspicious subjects. At that time inoculation
(soon to be superseded by vaccination) was a novel, risky procedure, so the Empress was
displaying both courage and modernism when she confided to Dimsdale: 'My life is my own
and I shall with the utmost cheerfulness and confidence rely on your care'. On 12th October
1768, later declared a day of national thanksgiving, Catherine was successfully inoculated,
shortly followed by the Grand Duke. Luckily for the Dimsdales' peace of mind, they had not
known of the relay of horses prepared for their escape from Russia had harm befallen the
Imperial persons. As it was, the modest doctor who had refused to charge for his services was
fêted and lavishly honoured. He was created a Baron of the Russian Empire, appointed
counsellor of state and physician to Her Majesty, given the sum of £10,000 and an annuity
to be paid in England and presented with miniatures of Catherine and Paul. According to
Dimsdale's account: 'Her Majesty was also graciously pleased to express her approbation of
my son's conduct, by . . . ordering him to be presented with a superb gold snuff box, richly set
with diamonds'. The box remained in the family until it achieved a world record price.

A detail of Pater's *Le Plaisir de l'Eté*, the source for the lid design (*left*).

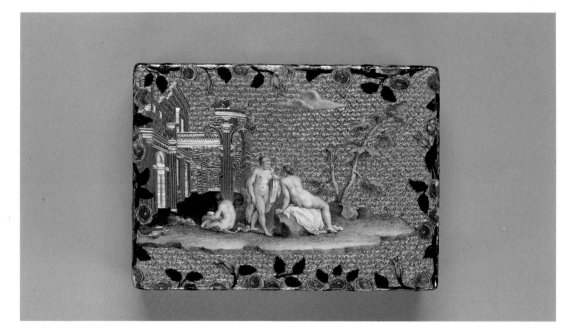

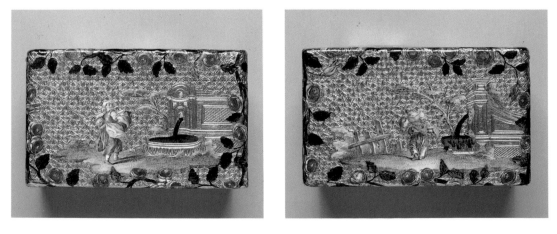

Fig. 1
A German gold and enamel snuff box, maker's mark of Daniel Baudesson, the enamel by Daniel Nikolaus Chodowiecki, Berlin, *circa* 1765, width 3¼in (8.1cm)
Geneva SF770,000 (£327,660:$550,000).
15.V.90
From the collection of the British Rail Pension Fund

Snuff boxes from the collection of the British Rail Pension Fund

Julia Clarke

Fig. 2
An English gold and enamel *étui*, maker's mark of George Michael Moser, London, mid eighteenth century, length 4¾in (12cm) Geneva SF484,000 (£205,957:$345,714). 15.V.90
From the collection of the British Rail Pension Fund

Gold boxes in the eighteenth century were not merely containers for snuff. They were symbols of their owners' artistic discernment, eye for novelty, social status and, of course, wealth. Boxes could be the gifts of kings to reward or celebrate an occasion; boxes were exchanged as New Year's *étrennes*; boxes were commissioned, collected, carried. Above all, the boxes were held in the hand, to be studied and admired. Goldsmiths responded to the demand for these works of art in miniature by concocting a seemingly endless multiplicity of shapes and styles in luxurious materials. Paris was the main centre for originality and quality in the creation of snuff boxes, as for so much else, although many other European courts, such as Dresden, Berlin, Naples or St Petersburg, inspired their craftsmen to invent their own specialities.

Contemporary collections of snuff boxes were made by passionate connoisseurs, both male and female, such as Frederick II of Prussia, Madame de Pompadour in France and Catherine the Great in Russia. For later collectors a snuff box could encapsulate the charm and quality of a lost pastoral world, a nostalgia inspired by the de Goncourt brothers. A sparkling cluster of objects of vertu and gold boxes would be imperative for serious collectors such as the 3rd Marquess of Hertford (whose boxes are now at the Wallace Collection) or the Rothschilds.

The British Rail Pension Fund Collection followed in the steps of these earlier amateurs in its search for objects which would demonstrate the best Parisian boxes and the best of those that were being produced in other European centres. The collection included boxes of chased, coloured or jewelled gold, enamel, mother-of-pearl, hardstones, ivory, tortoiseshell, porcelain, Japanese lacquer and its French imitation *vernis Martin*. Works by celebrated makers such as Ducrollay, Drais and Vachette of Paris, Baudesson of Berlin, Neuber of Dresden and Moser of London, were included. Inevitably, as well, many of the objects were either made for or have belonged to illustrious people. Yet, surprisingly, the two rarest items in the collection have no history before the middle of the twentieth century. The Berlin gold box of *circa* 1765, maker's mark of Frederick the Great's *Hofjuwelier*, Daniel Baudesson (Fig. 1), was enamelled by Daniel Chodowiecki with hedonistic scenes, that on the lid based on Pater's *Le Plaisir de l'Eté*. Curiously, one of the two original versions of the painting is known to have been in Frederick's possession at Sans Souci some twenty years before, but the time lapse involved makes it very unlikely that this is anything

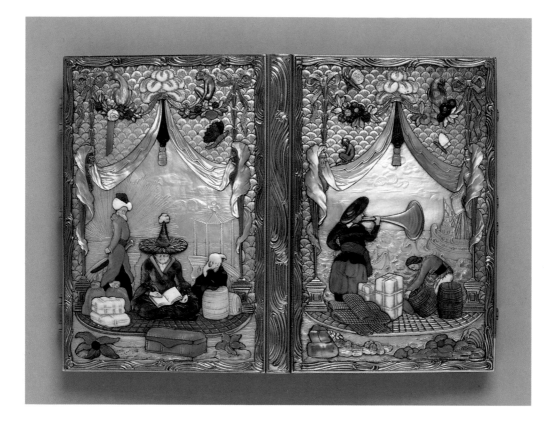

Fig. 3
A French gold, mother-of-pearl and shell *aide-mémoire*, maker's mark of Thomas-François Breton, Paris, 1747, height 3¾in (9.6cm) Geneva SF264,000 (£112,340:$188,571). 15.V.90
From the collection of the British Rail Pension Fund

more than a coincidence. The gold *étui* chased and enamelled by George Michael Moser (Fig. 2), the celebrated artist who worked in London for most of his life, is the only *étui*, and the only enamel other than a watch case, which he has signed. Its origins are lost but its future is assured. Purchased by a Swiss foundation, it is to be displayed in the museum at Schaffhausen, Moser's birthplace.

Again, we do not know who first owned the unusual French gold-mounted note-book cover (Fig. 3), encrusted in shells and variously-coloured mother-of-pearl depicting a meeting of East and West (Turkish, Chinese and Dutch traders meet on a quayside under canopies scaled by monkeys and insects). It subsequently belonged, however, to Beau Brummell, the celebrated British arbiter of fashion, who gave it in 1805 to the pretty Lady Harriet Villiers. Her descendants took the trouble to write the history in the notebook – and their scribbles animating the rest of the leaves add to our sense of the past.

In the case of a box which has excited the interest of many previous commentators (Fig. 4), the documentary evidence is as confusing as it is informative. The rim is inscribed 'Debèche . . . Pour le Cabinet de Sa Majesté . . . Année 1710' but the box was made in Paris by Pierre-François Drais in 1772. Enamelled in brilliant green over engraved decoration, it is set with six gold panels breathtakingly chased with classical scenes attributable to the flamboyant Flemish chaser Gérard Debèche. Debèche was as famed in folk-memory for his drunken debauchery as for his fine chasing, and is known to have worked with Drais and for the Court.

Opposite
Fig. 4
A French three-colour gold and enamel snuff box, maker's mark of Pierre-François Drais, inset with six gold plaques attributed to Gérard Debèche, Paris, 1772, width 3¼in (8cm) Geneva SF555,500 (£236,383:$396,786). 15.V.90
From the collection of the British Rail Pension Fund

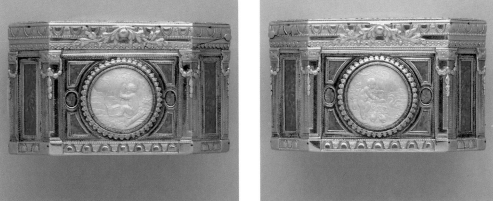

More often, however, the boxes do not carry inscriptions, and we must infer the identity of the original owner from clues in the decoration. The gold-mounted Meissen porcelain box painted with views of the castles and territories of Augustus III, Elector of Saxony and King of Poland (Fig. 5), is one of a small group of boxes quite evidently made for royal distribution. More subtly, methodical research into the pictorial sources of the miniatures painted by Jacques Charlier on a French box mounted by Jean Ducrollay in 1750 (Fig. 6), has suggested overwhelmingly that the box must have been made for Madame de Pompadour. The miniatures are all based on paintings by François Boucher and the two principal panels are after two pendants, *Les Deux Confidentes* and *Le Sommeil Interrompu*, signed and dated 1750, delivered to Madame de Pompadour and probably intended for the Château de Bellevue. Both paintings and the box are closely contemporary, and Madame de Pompadour was known to own boxes with miniatures by Charlier.

As Horace Townsend wrote of another collection dispersed in 1910:

. . . these boxes, one and all, possess historical association in its most comprehensive meaning. In their grace, their lavish ornamentation, and their incrusted jewels they are more eloquent than a chapter of Carlyle of the social conditions and causes which culminated in the French Revolution.

Fig. 5
A Meissen porcelain topographical snuff box with two-colour gold mounts, *circa* 1755–60, width 3¼in (8cm) Geneva SF396,000 (£168,511:$282,857). 15.V.90
From the collection of the British Rail Pension Fund

An engraving of Boucher's *Les Deux Confidentes*, the source for the lid design (*right*).

Fig. 6
A French gold *boîte à miniature*, maker's mark of Jean Ducrollay, mounted *à cage* with miniatures by Jacques Charlier after François Boucher, Paris, 1750, width 3¼in (8.2cm)
Geneva SF418,000
(£177,872: $298,571).
15.V.90
From the collection of the British Rail Pension Fund

Clocks and watches

A Louis XV ormolu and patinated bronze musical clock, the case by Jean-Joseph de Saint Germain and inscribed *St. Germain* and the movements signed by Pierre Gille, l'Ainé, mid eighteenth century, height 32½in (82.5cm)
New York $660,000 (£420,382). 3.XI.89
From a collection formed by Roberto Polo

Right
A Regency gilt-bronze mounted tortoiseshell, ebony and mother-of-pearl clock and stand, attributed to Jean-Pierre Latz, *circa* 1730, height 8ft 10¼in (270cm)
Monte Carlo FF2,220,000 (£223,116:$389,474). 16.VI.90
From the collection of Count Harrach

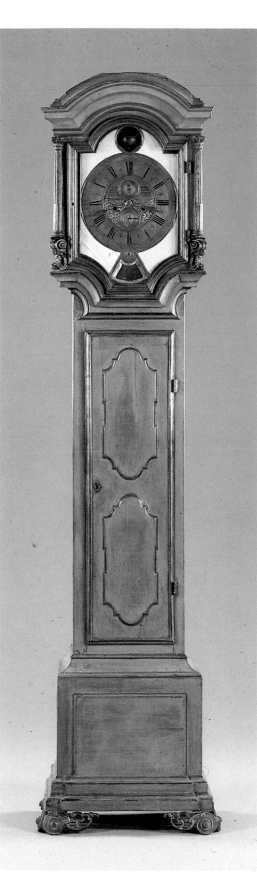

Right
A month going equation
calendar longcase clock
with duplex escapement by
Daniel Delander, inscribed
Tempus aequale, et inaequale:
horologio hoc indicatur.
Differentia est aequatio
temporaria Flamstedy,
circa 1710, height
7ft 11in (241.3cm)
London £104,500
($178,695). 5.X.89

Far right
A Queen Anne walnut
month going longcase clock
by Thomas Tompion,
inscribed *Tho. Tompion*
Londini Fecit and *Tho.*
Tompion & Edw. Banger
London, circa 1700, overall
height 8ft 4½in (255cm)
London £132,000
($225,720). 5.X.89

An ebony veneered quarter repeating bracket clock with oak travelling case by Thomas Tompion, inscribed *Tho. Thompion Londini Fecit*, *circa* 1700, height 15in (38cm)
London £165,000 ($298,650). 22.II.90

Below, left
A George II mahogany combination angle barometer, thermometer and mirror, probably by Edward Scarlett, with later signature *T. Blunt London*, *circa* 1730, height 44⅞in (114cm)
London £88,000 ($150,480). 5.X.89

Below
A Charles II walnut bracket clock by Joseph Knibb, inscribed *Joseph Knibb Londini Fecit*, *circa* 1865, height 13in (33cm)
London £46,200 ($82,236). 11.V.90

Right
A gold keyless lever minute repeating split seconds clockwatch with grande and petite sonnerie by Golay Fils & Stahl, with presentation inscription *Made for Joseph Beecham by Golay Sons & Stahl Geneva 1899*, diameter 2⅛in (5.4cm) London £31,900 ($56,782). 10.V.90

Far right
A gold openface split seconds chronograph with register by A. Lange & Sohne, *circa* 1906, diameter 2⅛in (5.5cm) Geneva SF82,500 (£35,106:$58,929). 15.V.90

A gold openface minute repeating tourbillon grande sonnerie clockwatch with perpetual calendar and moon phases by Charles Frodsham, inscribed *Chas. Frodsham of 27 South Moulton St., London*, 1917, diameter 3in (7.5cm)
New York $374,000 (£236,709). 30.X.89

A gold hunting cased minute repeating perpetual calendar keyless lever chronograph by S. Smith & Son, inscribed *S. Smith & Son, 9, Strand, London, No. 150-100*, 1899, diameter 2⅜in (5.9cm)
London £30,800 ($52,668). 5.X.89

A gold openface minute repeating split seconds chronograph with perpetual calendar and moon phases by Patek Philippe & Co., *circa* 1915, diameter 2⅛in (5.5cm)
New York $203,500 (£120,414). 7.VI.90

A gold keyless lever one minute tourbillon by Charles Frodsham, inscribed *Chas. Frodsham 09364 AD Fmsz*, 1910, diameter 2½in (6.5cm)
London £46,200 ($78,540). 14.XII.89

A gold and enamel hunting cased minute repeating watch by Patek Philippe & Co., *circa* 1910, diameter 2in (5cm)
Geneva SF52,800 (£20,545:$32,593). 14.XI.89

A gold openface watch with up and down scale and Guillaume balance by Patek Philippe & Co., 1910, diameter 2in (5cm)
Geneva SF71,500 (£30,425:$51,071). 15.V.90

Right, top to bottom
A gold wristwatch by Patek
Philippe & Co., 1954,
diameter 1⅜in (3.3cm)
London £16,500
($29,370). 10.V.90

A gold split seconds
chronograph with tach-
ometer and register by Patek
Philippe & Co., *circa* 1947,
diameter 1⅜in (3.5cm)
New York $330,000
(£198,795). 25.I.90

A platinum tonneau
minute repeating single-
button chronograph with
register, perpetual
calendar and moon phases
by James Schultz, *circa*
1930, length 1⅜in (3.5cm)
New York $539,000
(£341,139). 30.X.89

A gold chronograph with
tachometer and registers
by Audemars Piguet, *circa*
1942, diameter 1⅜in (3.3cm)
Geneva SF176,000
(£68,482:$108,642). 14.XI.89

Centre, top to bottom
A gold chronograph with
tachometer and telemeter
by Patek Philippe & Co., *circa*
1945, diameter 1⅜in (3.3cm)
Geneva SF209,000
(£81,323:$129,012). 14.XI.89

A gold double-dial rectangular reverso chronograph by
Movado, *circa* 1935, length
1¾in (4.4cm)
Geneva SF170,500
(£66,342:$105,247). 14.XI.89

Far right, top to bottom
A gold minute repeating
wristwatch by Patek Philippe
& Co., *circa* 1955, diameter
1⅜in (3.3cm)
New York $264,000
(£156,213). 7.VI.90

A platinum moonphase
calendar wristwatch by Patek
Philippe & Co., 1935,
diameter 1⅛in (3cm)
London £308,000 ($557,480).
22.II.90

Jewellery

An emerald, ruby, sapphire and diamond bracelet-watch by Cartier, 1929
Geneva SF748,000 (£288,803:$461,728). 15.XI.89

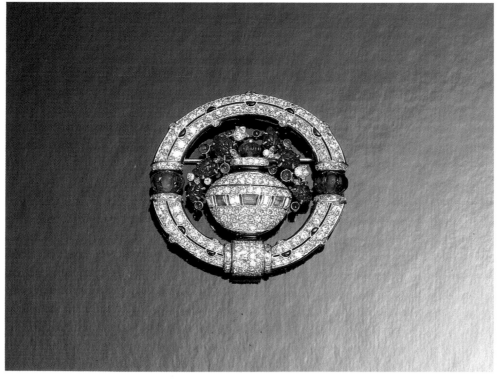

Top
An emerald, ruby, sapphire and diamond bracelet by Van Cleef & Arpels, 1939
Geneva SF275,000 (£106,178:$169,753). 15.XI.89

Above
A gem-set brooch by Van Cleef & Arpels, *circa* 1925, the hinged centre of *giardinetto* design concealing
a watch
London £39,600 ($67,716). 5.X.89

The jewels of Luz Mila Patiño, Countess du Boisrouvray

Nicholas Rayner

An emerald and diamond necklace by Cartier, London, 1937, $3,080,000 (£1,949,367)
A pair of emerald and diamond pendant-earclips, *en suite* with the necklace, by Cartier, London, 1937, $341,000 (£215,823)

These pieces from the collection of Luz Mila Patiño, Countess du Boisrouvray, were sold in New York on 26th October 1989.

The sumptuous jewels from the collection of the late Count and Countess Guy du Boisrouvray are the product of the unusual interest in gemstones of two men. Both the legendary Bolivian millionaire Simon Patiño and his son-in-law, Guy du Boisrouvray, were fascinated by the underground treasures of the earth.

Simon Patiño was born into a simple Bolivian Indian family. As a young man, he was first employed as an assistant in a local mining supply shop. One day a miner requested the loan of hand tools to work a small claim of tin ore in the nearby mountains. Having no funds, he lodged his claim certificate as a deposit. The miner was unsuccessful, and on returning the tools, he made over the claim certificate to Simon in lieu of payment. There was an old legend of tin in the area of the claim and Simon set off by himself to find it. After months of hard labour, using pick-axe and spade, he uncovered one of the richest veins of tin ever found in the Andes. This was the beginning of a story of mineral discovery which has been the dream of every prospector ever since.

Simon Patiño did not allow his vast new fortune to go to his head. He had married a pretty Bolivian girl from the local mining town of Oruro, whom he continued to adore through poor times and rich. But he also quickly learned to appreciate the best things in life. They had several grand houses and lived in a style befitting their fortune, surrounding themselves with beautiful furniture and works of art. Simon's greatest passion was for gems; as a miner, he was drawn to the rarest and the most beautiful minerals in the world, which he was able to appreciate more than most people.

The stone he preferred was the emerald for which South America is so famous. His was the eye that chose the extraordinary emerald necklace, which is composed of a superbly mounted row of Colombian stones of the 'old-mine material' often associated with the Muzo mine near Bogota. The necklace was made up for him by Cartier, London, in 1937 and originally supported a cross carved from a single emerald which had belonged in succession to Queen Isabella II of Spain, Empress Eugenie, Queen Victoria, Princess Beatrice and Queen Victoria Eugenie of Spain from whom Cartier bought it.

The lady to whom Simon Patiño presented it, his beloved wife, is remembered with great affection by the family. In her later life when she was an elderly widow, she lived in the Georges V Hotel in Paris. Every day, one of her children visited her for lunch or tea. At one point, her youngest daughter, Luz Mila, was robbed of her jewels, all except for a pair of sapphire and diamond earclips, which had been rolled up in cotton-wool at the back of a drawer. The next day, when it was Luz Mila's turn to come to lunch, Mrs Patiño took the news of the theft in her stride. When the

A ruby and diamond swirl brooch by Van Cleef & Arpels, New York
New York $1,100,000 (£696,203). 26.X.89
From the collection of Luz Mila Patiño, Countess du Boisrouvray

A ruby weighing 32.08 carats, mounted as a ring with two diamonds by Chaumet, Paris
New York $4,620,000 (£2,924,051). 26.X.89
From the collection of Luz Mila Patiño, Countess du Boisrouvray

A ruby and diamond pendant-brooch/necklace by Van Cleef & Arpels, New York, the detachable
pendant centred by a ruby weighing 24.20 carats
New York $3,080,000 (£1,949,367). 26.X.89
From the collection of Luz Mila Patiño, Countess du Boisrouvray

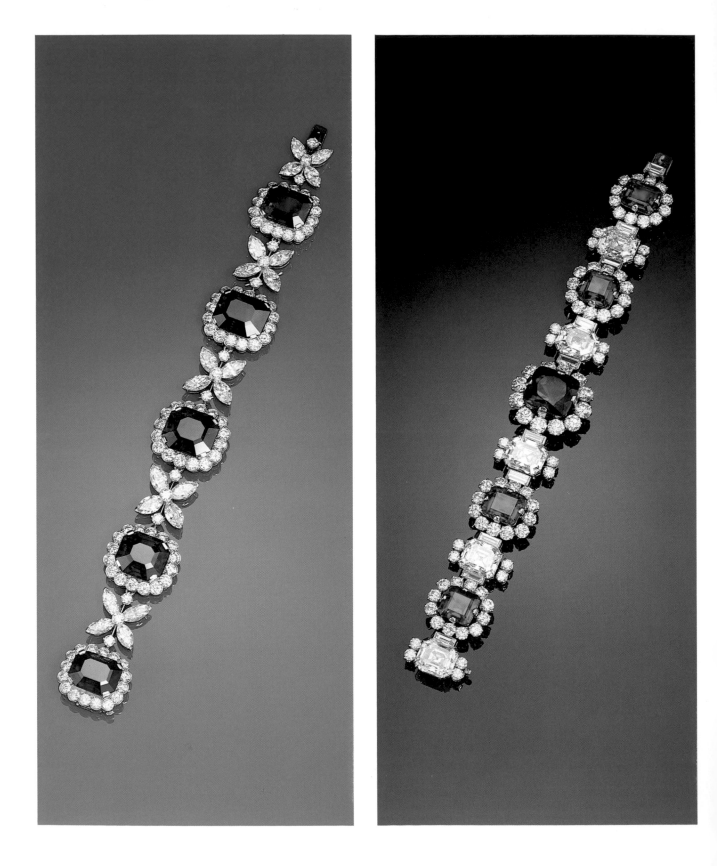

time came for Luz Mila to leave, she pressed something rolled up in cotton-wool into her hand. At home, Luz Mila discovered a wonderful jewel from her mother's collection. On many of her subsequent visits, Luz Mila was treated with the same extraordinary generosity, each time receiving on her departure a little package of rolled up cotton-wool with its precious contents. It was thus that many of the older jewels of the collection, including the emerald necklace, were handed down.

Luz Mila married a clever and charming Frenchman, Guy du Boisrouvray. Guy had also started his career in the rugged world of mining. Having finished his studies at the Ecole Centrale, possibly the most prestigious (and most difficult) school for mining engineers in Europe, he left for French Equatorial Africa. There he worked for eight years in a mining camp in the bush, with a company that was prospecting for gold. Among other things, he discovered diamonds for them. His mining education and his early prospecting experience gave Guy a common bond with his father-in-law. But, more relevant to this collection, it gave him a knowledge of the science of minerals and an exquisite taste for gemstones themselves.

The Boisrouvrays lived much of their early married life in New York where Guy was able to share his passion for gems with his great friend Louis Arpels, in those days the doyen of the New York jewellers. He was known in the family as Uncle Louis, and formal tea parties in the plush salons of the Fifth Avenue shop were often the order of the day, when jewels and gemstones were examined and compared by the two connoisseurs together with Luz Mila. Louis Arpels always stood his friends in good stead, never allowing them to buy anything but the finest, as is apparent from the extraordinary quality of the stones set in the classical designs of Van Cleef & Arpels of the 1940s and 50s in their collection. In those days, certificates of the country of origin of coloured gemstones were not required, and indeed, very often, the science of gemmology was not sufficiently advanced to prove origin. It is thus all the more remarkable that four of the five sapphires in one truly fabulous necklace are Kashmir stones.

Like his father-in-law, Guy covered his wife in the magnificent jewels he admired so much. But Luz Mila mostly dreamed of other things; her great passion in life was music. She graciously wore these gifts more to please her husband than herself. Her favourite stones were two superb rubies. During their later years, their style remained formal: they always dressed for dinner, even when they dined alone, and Guy du Boisrouvray had frequent occasion to contemplate his wife in her lustrous gems. He himself wore jewels as much as modern convention would allow. His dress-sets of rubies, sapphires and emeralds are exquisite. He used his gold toggles set with rare fancy coloured diamonds, for holding the scarves which he invariably used to wear, instead of a black-tie, with his velvet evening jacket.

Guy du Boisrouvray and Simon Patiño used their mineralogical knowledge to choose the best gems available to them. Their mining experiences and mutual passion for jewels have produced the finest group of coloured gemstones to appear on the market in the last two decades. The auction of this magnificent collection is a landmark event in the history of jewellery.

The jewels of Luz Mila Patiño, Countess du Boisrouvray were auctioned in New York in October 1989, and the proceeds were used to endow a foundation in memory of François-Xavier Bagnoud, her only grandson.

Opposite, far left
A sapphire and diamond bracelet by Van Cleef & Arpels, New York, $797,500 (£504,747)

Left
An emerald and diamond bracelet by Van Cleef & Arpels, New York, $1,265,000 (£800,633)

These bracelets, from the collection of Luz Mila Patiño, Countess du Boisrouvray, were sold in New York on 26th October 1989.

Opposite
A diamond brooch by Van Cleef & Arpels, 1951
SF165,000
(£70,213:$117,857)
An invisibly-set ruby and diamond brooch by Van Cleef & Arpels, 1951
SF264,000
(£112,340:$188,571)

These brooches were sold in Geneva on 16th May 1990.

A ruby and diamond ring by Van Cleef & Arpels, New York, weight of ruby 8.14 carats
New York $990,000
(£603,658). 24.IV.90

An Art Deco ruby, diamond, emerald and black onyx double rose brooch by Van Cleef & Arpels, *circa* 1925
New York $280,500
(£171,037). 24.IV.90

The original design for this brooch won a prize for Van Cleef & Arpels at the International Exhibition of Decorative Arts in Paris in 1925. During this period the firm featured jewels celebrating the beauty of the flower.

Opposite, above
A diamond and coloured stone Egyptian-Revival
bracelet by Lacloche Frères, Paris, *circa* 1925
St Moritz SF308,000 (£121,260:$205,333). 24.II.90

Below
An emerald and diamond brooch by Harry Winston,
weight of emerald 16.10 carats
New York $308,000 (£191,304). 26.X.89
From the collection of Mrs Severance A. Millikin

Right
A fancy pink diamond weighing 20.62 carats,
mounted as a ring
St Moritz SF7,040,000 (£2,771,654:$4,693,333).
24.II.90

Below, right
A diamond weighing 25.06 carats, mounted as a ring
Geneva SF1,265,000 (£538,298:$903,571). 16.V.90

Below
A pear-shaped diamond weighing 21.10 carats
Geneva SF1,100,000 (£424,710:$679,012). 15.XI.89

A fancy yellow diamond weighing 43.08 carats, mounted as a ring
New York $1,210,000 (£751,553). 26.X.89

A brilliant-cut diamond weighing 18.42 carats
Geneva SF1,760,000 (£679,537:$1,086,420). 15.XI.89

Right to left
A fancy pink diamond weighing 6.09 carats, mounted as a ring
New York $907,500 (£553,354). 24.IV.90

A fancy greyish-blue diamond weighing 4.20 carats,
mounted as a ring
New York $440,000 (£268,293). 24.IV.90

A fancy blue diamond weighing 7.78 carats, mounted as a ring
New York $1,705,000 (£1,059,006). 26.X.89

Opposite
A cultured pearl and diamond necklace
New York $2,200,000 (£1,341,463). 24.IV.90

A sapphire and diamond necklace by Van Cleef & Arpels, 1960
SF1,870,000 (£795,745:$1,335,714)
A diamond weighing 20.79 carats, mounted as a ring by Cartier
SF1,650,000 (£702,128:$1,178,571)

These jewels were sold in Geneva on 16th May 1990.

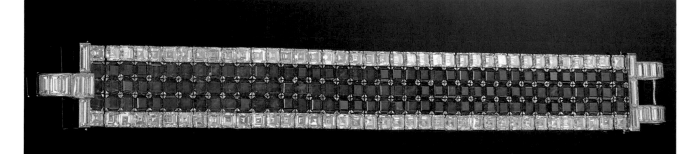

Above
A sapphire and diamond ring by Meister,
weight of sapphire 26.11 carats
Geneva SF660,000 (£254,826: $407,407).
15.XI.89

Top
A sapphire and diamond bracelet by Van
Cleef & Arpels
St Moritz FF198,000 (£77,952: $132,000).
24.II.90

Right
A *devant-de-corsage* by Boucheron, *circa* 1900
Geneva SF93,500 (£39,787: $66,786).
16.V.90

A diamond necklace by Cartier, *circa* 1904
London £154,000 ($280,280). 21.VI.90
From the collection of the late Countess of Brecknock, DBE

This jewel was made by Cartier, Paris and bought by Lady Brecknock's great uncle,
Sir Ernest Cassel, the private financial adviser and friend of Edward VII.

A diamond necklace by Harry Winston
New York $528,000 (£321,951). 24.IV.90

An emerald-cut diamond weighing 52.16 carats, mounted as a ring
New York $4,730,000 (£2,884,146). 24.IV.90

Opposite
A diamond necklace
New York $253,000 (£154,268). 24.IV.90

The central emerald-cut diamond in this necklace, from the collection of Paulette Goddard,
was formerly her engagement ring from Charlie Chaplin.

Silver

A Queen Anne silver-gilt cup and cover, maker's mark
of Benjamin Pyne overstruck by that of Henry Lyon,
London, 1705, height 10⅝in (27cm)
London £121,000 ($210,540). 3.V.90

Opposite
Four late-seventeenth-century silver-gilt cups, covers and stands,
from a set of six, two with maker's marks of David Willaume,
London, 1700, heights of the cups and covers 4½in (11.5cm)
London £198,000 ($336,600). 24.X.89
From the collection of Mrs David Bowes-Lyon

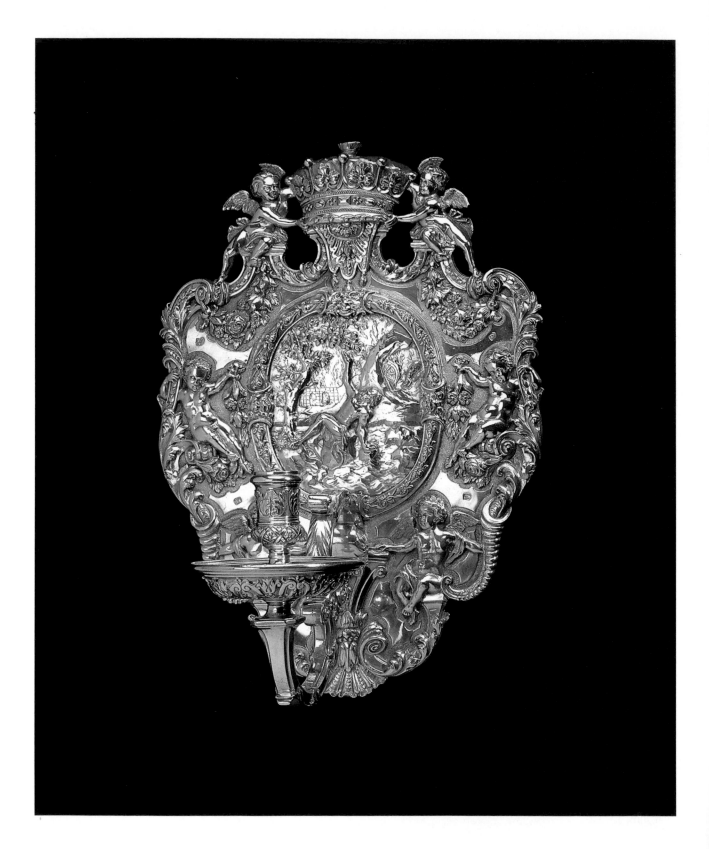

The Dunham Massey sconces

John Culme

'A Weakness in my Hand almost disables me to hold my pen,' apologised George Booth, 2nd Earl of Warrington, in a letter of 1756. He was then over eighty and daily expecting the dissolution of his 'old decaying Life.' With commendable foresight, however, he had already put his earthly affairs in order and in 'The Particular of my Plate and its Weight' which he compiled six years earlier, twenty-six and a half thousand ounces of silver are detailed. The large quantity of pieces which have survived tell that it was indeed a remarkable collection amassed, one suspects, for investment and display, rather than for the pure delight of the silver itself.

Among the more important items listed in 'The Particular' were the set of six wall sconces made in 1730–31, for 'the Great Bedchamber' at his seat, Dunham Massey, in Cheshire and transferred four years later to the Earl's Staffordshire property, Enville Hall. From here they were eventually removed by his descendants for sale in 1921 and realised the then impressive figure of £3,100 or £4 18s an ounce.

The Earl and Countess of Warrington's antipathy for one another is well known. The antiquary Philip Bliss records that 'they quarrell's & lived in the same house as absolute strangers to each other at bed and board.' As a result, the Earl published a pamphlet in 1759 advocating divorce on the grounds of incompatibility. The sole occupant of the Great Bedchamber at Dunham would have had plenty of time to contemplate the sconces' decoration. Their borders, inspired by late-seventeenth-century examples but with an architectural boldness reminiscent of William Kent's designs, each enclose a mythological scene. On one Narcissus gazes into a pool, ignoring poor Echo; another shows Tantalus after murdering his son, punished forever to strain for tempting fruit beyond his grasp, while Ixion (at a distance) roasts on a blazing wheel and Sisyphus stumbles under the weight of a boulder; upon a third, Perseus rescues Andromeda; reckless Phaeton plunges to his destruction on another; and on a fifth Prometheus writhes in torment as an eagle pecks at his liver, deemed in antiquity to be the seat of the emotions. The encounter, on the sixth sconce, between Diana and the hapless, horn-sprouting Actaeon brings to a close this cycle of stirring old tales.

If the Earl saw himself in the light of Actaeon to his lady's vengeful Diana, then he could rejoice in at least two compensations. The first was the £40,000 dowry which his bride brought with her. The second was their only child Mary, the Earl's sole heir. Their fond relationship, hinted at in a charming double portrait which hangs to this day at Dunham Massey, was unsevered even after Mary's marriage in 1736 to her very own Perseus, Harry Grey, 4th Earl of Stamford.

A George II wall sconce depicting Tantalus with Ixion and Sisyphus, from a set of six, maker's marks of Peter Archambo, London, 1730, each engraved with the monogram and coronet of George Booth, 2nd Earl of Warrington (1675–1758) who commissioned them for Dunham Massey, Cheshire, heights 16⅛in (41cm) London £1,155,000 ($2,009,700). 3.V.90

A George I two-handled wine cistern, maker's mark of Jacob Margas, London, 1714,
height 18¼in (46.4cm)
New York $638,000 (£406,369). 3.XI.89

Opposite
One of a pair of George II three-light candelabra, maker's marks of Charles Frederick Kandler,
London, 1738, heights 18¾in (47.6cm)
New York $1,540,000 (£980,892). 3.XI.89
Formerly in the collection of HRH The Duke of York (1763–1827)

The bases are cast with four putto heads representing the continents within cartouches
linked by emblems of the seasons applied and modelled in full relief. The stems are formed as
figures of Cupid and Psyche seated on a scrolled pediment covered with a lion pelt. The
modelling of the figures is reminiscent of the Daphne and Apollo candlesticks attributed to
George Michael Moser, in the collection of the Victoria and Albert Museum, London.

Opposite
A Louis XV toilet mirror,
maker's mark of Antoine-
Sebastien Durand, Paris,
1764, height 28¾in (73cm)
New York $275,000
(£175,159). 3.XI.89

A carved nautilus shell and
coral cup, with German
silver-gilt cover and mounts,
maker's mark *PH*, possibly
Lauenburg, *circa* 1630–40,
height 16½in (42cm)
Geneva SF660,000
(£256,809:$407,407).
13.XI.89

Above
A pair of French wine coolers, with maker's marks of Jean-Baptiste de Lens, Paris, 1732, heights 7½in (19.2cm)
Geneva SF1,815,000 (£706,226:$1,120,370). 13.XI.89

Left
A French soup tureen, cover and liner, with maker's mark of Jean-Baptiste de Lens, Paris, 1732, with a stand by Guillaume Hannier, Paris, 1747, width 18¼in (46.5cm)
Geneva SF1,155,000 (£449,416:$712,963). 13.XI.89

Opposite
A pair of Belgian oval toilet boxes, with maker's marks of Hubert Horion-Doré, Mons, 1678–79, widths 7⅝in (19.5cm)
Geneva SF605,000 (£257,447:$432,143). 14.V.90

Ceramics and glass

An English delftware 'fox' charger, *circa* 1670–80, diameter 13in (33cm)
London £36,300 ($64,977). 5.VI.90

Opposite
A faenza tin-glazed earthenware aquamanile, late fifteenth century, height 13½in (34.3cm)
New York $236,500 (£142,470). 9.I.90

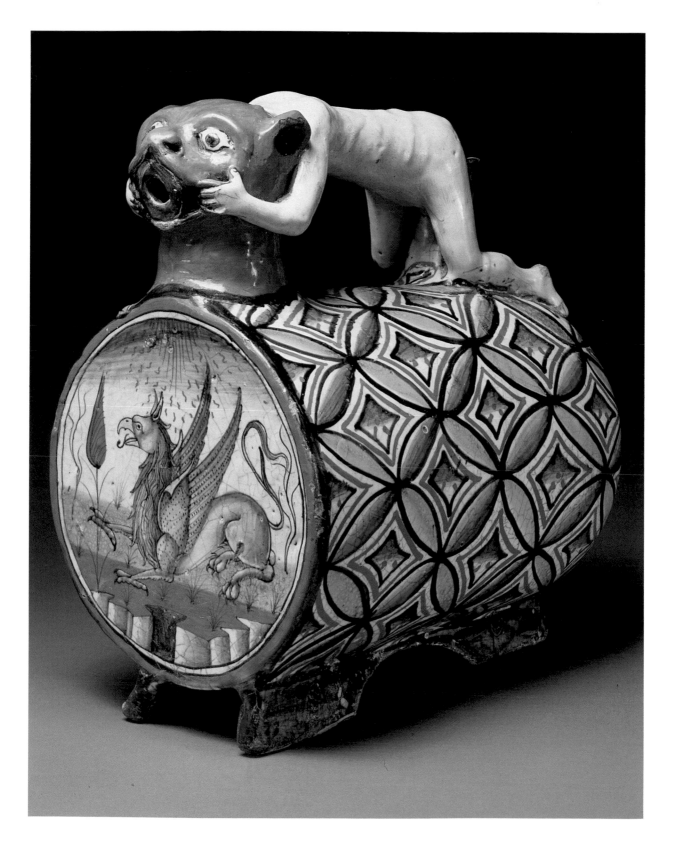

A pair of Naples ormolu-mounted wine glass coolers from the 'Servizio Ercolanese', Fabbrica Real
Ferdinandea, *circa* 1781–82, widths 10¾in (27.3cm)
New York $220,000 (£129,412). 26.IX.89.
From the collection of Frederick J. and Antoinette H. Van Slyke

The 'Servizio Ercolanese' was commissioned in 1781 by Ferdinand IV, King of the Two
Sicilies, as a gift for his father Charles III, formerly King of Naples and Sicily, and then King
of Spain. As one of the first major projects of the Fabbrica Real Ferdinandea under its new
director Domenico Venuti (formerly the General Superintendent of Antiquities for the city
of Naples), it reflects classical tastes revived by the excavations at Herculaneum (1738) and
Pompeii (1740), which had begun under Charles III and were continuing under Ferninand
IV. The figures and landscapes around the coolers, depicting sacrifices to Bacchus, were
inspired by prints of the wall paintings discovered at Herculaneum, published in *Le Antichità
di Ercolano esposte* (see below). Sadly, Charles III received the service indifferently, perhaps
because it reminded him too much of his former reign. The pieces are now scattered, but
each witnesses the impact of the classical discoveries on the fine and decorative arts during a
century that progressed from rococo exuberance to a new sense of order and proportion.

The collection of Frederick J. and Antoinette H. Van Slyke

Never was there a better illustration of the axiom that 'good things come in small packages'. Approaching the Van Slykes' tiny house in Townson, Maryland, a rambling suburb of Baltimore, one could hardly have been tempted to imagine the riches within, had it not been for an old, 600-item insurance inventory and ten curling photographs of Chinese and European porcelain, taken while the pieces were on loan to the Baltimore Museum of Art during the 1960s. Once inside the house, however, it was readily apparent that the inventory had been somewhat modest.

Remarkably little is known of the Van Slykes, and the story of the formation of their collection can be reconstructed only from a small carton of records discovered during the process of clearing out the house. It would seem that in the early 1940s the Van Slykes began to make excursions to New York, where they were drawn to 57th Street with its brigade of grand antique shops flanking Parke Bernet Galleries, recently re-installed at 30 East 57th Street. It is possible that the excursions and the concomitant collecting were the direct result of the legendary sale in April 1941 of the great collections of Mr and Mrs Henry J. Walters of Baltimore, whose local and international celebrity as collectors could have been a genuine inspiration to the Van Slykes. Among their first recorded purchases were fourteen lots of Chinese porcelain bought at the Walters sale for a total of $767.50. In the succeeding years, the Van Slykes continued to buy at Parke Bernet, while at the same time establishing a rapport with major dealers in ceramics in New York.

In his lifetime, Frederick Van Slyke, a lawyer, aspired toward the creation of a collection and its attendant celebrity that would elevate him to the ranks of J. Pierpont Morgan, William Randolph Hearst and other historic American collectors who had enjoyed public acclaim. To that end, he loaned pieces to special exhibitions at the Walters Art Gallery and for general display at the Baltimore Museum of Art. Mrs Van Slyke had no such ambition – after her husband's death in 1968, she reclaimed the pieces from the Baltimore Museum, sold a small collection of early Continental silver, and closed the door on acquisitions, allowing the porcelain to recede from the public eye.

In doing so, Mrs Van Slyke unintentionally fulfilled her husband's hopes for immortality. When the collection of almost 700 lots appeared at auction in New York, the Van Slyke name became synonymous with triumph. Formed during the dark years of World War II and its succeeding decade of recovery, a time when great objects were still abundantly available, often from very private sources, the Van Slyke Collection, in its magnitude, quality and originality, took the delighted ceramics market by complete surprise – a fairy tale in the annals of collecting. The sales produced slightly over $8.5 million for the family heirs.

Opposite
A Meissen Böttger
stoneware quadrangular
bottle, 1711–13, height
7¾in (19.7cm)
New York $85,250
(£50,147). 26.IX.89
From the collection of
Frederick J. and Antoinette
H. Van Slyke

A Meissen celadon-ground
bottle, *circa* 1730, height
7⅝in (19.5cm)
New York $40,700
(£23,941). 26.IX.89
From the collection of
Frederick J. and Antoinette
H. Van Slyke

A Fulda group of 'The Sleeping Shepherd', modelled by Georg Ludwig Bartholomé, *circa* 1780,
height 6⅝in (16.7cm)
New York $37,400 (£22,000). 26.IX.89
From the collection of Frederick J. and Antoinette H. Van Slyke

Opposite
A Frankenthal allegorical *déjeuner*, comprising an ovoid teapot and cover, a three-footed milk jug, a
small circular sugar bowl, a coffee cup and saucer and an oblong tray, dated *1777*, height of teapot
5¼in (13.3cm), length of tray 13in (33cm)
New York $49,500 (£29,118). 26.IX.89
From the collection of Frederick J. and Antoinette H. Van Slyke

Opposite
A Meissen soup tureen and cover from the Swan Service, modelled by J. J. Kändler and F. Eberlein, *circa* 1739, height 17⅜in (44cm) London £63,800 ($107,184). 17.X.89

A William Morris and de Morgan tile-panel, *circa* 1876, 64¾in by 35⅝in (163.5cm by 90.5cm) London £46,200 ($78,540). 19.XII.89

Commissioned by the architect George Devey for Membland Hall, Devon, this is one of six known surviving panels, two of which are in the Victoria and Albert Museum, London and the William Morris Art Gallery, Walthamstow.

Opposite
The Clichy Magnum
basket weight, diameter
$4\frac{1}{4}$in (10.8cm)
New York $258,500
(£148,563). 26.VI.90

A stipple engraved portrait
glass by David Wolff, with
the bust of William V of
Holland, *circa* 1780,
height $5\frac{5}{8}$in (14.4cm)
London £13,200
($23,628). 5.VI.90

Furniture

Two from a set of four George III painted and parcel-gilt armchairs, attributed to Thomas
Chippendale, *circa* 1770
New York $253,000 (£161,146). 23.IX.89

Opposite
One of a set of four painted and giltwood circular roundels based on designs by Thomas Hope,
circa 1810, diameters 15in (38cm)
London £66,000 ($125,400). 6.V11.90

A George III ormolu-mounted inlaid and engraved satinwood and yew wood tambour ladies' writing
desk, 1775–80, height 37in (94cm)
New York $198,000 (£126,115). 23.IX.89

Opposite
A Queen Anne walnut bureau bookcase, *circa* 1700, height 8ft 1⅝in (248cm)
London £96,800 ($174,240). 23.II.90

Two from a set of six George II gilt-decorated and japanned side chairs, *circa* 1735
New York $352,000 (£222,785). 21.X.89
From the collection of John T. Dorrance, Jr

Opposite
One of a pair of George II giltwood armchairs, *circa* 1755
London £88,000 ($146,960). 17.XI.89

A marquetry chest-on-stand, stamped with monogrammed *AT* for the Comte d'Artois and *G.M.* for
his Garde-Meuble, the giltwood stand stamped *G. Jacob*, supplied by Delaroue, Jacob and Rode for the
Comte d'Artois' bed chamber at Bagatelle, 1778, width 4ft ⅜in (123cm)
London £165,000 ($298,650). 15.VI.90

Opposite
A Louis XVI rosewood *secrétaire à cylindre* by Jean-François Leleu, stamped, inscribed *Stadler*, probably
supplied for the Prince de Condé at Chantilly, height 3ft 5¾in (106cm)
Monte Carlo FF3,996,000 (£401,608:$701,053). 16.VI.90

A Louis XVI two-tone giltwood console, formerly at Fontainebleau, last quarter eighteenth century,
width 5ft 10½in (179cm)
New York $1,320,000 (£840,764). 3.XI.89
From a collection formed by Roberto Polo

Above
A Louis XV/XVI ormolu-mounted tulipwood, fruitwood and sycamore marquetry commode by Roger Vandercruse, called Lacroix, stamped *R.V.L.C., JME*, supplied for the Comtesse de Provence at Fontainebleau, 1771, width 4ft 5½in (136cm) New York $687,500 (£437,898). 3.XI.89 From a collection formed by Roberto Polo

Right
A Louis XV bureau plat by Bernard II Vanrisamburgh, stamped *B.V.R.B., circa* 1750, length 4ft 11½in (151cm) Monte Carlo FF4,440,000 (£453,061:$765,517). 3.III.90

An Italian *pietra dura* table top attributed to Cosimo Castrucci, depicting an Italian landscape with the Temple of Sybilla in Tivoli and Christ with the pilgrims of Emaus, Prague, early seventeenth century, mounted on a mid-nineteenth-century table, the panel $23\frac{1}{4}$in by $17\frac{3}{8}$in (59cm by 44cm)
Monte Carlo FF3,663,000 (£373,775:$631,552). 3.III.90

This is one of a pair of *pietra dura* table tops attributed to the Castrucci workshop, formerly in the collection of Baron Robert de Rothschild. The other panel, also sold on 3rd March 1990, depicts a view of Florence, with a child being saved from drowning in the foreground.

Opposite
A Louis XIV marquetry cabinet-on-stand attributed to Pierre Gole, *circa* 1670, height 6ft 2in (188cm)
London £363,000 ($657,030). 15.VI.90

This cabinet is now in the Rijksmuseum, Amsterdam.

A Louis XV ormolu-mounted Chinese porcelain pot pourri, mid eighteenth century,
height 16½in (42cm).
New York $253,000 (£161,146). 4.XI.89

One of a pair of Italian marble and giltwood centre tables by Giacomo Raffaelli and Giuseppe
Leonardi, Rome, *circa* 1815, width 5ft 1⅜in (156cm)
London £418,000 ($698,060). 8.XII.89
From the collection of John Chichester-Constable, Burton Constable

Rafaelli was the most celebrated marble inlayer and mosaicist in Rome in the late eighteenth
century. In 1804, he went to work at the Napoleonic court in Milan, returning in 1814. As
well as geometric work, his *œuvre* includes a monumental mosaic mural of Leonardo's *Last
Supper*. The present tables are recorded at Burton Constable in 1841, having been
commissioned by William Constable.

'The Story of the Emperor of China', probably representing the Emperor Kangxi (1661–1721), may illustrate as many as ten subjects. It was designed by Guy-Louis Vernansal, Jean-Baptiste Belin de Fontenay and 'Baptiste' (probably Jean-Baptiste Monnoyer). It is likely that the series was woven in the workshop of Philippe Behagle, director of the Beauvais factory, or that of his son or widow.

Rugs and carpets

A Tekke bird *asmalyk*, West Turkestan, early nineteenth century, approximately 4ft 6in by 2ft 10in
(137.2cm by 86.4cm)
New York $115,500 (£70,427). 20.I.90

Opposite
An Ottoman court prayer rug, late sixteenth – early seventeenth century, 5ft 2in by 3ft 11in
(158cm by 119cm)
London £143,000 ($248,820). 7.III.90

A Star from the East

The 'Star' Kazak rugs are believed to be the earliest Kazak weavings to survive, and have been described as 'the pinnacle of Caucasian rugs, admired for their spectacular, unambiguous designs and their splendidly inscrutable ornaments in bold blocks of solid colours on a milk-white ground.'

This rug, from the late eighteenth century, is one of five examples all featuring an unusually narrow border, allowing for a more open arrangement of the basic design of deep blue stars and softer red medallions on the milky-white ground. The narrow border may be a Caucasian interpretation of those found on fifteenth- and sixteenth-century Anatolian carpets, which leads to the suggestion that these are the earliest of the Kazak weavings. The present example incorporates a particularly lively array of decorative elements. The deep, saturated blue stars with the softer, salmon-red medallions are in turn flanked by aubergine darts and blue-green diagonal polygons, all meticulously balanced on the neutral-coloured field. This sophisticated design is then 'embroidered' with whimsical decorations – birds and abstract foliate motifs – all of which are barely contained by the narrow border, as though the weaver became so enamoured with the strength of the design that she left its power undiluted in a minimal frame. The weaver has also left ample space between these decorative elements, so that the rug appears much more balanced and unencumbered than its contemporaries.

The origins of the bold repeat design of Star Kazak rugs remain unclear, but most experts believe they evolve from earlier eighteenth-century Caucasian rugs and embroideries. The pattern of large medallions flanked by diagonal emblems, and the interior decorative motifs of stars and polygons, as well as the attenuated latchhooks issuing from the medallions, are similar to those found in earlier embroideries.

Although many of the present Star rug's design elements, and its basic colour scheme, also appear in later Kazak weavings, their spontaneity, variety and sparkling clarity here make it unrivalled in the tradition of Caucasian carpets.

Opposite
A Star Kazak rug, south-west Caucasus, late eighteenth century, approximately 8ft 2in by 5ft 10in (249cm by 178cm)
New York $286,000 (£174,390). 20.I.90

Nineteenth-century decorative arts

A William IV red tortoiseshell, mother-of-pearl, walnut and gilt centre or library table, in the manner of Morel and Seddon, *circa* 1835, length 5ft 5¾in (167cm)
London £63,800 ($109,098). 16.III.90

This table belongs to the rococo revival largely pioneered by the Wyatt family of architects. The use of the 'Boulle' technique, cutting brass and pewter into a tortoiseshell ground, was a popular contemporary feature. The restoration of the French monarchy in 1814 revived old monarchical styles, and 'Boulle' furniture also became popular in England. It was termed 'Buhl' in the 'Louis Quatorze' style, often mixing Louis XIV with Louis XV rococo.

Opposite
One of a pair of early Victorian porcelain-mounted display cabinets by Edward Holmes Baldock, each with a printed label bearing the arms of the Earl Shelburne, one stamped *E.H.B.*, London, *circa* 1840, heights 4ft 11¼in (150.5cm)
London £39,600 ($67,716). 16.III.90

Edward Holmes Baldock (1777–1845) was 'purveyor of earthenware and glass' to King William IV from 1832 to 1837 and 'purveyor of China' to Queen Victoria from 1838 to 1845. He supplied modern furniture in his distinctive French style to several notable Scottish houses.

One of a pair of Napoléon III *premier* and *contre-partie* cut-brass and brown tortoiseshell 'Boulle'
commodes by Winckelsen of Paris, stamped under the marble top *CHles Winckelsen . . . St Louis* within
an oval, *circa* 1860, widths 4ft 1¼in (125cm)
London £187,000 ($319,770). 16.III.90

Charles-Guillaume Winckelsen (1812–71) was *ébéniste* and *bronzier* established in Paris in
1854. These commodes are copies of a pair by André-Charles Boulle commissioned in
1708–1709 for Louis XIV's bedroom at the Trianon.

Opposite
A pair of Spanish gold damascened and silver vases, by Plácido Zuloaga of Madrid, each signed with
initials, *circa* 1880, heights 14½in (37cm)
London £34,100 ($56,947). 3.XI.89

One of a set of six gilt-bronze wall lights by Henri Dasson, after an early Louis XV design, Paris, signed and dated *1880*, heights 37in (94cm)
London £24,200 ($40,414). 3.XI.89

A pair of French patinated and gilt-bronze-mounted earthenware nine-light candelabra, in the style of Louis XVI, *circa* 1880, heights 5ft 8in (172.7cm)
New York $77,000 (£49,045). 3.XI.89
From a collection formed by Roberto Polo

A Napoléon III gilt-bronze-mounted marquetry commode, in the style of Louis XV, Paris, *circa* 1870, width 4ft 10¼in (148cm)
London £29,700 ($50,787). 16.III.90

Only a few French pieces from this period were signed. Nothing is known about the maker of this distinctive commode, and no parallels can be drawn with other documented pieces.

Twentieth-century decorative arts

A Gallé carved cameo and enamelled glass vase, engraved *Gallé 1894* within an etched butterfly motif
on the underside, height 6⅛in (15.5cm)
London £121,000 ($210,540). 2.V.90

A pair of oak high-back chairs designed by Charles Annesley Voysey for W. Ward Higgs, 1898,
heights 54in (137cm)
London £59,400 ($103,356). 2.V.90

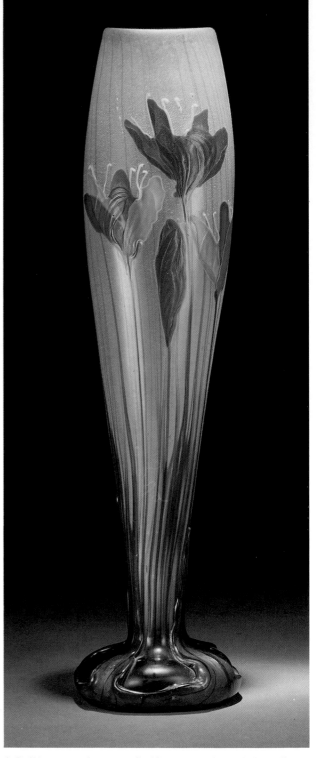

A Tiffany favrile glass, French gilt-bronze and lapis-lazuli exhibition vase, inscribed with the mark and number of Louis C. Tiffany, the base inscribed with the mark of Escalier de Cristal and Pannier Frères, Paris, *circa* 1900, height including base 26in (66cm)
New York $220,000 (£141,026). 2.XII.89

A Gallé *marqueterie sur verre* floriform vase, signed in intaglio, *circa* 1900, height 17⅜in (44.1cm)
New York $187,000 (£119,872). 2.XII.89

A Tiffany favrile glass and bronze trumpet vine lamp, the base impressed with the mark and numbering
of Tiffany Studios, New York, 1899–1920, height 26¾in (68cm)
New York $440,000 (£282,051). 1.XII.89
From the collection of Arnold R. King and Hank Helfand

'Les Coprins'

Philippe Garner

Fig. 2
A photograph showing
Emile Gallé's factory,
from a volume of 47
photographs, bound in
green and gilt morocco,
inset with a panel bearing
a facsimile *Gallé* signature
New York $41,250
(£26,442). 2.XII.89

Fig. 1
An internally decorated
and intaglio-carved glass
and wrought-iron lamp,
'Les Coprins', by Emile
Gallé, *circa* 1902,
height 31⅞in (81cm)
New York $1,100,000
(£705,128). 2.XII.89

A glass table lamp in the form of three greatly over-scaled mushrooms (Fig. 1) was sold in New York in December 1989 for $1,100,000. This remarkable object, at once an imaginative and curiously unnerving artistic achievement and a *tour de force* of glass-working virtuosity, was conceived by Emile Gallé, around 1902, and executed under his supervision in his glassworks at Nancy in north-eastern France.

The high price achieved is a reflection of the considerable esteem in which Gallé's artistry is held, present day collectors echoing the acclaim which Gallé enjoyed during his own lifetime. His position as one of the foremost artist craftsmen of his day is evidenced in the prestigious commissions which he received from the state, and from the most distinguished of patrons; it is confirmed by his election to the *Légion d'Honneur* and by the numerous awards bestowed upon him at major exhibitions. The acquisition during his lifetime of a substantial number of his pieces by national museums confirms his achievements in contemporary craft.

A presentation album of contemporary photographs appeared as the subsequent lot in the same sale. Bound in green morocco enriched with the name 'Gallé' applied in elaborate facsimile script in silver, the collection included shots of Gallé's work-shops, of individual pieces and of interior schemes, including one of a bedroom featuring two variants of the mushroom lamp. Several of the photographs seem very much at odds with the image of an inspired artist concentrating his creative resources and technical experience in the production of complex works of art in glass. The photographs reveal a factory (Fig. 2) rather than a studio, with large brick halls and slender chimneys where rows of artisans work away at the decoration of serried ranks of production-line vases. Between these two extremes – a rare and remarkable lamp fetching $1,100,000 and the rows of decorative but often artless vases produced by a factory which, at its peak, employed some three hundred workers – lies the full story of Emile Gallé's career.

During the 1870s Gallé gradually assumed full creative and managerial responsibility for the successful family business, creating decorative faïence and glass wares. These were often in traditional style, derived from eighteenth-century models. During his years of education and apprenticeship Gallé had been able to develop his artistic sensibilities and technical knowledge of the complex science of faïence and glass production. His ambition was to raise both crafts, and particularly that of glass-making, to new heights, elevating the medium to hitherto unimagined artistic status. In this, he succeeded most impressively, and throughout thirty years of experimentation, until his death in 1904, he devised ever more challenging possibilities for this most difficult of media. He created a wide palette of colours, with rich internal and surface effects; he evolved brilliant polychrome enamels, new techniques of inlaying glass and of working it, partly at the furnace and partly with cold bench work, into sculptural forms with high-relief decoration. Gallé imbued glass with the qualities of semi-precious stones. He created glass resembling jade or agate, and opalescent glass capable of changing its colour and character in different lights.

Fig. 3
A detail of an enamelled vase by Emile Gallé showing an early version of the three mushrooms motif.

The surviving records of Gallé's *envois* to the major Paris exhibitions include detailed descriptions of his researches into the chemistry of glass and of his never-ending pursuit of the infinite variety of the medium. In his notes on his submission to the 1889 'Exposition Universelle' he lists 'Imitations of semi-precious stones. Glass resembling smokey quartz and amethyst quartz', 'iridescent air bubbles', 'copper *flambés*' as well as 'imitation of jade' and of various agates. A display furnace at the Paris 'Exposition Universelle' of 1900 bore the inscription 'Mais si les hommes son méchants, faussairs et prévaricateurs,/A moi les mauvais démons du feu! Eclatent les vases! Croule le four!/Afin que tous apprennent à pratiquer la justice.' ('But if men should be wicked, perverters of truth and justice, come to my help o ye demons of fire, let vases burst and let furnaces crumble so that all men learn to be just.')

This heroic invocation, and the litter of broken masterpieces on the ground, vases fractured during their risky exposures to the fierce heat, or which had not survived the equally hazardous cooling process, bear witness to the nature of the challenge which Gallé undertook in his confrontation with this treacherously difficult medium.

Impressive though they were, however, his technical successes alone would not have earned him the esteem he enjoyed, for technical mastery was only the means to an end. His primary aims were artistic. He defined his purpose as creating for glass '. . . des rôles tendres ou terribles'. Steeped in the work of the French symbolist poets, Gallé saw himself as a symbolist, and glass as a medium full of mystery and magic capable of conveying his poetic ideas. The literary basis of so much of his work can be seen in his *verrerie parlante*, glass vessels engraved with lines of verse which served as the inspiration for their form and decoration.

On 17th May 1900 Gallé read a paper to the Académie Stanislas, *Le Décor Symbolique*, which is perhaps his most important statement on his artistic ideals and creative processes. It is a passionate credo at the very basis of which is a mystical fascination with nature and a belief in the rich, potentially symbolic value of motifs drawn from nature. Well versed in the styles of past centuries and distant cultures, Gallé nonetheless found his greatest inspiration quite literally in his own back yard. He was a keen and highly knowledgeable botanist and horticulturalist who turned to plants, flowers and insects as the lexicon of his art. He had the motto 'Ma racine est au fond des bois' carved into the large oak doors of his factory.

It was within this factory that he built up a hugely successful industry, manufacturing the acid-etched cameo vases which ensured his commercial success and financed the costly experimentation allowing him to create the expressive works of art which are so highly prized by collectors. At least one contemporary, Count Robert de Montesquiou, a friend and patron, was deeply critical of Gallé for having debased his art through the commercialisation of his ideas. He accused him of having 'fait pipi à l'esthétique' (literally, 'pissed on his aesthetics'). But Gallé was an industrialist as well as an artist and he was willing to produce a dilute version of his art at the factory.

Gallé used a very wide range of motifs derived from nature, though certain favourite recurrent motifs have come to be closely associated with him. He was evidently fascinated by pond life, particularly by waterlilies and dragonflies which are common features in his repertoire. He exploited the graphic potential of the ombellifers which grew in abundance around Nancy, and the silhouette of cow parsley became a leitmotif in his work.

Another favoured motif was the mushroom, most usually represented in clusters. The graphic motif of three mushrooms features on an early faïence plate. It appears again as a minor feature on an enamelled vase (Fig. 3), and is recorded as a two-dimensional design within a series of decorative motifs in a portfolio of designs lodged with the copyright registry office. Another design made for copyright registration shows an elaborate trade mark, incorporating a facsimile signature and a mushroom (Fig. 4).

As was often the case with Gallé an idea would be developed over a period of years, and an apparently simple motif would be exploited until its full symbolic potential was expressed. No better example of this process exists than the large mushroom lamp, known as 'Les Coprins' (Fig. 1). Here is the ultimate exploitation of an idea. The simple motif of three mushrooms has been worked into an object potent with symbolism. The glass mushrooms suggest a forceful voluptuousness. Representing three stages of growth, they invite interpretation as symbols of the life-cycle. They are imbued with an extraordinary vitality and a strangely sinister sensuality. They have been described as surrealist objects, reviled as examples of art nouveau decadence or dismissed as vulgar kitsch. But 'Les Coprins' cannot be ignored. The work is an evocative artistic statement which has an enigmatic, mysterious quality.

Emile Gallé had considerable influence on many of his contemporaries. Most importantly he played a crucial role in drawing together the artists and craftsmen of Nancy to identify a unity of vision which made the city an artistic centre to rival Paris. Foremost amongst the group of artists whom Gallé brought together under the official banner of the 'Alliance Provinciale des Industries d'Art' in 1909, were Auguste Daum, who turned a traditionalist glass factory into a *verrerie d'art* to rival that of Gallé himself, and Louis Majorelle, a cabinet-maker who, under Gallé's influence, adapted the principles of organic growth to the creation of sculptural forms for furniture.

The fine three-branch flower-form bronze and glass lamp (Fig. 5) which sold in New York was an exceptional example of the collaboration of Daum and Majorelle, and should perhaps also be acknowledged as a tribute to their mentor and guiding light, Emile Gallé.

Fig. 4
An elaborate trade mark designed by Emile Gallé and lodged with the copyright registry office, incorporating a facsimile signature and a mushroom emblem.

Fig. 5
A wheel-carved cameo glass and bronze three-branch lotus lamp by Auguste Daum and Louis Majorelle, the shade signed *Daum/Nancy* and the base inscribed *Majorelle/Nancy, circa* 1902, height 31⅞in (81cm)
New York $1,760,000 (£1,128,205). 2.XII.89

A Lalique moulded glass box with silver-plated brass scarab mounts, signed in intaglio, *circa* 1923,
length 7½in (18.9cm)
New York $225,500 (£144,551). 2.XII.89

Opposite
A silver- and nickel-plated, marble and glass clock designed by Jean E. Puiforcat, *circa* 1927,
height 11¼in (28.6cm)
Monte Carlo FF732,600 (£69,771:$112,708). 15.X.89

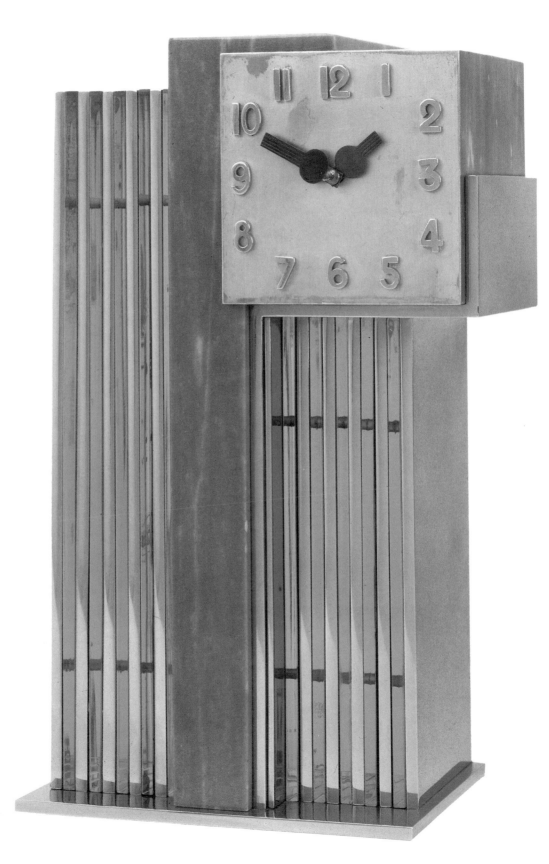

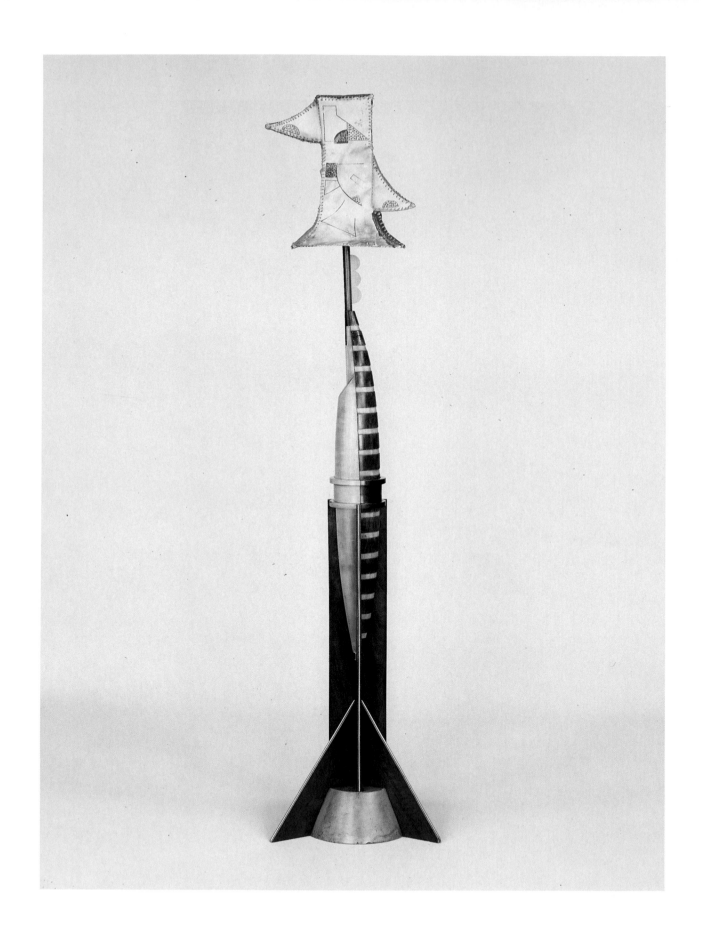

A palmwood cabinet by Eugène Printz with dinanderie doors by Jean Dunand, signed with monogram, *circa* 1930–35, width 78¾in (200cm)
Monte Carlo FF1,609,500 (£173,065:$282,368). 22.IV.90

Opposite
A wood and decorated vellum floor lamp by Eileen Gray, *circa* 1919–23, height 6ft ½in (184.2cm)
New York $154,000 (£98,718). 2.XII.89

A version of this lamp featured as part of a bedroom design by Eileen Gray, presented at the 'Salon des Artistes Décorateurs' in Paris in 1923.

Right
An ebony, walnut and ivory console table designed by Emile-Jacques Ruhlmann, *circa* 1925–30 length 59in (150cm)
Monte Carlo FF1,054,500 (£100,429:$162,231). 15.X.89

American decorative arts

A Chippendale carved mahogany block-front bonnet-top chest-on-chest,
Boston, Massachusetts, *circa* 1760, height 6ft 6in (198cm)
New York $110,000 (£63,218). 28.VI.90
From the collection of Mr and Mrs Vivian Ridler

A Queen Anne walnut tallcase clock, the works by
Thomas Hughes, London, the case signed by George
Glinn, Boston, *circa* 1750, height 8ft 4in (254cm)
New York $236,500 (£135,920). 28.VI.90

A Chippendale carved and inlaid cherrywood bonnet-top serpentine-front chest-on-chest attributed
to Cotton White, Hatfield, Massachusetts, *circa* 1790, height 7ft 3in (221cm)
New York $319,000 (£193,333). 26.I.90

A Chippendale carved and figured mahogany card table attributed to Thomas Affleck, Philadelphia,
circa 1770, width 36in (91.4cm)
New York $264,000 (£160,000). 26.I.90

Opposite
A Bonnin and Morris porcelain shell-form sweetmeat stand, 1771–72, height 5⅝in (14.3cm)
New York $82,500 (£50,000). 24.I.90

A moulded and gilded copper and zinc horse and rider weathervane stamped *J. Howard & Co.*,
West Bridgewater, Massachusetts, *circa* 1860, height 3ft 6in (106.7cm)
New York $770,000 (£463,855). 27.I.90
From the collection of the late Bernard M. Barenholtz

Opposite
A silver and other metals 'Japanese Style' five piece *tête à tête* tea and coffee set by Tiffany & Co.,
New York, *circa* 1880, height of kettle including stand 10¾in (27.3cm)
New York $93,500 (£53,736). 27.VI.90

Musical instruments

Far left
A violin by Joachim Tielke,
Hamburg, *circa* 1684,
length of back 14in (35.6cm)
London £33,000
($54,780). 23.XI.89

Left
A violin by Giovanni
Battista Guadganini,
Turin, 1780, length of back
14in (35.6cm)
London £143,000
($260,260). 14.VI.90

Opposite, left
A bass from a quartet of
ivory recorders by Johann
Benedikt Gahn,
Nuremberg, *circa* 1700,
length 39¾in (101cm)
London £33,000
($54,780). 22.XI.89

The quartet was probably
made for the Oelighausen
monastery, near Arnsberg,
Westfalen.

Centre
A sixteen-keyed ebony
bassoon by Charles Joseph
Sax, stamped *Sax, Facr. du
Roi à Bruxelles*, Brussels,
circa 1830, length 49⅛in
(124.8cm)
London £27,500
($45,650). 22.XI.89

Right
A violoncello by Carlo
Giuseppe Testore, Milan,
circa 1690, length of back
29½in (75cm)
London £126,500
($209,990). 23.XI.89

Arms and armour, medals and sporting guns

A cased Russian percussion revolver embellished with gold, inscribed in cyrillic *By The Tula Gunmakers, circa* 1850, case dimensions 12½in by 8in by 2⅝in (31.7cm by 20cm by 6.7cm)
London £7,700 ($14,245). 28.VI.90

Opposite
A German composed fluted 'Maximillian' full armour of bright steel, *circa* 1525–30, the helmet earlier, *circa* 1510–20
New York $77,000 (£46,385). 10.I.90

A powder flask with chiselled
and gilt iron mounts, possibly
Italian, late sixteenth century,
height 8⅞in (22.5cm)
London £6,600
($11,748). 3.VII.90
From the Visser Collection

Below
A pair of Saxon silver-mounted
wheel-lock 'puffer' pistols for the
Trabanten-Leib guard, *circa*
1590, overall length 24⅜in
(62cm)
London £45,100
($80,278). 3.VII.90
From the Visser Collection

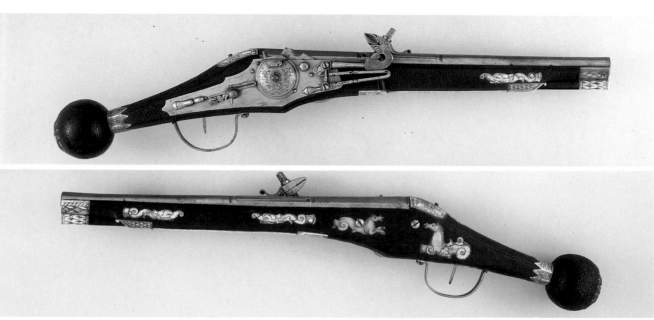

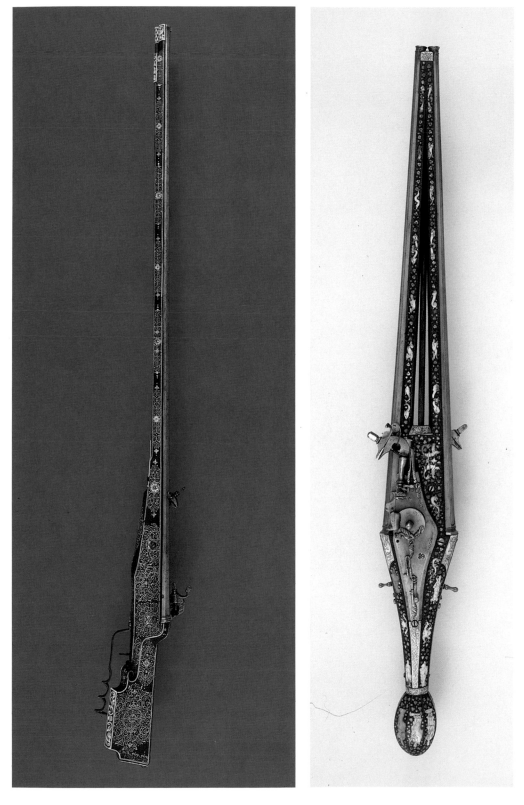

Right
A German wheel-lock
superimposed-load
sporting rifle, *circa* 1600,
overall length 54⅛in
(137.5cm)
London £38,500
($68,530). 3.VII.90
From the Visser Collection

Far right
An Alsatian
double-barrelled over-and-
under wheel-lock pistol,
Sedan, *circa* 1600, overall
length 30½in (77.5cm)
London £67,100
($119,438). 3.VII.90
From the Visser Collection

Naval Gold Medal Group, awarded to Admiral of the Fleet Sir Francis Austen, GCB, brother of the famous novelist, Jane Austen
London £29,700 ($54,945). 28.VI.90

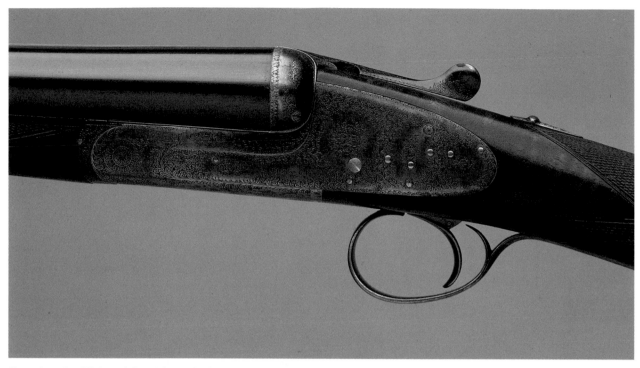

One of a pair of lightweight 12-bore single-trigger assisted opening round-bodied side-lock ejector guns
by Boss & Co., numbered *8377* and *8378*, overall length 14½in (36.8cm)
London £38,500 ($61,600). 19.XII.89

One of a pair of hunt-engraved 12-bore single-trigger self-opening side-lock ejector guns, numbered
27913 and *27914*, overall length 15⅜in (39cm)
London £78,100 ($127,303). 2.IV.90

Postage stamps

Left
British Guiana, 1856 4*c*. black on deep blue, coloured through
London £26,400 ($51,216). 18.VII.90
From the 'Dallas' Collection

Below
Cape of Good Hope, 1861 4*d*. vermilion error of colour in a block
with three 1*d*. vermilion
London £104,500 ($172,425). 9.IX.89
From the 'Maximus' Collection

Above, left to right

Barbados, 1875–78 Perf. 14 x 12½, 4*d*. red; £8,800 ($17,072)
Hong Kong, 1863–71 96*c*. olive-bistre; £5,060 ($9,816)
Northern Nigeria, 1904 £25 green and carmine; £15,950 ($30,943)
Tobago, 1879 £1 mauve; £5,775 ($11,204)

These four stamps from the 'Dallas' Collection were sold in London on 18th July 1990.

Above, left to right

Jamaica, 1919–21 1*s*. orange-yellow and red-orange, frame inverted; £14,850 ($28,809)
Great Britain, 1902–1904 Inland Revenue £1 dull blue-green; £9,350 ($18,139)
Malaya – Straits Settlements, 1912–23 $500 purple and orange-brown; £14,300 ($27,742)

These three stamps from the 'Dallas' Collection were sold in London on 18th July 1990.

Above, left to right

Newfoundland, 1860 1*s*. orange-vermilion on vertically laid paper; £9,350 ($18,139)
Sierra Leone, 1897 2½*d*. on 2*s*. dull lilac, type B; £20,900 ($40,546)
Newfoundland, 1927 'De Pinedo' 60*c*. black; £13,750 ($26,675)

These three stamps from the 'Dallas' Collection were sold in London on 18th July 1990.

Collectors' sales

A French musical automaton of 'The Drunkard' by Gustav Vichy, 1900, height 22in (55.9cm)
New York $23,100 (£14,348). 15.XII.89

Above
A French bisque harpist by Roullet et Decamps, *circa* 1880, impressed *10* and stamped in red *Déposé TETE JUMEAU Bte. S.G.D.G.*, height 29½in (75cm)
London £16,500 ($29,700). 18.V.90

An English admiralty model of a sixth-rate ship-of-the-line, early eighteenth century, length 26¾in (68cm)
London £126,500 ($216,315). 5.X.89

Above
A presentation 'gold' disc for
'I Want to Hold Your Hand',
inscribed, *Presented to The Beatles*
to commemorate the sale of more than
one million copies, 16⅞in by 13in
(43cm by 33cm)
London £6,380 ($10,718).
22.VIII.89

Jimi Hendrix's Fender
Stratocaster guitar, *circa* 1968,
length 25⅜in (64.5cm)
London £198,000 ($344,520).
25.IV.90

Buddy Holly's Gibson J-45 country-style acoustic guitar
with custom leather covering, designed and hand tooled by
Buddy Holly, *circa* 1945,
New York $242,000 (£139,884). 23.VI.90

Left
A French bisque doll by Jumeau, *circa* 1875, impressed *5*,
stamped in blue *JUMEAU Medaille d'Or Paris* and incised *5 L.I*,
height 16⅛in (41cm)
London £6,270 ($11,286). 18.V.90

Right
A German cloth doll by Kathe Kruse, *circa* 1905, marked *Kathe
Kruse*, height 16½in (41.9cm)
New York $3,850 (£2,391). 15.XII.89

Opposite
A French swivel-head bisque doll, *circa* 1860, height 18⅛in (46cm), £37,400 ($62,832)
An Italian Directoire-style painted miniature armchair, *circa* 1900, height 18½in (47cm), £2,530 ($4,250)

These pieces, from the collection of the late Mrs Marianne Bodmer, were sold in London on 8th and
9th November 1989.

Left
A German dual-plush teddy bear by Steiff, *circa* 1920,
height 24⅜in (62cm)
London £55,000 ($91,850). 19.IX.89

Below
A German teddy bear by Steiff, *circa* 1912, height 18⅞in (48cm)
London £24,200 ($43,560). 18.V.90

Left
A German tinplate clockwork 'Mickey Mouse' barrel organ
toy, probably by Distler, *circa* 1930, height 8¼in (21cm)
London £2,420 ($4,356). 18.V.90

Below
A Walt Disney black and white celluloid from *The Mail
Pilot*, 1933, 8in by 10¾in (20.3cm by 27.3cm)
New York $115,500 (£67,151). 21.VI.90

Opposite, above
Three original Lanvin
studio fashion drawings,
from a group of
twenty-three albums
depicting fashion and
theatrical designs by
Jeanne Lanvin, collected
by Dolores Valenti,
Director of Lanvin in
Spain, *circa* 1922–24, sheet
sizes from approximately
9⅞in by 5½in (25cm by
14cm) to 15¾in by 12¼in
(40cm by 31cm)
London £220,000
($367,400). 19.IX.89

The Rick Carroll Collection

Ronald Varney

In 1962, as a young insurance agent just starting his own business in South Florida, Rick Carroll acquired a run-down 1927 Model T touring car and set about restoring it. From that modest beginning, Mr Carroll moved on to more exotic cars, and more elaborate restorations. During the next twenty-seven years he acquired hundreds of automobiles – obscure Mercers, Jewetts, Wintons and Thomas Flyers, as well as the more fabled Auburns, Cords, Packards and Stutz Bearcats, V16 Cadillacs from the early 1930s and even a 1926 Isotta Fraschini built for Rudolph Valentino. The one constant was Mr Carroll's passion for authenticity: he immersed himself in the technical and romantic lore of every car he owned.

Collecting Rolls Royces and other luxury automobiles is not an enterprise for the faint-hearted, but it was perhaps inevitable that Rick Carroll would eventually move up and assemble one of the greatest private collections of Rolls-Royces, encompassing both pre-1910 models and the big P-III's of the late 1930s. Of particular note were a pair of 1907 Silver Ghosts that have shadowed each other over the years. Chassis number 553 was delivered in May 1907 to Samuel Stevens, vice-president of the Rome-Merchant Iron Mill in Rome, New York. A Harvard man and a keen racing enthusiast, Mr Stevens used the car extensively for local rallies before parting with it. Chassis number 565 (see opposite) was also delivered to Mr Stevens, sometime in June 1907, and saw rather less active service, as transportation for his mother. It later passed into the hands of Nelson Rockefeller, and then Winthrop Rockefeller. Rick Carroll finally reunited these sister cars in his own collection.

Beyond the Rolls-Royces, the Carroll Collection was filled with show-stoppers. There was the very rare 1955 Corvette, one of only seven hundred built and among the first with a V8 engine, as well as the Bentley Freestone and Webb convertible with the jazzy 'Batmobile' fins popular in the 1950s. Of the two Carroll Packards, the rare 1930 Speedster Runabout Boat Tail (model 734) is generally considered among the most interesting and attractive models the Packard Motor Company ever built, the very essence of elegance and speed, and perfect for motoring along the ocean boulevards of Newport and Palm Beach.

Rick Carroll's favourite marque was the Duesenberg, a car demanding nothing short of perfection from the restorer's hand – at one point, he owned as many as seventeen models. Perhaps the one that best captured the freewheeling spirit of the Carroll Collection is the alluring 1931 Duesenberg Mudd Coupé (J212), with the sweeping black aero-style body and the stunning fabricord roof. Lighter by far than other model J's, the supercharged Mudd Coupé (named after a former owner, Dr Seeley Mudd of California) was probably one of the fastest Duesenbergs in the world.

A 1907 Rolls-Royce Silver Ghost 40/50 hp tourer, chassis number 60-565 Palm Beach $2,860,000 (£1,702,381). 12.V.90 From the Rick Carroll Collection

Opposite, above
A 1926 Rolls-Royce
Phantom 1 40/50hp
two seat coupé,
chassis number 21 SC
Paulerspury £143,000
($258,830). 15.VI.90

Opposite, below
A 1934 Mercedes-Benz
500K cabriolet 'A'
Cleveland $660,000
(£400,000). 31.III.90
From the collection of the
Frederick C. Crawford
Auto-Aviation Museum

Right
An 1896 Lutzmann 3hp
Victoria motor carriage
Hendon £86,900
($151,206). 5.V.90
From the Sullivan
Collection

Below
A 1937 Bugatti type 57S
drophead coupé,
chassis number 57513
Hendon £715,000
($1,337,050). 2.VII.90
From the collection of the
late T.A. 'Bob' Roberts

The 1962 Ferrari 250 Gran Turismo Berlinetta Competition 'GTO', chassis number 3607 GT
Monte Carlo FF59,940,000 (£6,445,161:$10,515,789). 21.V.90

The 1962 Ferrari 250 Gran Turismo Berlinetta Competition 'GTO'

We are now travelling fast, about 150 miles an hour. The sound is glorious, the ride is smooth, the handling absolutely perfect and secure. The exhaust, motor, gearbox and differential all join in the concert, but each keeps its distinctive voice. Meanwhile, the water temperature is still 85, the oil near 70, the oil pressure 7 kg and the gas mileage around 20 to 22 litres for 100 km. Amazing!

This was the Ferrari historian, Jess Pourret's description of the 250 GTO, unveiled on 24th February 1962, at the Ferrari factory at Maranello. Designed by Giotto Bizzarini, the car was the latest development in the GT series that had included such famous models as the 250 Sport. These cars were docile enough for touring use, but were in their element in competition, winning the Tour de France four times in a row. The new GTO lived up to its pedigree – coming first, second and third in the 1962 British Touring Trophy, and second overall at Le Mans in the same year.

Eye-catching coachwork and the ultimate 3-litre, 250 GT engine brought customers clamouring, and there is little doubt that new owners were closely vetted. Buyers were in any case strictly limited as only thirty-nine GTOs were built – thirty-six with the 250 GT engine, and three 4-litre cars. 'Everything in a GTO works in harmony', said Jess Pourret. 'It needs only a driver who understands this harmony and works with it, not against it.' Pourret owned the present model himself for over twenty years, acquiring it from Pierre Bardinon's 'Mas du Clos' collection whence it retired after three years in the famous Scuderia Serenissima Venezia of Count Volpi de Misurata, where it won the GT class of the 1965 Paris Grand Prix. Before that, in the hands of the Italian Pagliarini, the car saw action at Bologna and Monza as well as the 1962 Coppa Fagioli. This model, chassis number 3607 GT, was also one of the few GTOs to race in Africa, competing there in the Angola Grand Prix.

After 'retiring' in 1965, the car was meticulously cared for. In Pourret's hands, its absolute originality was painstakingly maintained before it passed into the collection of Robert M. Rubin, proprietor of the historic Bridgehampton Motor Racing Circuit on Long Island. Rarely does a racing car of this provenance survive more than twenty-five years with no modifications – its condition would have delighted Enzo Ferrari himself.

Garden statuary

One of a pair of white marble urns, commissioned in France for Lynford Hall, Norfolk, the bases
inscribed and dated *J.C. Geslin Arch. my. ca. dir. A. Thabard Ft. 1868*, heights 63in (160cm)
Billingshurst £61,600 ($103,303). 31.V.90

Opposite
A lead figure of Neptune, mid eighteenth century, height 62in (158cm)
Billingshurst £39,600 ($67,003). 30.V.90

The Villa Cornaro

John Wilton-Ely

Opposite
Fig. 1
The garden elevation of the Villa Cornaro at Piombino Dese, designed by Andrea Palladio for the Cornaro family *circa* 1551–52, and completed in 1613
London £1,265,822 ($2,000,000). 31.X.89

Few periods in western architecture have produced such masterpieces of domestic building as the late Italian Renaissance. Finely designed and closely related to its landscape setting, the Palladian villa has rarely been bettered as a solution for elegant living.

The Renaissance villa reached its peak of perfection during the sixteenth century, as part of the self-conscious Italian revival of classical civilization. While the villas of the Medici around Florence and those of the great papal families near Rome were devised as places of relaxation away from the oppressive summer heat of the city, a completely new architectural formula was introduced in the Veneto, in response to economic as well as social needs. As the mercantile nobility of Venice found their sources of maritime trade in decline, they turned landward to their estates on the *terra firma* as a fresh means of wealth. An agrarian revolution followed, involving improved cereal crops and vast schemes of land reclamation. Between 1510 and 1580, the tax yield from these properties alone increased by four hundred per cent.

Fig. 2
The ground floor *salone* of the Villa Cornaro, showing two of the room's four Ionic columns, and two of the four niches containing sculptures of eminent Cornaro family members.

Fig. 3
Biblical frescoes by Mattia Bartoloni, and decorative plaster-work by Bartolomeo Cabianca, carried out at Villa Cornaro in 1716–17. The ground-floor rooms contain Old Testament scenes, with New Testament scenes on the upper floor.

In order to supervise this dramatic change, aristocratic landowners needed to spend long periods based on their estates, away from their palaces in Venice. A new type of villa, combining the practical functions of the farmyard with the grandeur and sophistication of the palace, was required. It fell to the young architect Andrea Palladio to create the perfect synthesis. By his death in 1580, over twenty such villas had been built and a further twenty remained as projects. Each design was individual and distinct, but was conceived within a system of planning principles and laws of harmony and proportion, as defined in Palladio's illustrated treatise *I Quattro Libri dell'Architettura*, published in Venice in 1570. The agricultural lands of the Cornaro family at Piombino Dese – situated some twenty miles from Venice between Padua and Castelfranco – can be traced back to 1422. When Giorgio Cornaro died in 1551, the inheritance was divided between his two sons Marco and Girolamo, and it was the latter who commissioned a villa from Palladio for his portion (Fig. 1). Construction began in 1552 and, although the building was inhabitable by 1554, it was not completely finished until 1613.

Palladio's earlier country villas generally consisted of a single-storey residential block over a raised kitchen basement, linked by arcades to service wings containing stables and granaries on either side. However, Villa Cornaro was given a more vertical and monumental form, with both façades centred on a majestic pair of Ionic and Corinthian loggias beneath temple pediments. As the *Quattro Libri* informs us, the kitchens and storerooms were located in the flanking blocks. Since these were normally situated in the basement, the Cornaro design may have been intended to cope with a swampy area liable to periodic flooding. (A map of 1613 shows a separate arched stable block to the west of the villa, leading to a courtyard in line with a garden and a vine pergola.) Be that as it may, the effect of the villa's tiered porticoes magnificently recalls certain buildings drawn by Palladio during his visit to Rome in 1541, particularly the Temple of Jupiter which he believed had similarly superimposed Ionic and Corinthian colonnades inside.

The eighteen major rooms inside the villa have recently been the subject of a faithful programme of restoration by Professor and Mrs Richard H. Rush, and are organised on both floors in identical plans (Fig. 4). A heirarchy of rooms reflecting various functions is grouped around an impressive hall or *salone*. On the lower level, the hall (Fig. 2) is enhanced by four impressive Ionic columns at the corners, together with a series of niches, later filled by six over-life-sized statues by Camillo Mariani representing illustrious members of the family. Besides Giorgio himself, as a Venetian admiral, they include his celebrated ancestor, Caterina Cornaro who, as Queen of Cyprus, brought that territory within the control of the *Serenissima*. Later still, frescoes were added to all major rooms, with Old Testament subjects on the lower floor and New Testament ones on the upper floor. These were carried out in 1717 by Mattia Bartoloni. Over 114 separate compositions are involved, together with superb decorative stucco work on the walls and ceilings by Bartolomeo Cabianca (Fig. 3).

Palladio's work here is pervaded by a great sense of harmony, but it avoids becoming static by creating a sequence of spaces and levels that amplify the senatorial status of the villa. Approaching the north front along its main axis from the entrance gates, the visitor enters the Ionic portico via a gently ramped staircase. Passing through the main door, we reach the *salone,* flooded with natural light from eight windows ranged around the garden door facing the entrance. This leads out to the south front (Fig. 1), where another central flight of steps descends to symmetrically-laid formal gardens extending to the back gates. These lead straight out into the fields – the source of Cornaro's wealth, and the villa's *raison d'etre.* Inside the villa, two stately oval staircases rise to the Corinthian loggia on the first floor, giving superb views over the fertile surroundings and providing access to the upper *salone* and adjacent rooms.

Palladio, of course, has had an enormous impact on European and American architecture. Woodcuts of the *Quattro Libri* helped spread the fame of his villas, as did first-hand studies by Inigo Jones and Lord Burlington. During the eighteenth century, the double-tiered porticoes of the Villa Cornaro influenced designs as diverse as the interior of the Bath Assembly Rooms and the garden front of West Wycombe Park in Buckinghamshire. Most remarkably, they are also echoed in Thomas Jefferson's earliest ideas for his house at Monticello, and for the Capitol in Washington.

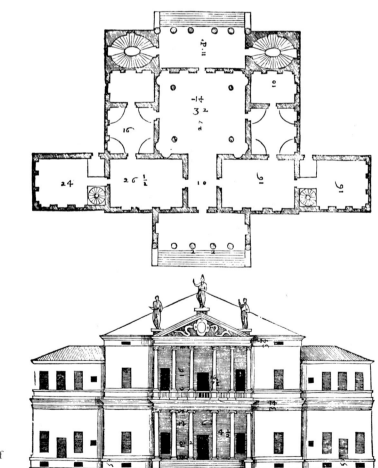

Fig. 4
A page from Andrea Palladio's illustrated treatise *I Quattro Libri dell'Architettura* (Venice, 1570), showing the floor plans and one elevation of the Villa Cornaro.

Massandra wines

David Molyneux-Berry

It is difficult to believe that one of the world's most fabulous cellars could have remained hidden although still in active production, but such is the case with Massandra. Once the private cellar and winery of Tsar Nicholas II, its excellent produce has been unobtainable even in Moscow.

Massandra is located on the south coast of the Crimea. It is a small hamlet, a stone's throw from Yalta, which was once a highly fashionable summertime resort. However, it was not until Count Mikhail Worontsov was appointed Governor General of Nova Rossiya in 1823, and began the construction of the Alupka palace, that the area took on the beauty it has today. The palace took twenty years to build at the cost, it is said, of 20,000 serfs' lives. The Tsar, too, had his own local palace, Livadia. To supply it, Nicholas II decided to have constructed the world's most impressive winery, Massandra, built between 1894 and 1897.

So how was it that Sotheby's stumbled upon this best-kept secret, unknown to the Russian populace following the revolution, and undisturbed by the invading German army in 1941? The wine department was first approached in the 1970s when it was asked whether it would be interested in an important cellar in Russia. There were doubts over the condition of such a cellar even if it existed, and a polite decline was made, but a decade later, the temptation was too great and this time the invitation was accepted. There were enormous logistical problems which had to be overcome. First the wines had to be labelled – a major task in itself – then packed. The greatest problem, however, was the shipment itself as overland travel was considered to be too risky. Eventually, thirteen Russian railway containers were commandeered. These were taken overland from Yalta to Odessa before being loaded onto a passenger liner destined first for Yugoslavia, then Southampton.

How do the wines compare with typical modern styles? It should be noted that they are all either sweet or fortified or both. The Tsar had a sweet tooth and demanded the finest, to compare with the great dessert wines of western Europe. Perhaps the greatest of all are the brilliant white and rose muscats, which must be among the finest produced anywhere – intensely sweet, yet beautifully fragrant and long on the finish. Ask a Russian which is his favourite, however, and it will invariably be the red 'port' – a product made solely for the Tsar, his family and the court, and now considered to be the Crimea's greatest delicacy.

A view of the cellars of West Green House, Hartley Wintney, which comprised over 7,000 bottles
including 1988 Pomerols, Château d'Yquem 1956 and 1960 CB, and outstanding red and white
Burgundies, as well as vintage ports, madeiras and whiskies
West Green House £243,745 ($409,246). 17.V.90

Left to right
One of three bottles of Château d'Yquem (White) 1947, £1,320 ($2,297)
One of three bottles of Château d'Yquem (White) 1941, £638 ($1,110)
One of two bottles of Château d'Yquem (White) 1929, £990 ($1,723)

These eight bottles were sold in London on 7th March 1990.

Principal officers and experts

Michael Ainslie
President and Chief Executive, Sotheby's Holdings, Inc.
The Rt.Hon. The Earl of Gowrie
Chairman, Sotheby's UK & International
John L. Marion
Chairman, Sotheby's North America
Julian Thompson
Deputy Chairman, Sotheby's UK & International (Asia)
Diana D. Brooks
President, Sotheby's North America
Timothy Llewellyn
Managing Director, Sotheby's UK & International
Simon de Pury
Deputy Chairman, Sotheby's UK & International (Europe)

American decorative arts and furniture
Leslie B. Keno *New York, 606 7130*
William W. Stahl, Jr *606 7110*
Wendell Garrett

American folk art
Nancy Druckman *New York, 606 7225*

American Indian art
Dr Bernard de Grunne *New York, 606 7325*

American paintings, drawings and sculpture
Peter B. Rathbone *New York, 606 7280*

Antiquities and Asian art
Richard M. Keresey *New York, 606 7328*
Felicity Nicholson (Antiquities) *London, 408 5111*
Brendan Lynch (Asian) *408 5112*

Arms and armour and medals
Michael Baldwin *London, 408 5318*
David Erskine-Hill (medals) *408 5315*
Florian Eitle *New York, 606 7250*

Books and manuscripts
Roy Davids *London, 408 5287*
David N. Redden *New York, 606 7386*
Paul Needham
Dominique Laucournet *Paris, 33 (1) 42 66 40 60*

British paintings 1500-1850
James Miller *London, 408 5405*
David Moore-Gwyn *London, 408 5406*
Henry Wemyss (watercolours) *408 5409*

British paintings from 1850
Simon Taylor (Victorian) *London, 408 5385*
Janet Green (twentieth-century) *408 5387*

Ceramics
Peter Arney *London, 408 5134*
Letitia Roberts *New York, 606 7180*

Chinese art
Carol Conover *New York, 606 7332*
Arnold Chang (paintings) *606 7334*
Julian Thompson *London, 408 5371*
Colin Mackay *408 5145*
Mee Seen Loong *Hong Kong, (852) 524 8121*

Clocks and watches
Tina Millar (watches) *London, 408 5328*
Michael Turner (clocks) *408 5329*
Daryn Schnipper *New York, 606 7162*

Coins
Tom Eden (Ancient and Islamic) *London, 408 5313*
James Morton
(English and paper money) *408 5314*
Mish Tworkowski *New York, 606 7391*

Collectables
Dana Hawkes *New York, 606 7424*
Hilary Kay *London, 408 5205*

Contemporary art
Hugues Joffre *London, 408 5400*
Lucy Mitchell-Innes *New York, 606 7254*

European works of art
Florian Eitle *New York, 606 7250*
Elizabeth Wilson *London, 408 5321*

Furniture
Graham Child *London, 408 5347*
George Read (English) *New York, 606 7577*
Thierry Millerand (French and Continental) *606 7213*
Robert C. Woolley *606 7100*
Alexandre Pradère *Paris, 33 (1) 42 66 40 60*

Glass and paperweights
Lauren Tarshis *New York, 606 7180*
Perran Wood *London, 408 5135*

Heritage Sales
Timothy Sammons *London, 408 5335*

Impressionist and modern paintings
David J. Nash *New York, 606 7351*
John L. Tancock *606 7360*
Marc E. Rosen (drawings) *606 7154*
Michel Strauss *London, 408 5389*
Julian Barran *Paris, 33 (1) 42 66 40 60*

Islamic art and carpets
Richard M. Keresey (works of art) *New York, 606 7328*
William F. Ruprecht (carpets) *606 7380*
Professor John Carswell *London, 408 5153*

Japanese art
Neil Davey *London, 408 5141*
Nyr Indictor *New York, 606 7338*

Jewellery
David Bennett *Geneva, 41 (22) 732 85 85*
John D. Block *New York, 606 7392*
Alexandra Rhodes *London, 408 5306*

Judaica
Jay Weinstein *New York, 606 7387*

Latin American paintings
Grace Lowe Russak *New York, 606 7290*

Musical instruments
Charles Rudig *New York, 606 7190*
Graham Wells *London, 408 5341*

Nineteenth-century European furniture and works of art
Christopher Payne *London, 408 5350*
Elaine Whitmire *New York, 606 7285*

Nineteenth-century European paintings and drawings
Alexander Apsis *London, 408 5384*
Nancy Harrison *New York, 606 7140*
Pascale Pavageau *Paris, 33 (1) 42 66 40 60*

Old master paintings and drawings
Julien Stock *London, 408 5420*
Elizabeth Llewellyn (drawings) *408 5416*
George Wachter *New York, 606 7230*
Nancy Ward-Neilson *Milan, 39 (2) 78 39 11*
Etienne Breton *Paris, 33 (1) 42 66 40 60*

Oriental manuscripts
Nabil Saidi *London, 408 5332*

Photographs
Philippe Garner *London, 408 5138*
Beth Gates-Warren *New York, 606 7240*

Portrait miniatures, objects of vertu, icons and Russian works of art
Julia Clarke (vertu) *London, 408 5324*
Haydn Williams (miniatures) *408 5326*
Heinrich Graf von Spreti *Munich, 49 (89) 22 23 75*
Gerard Hill *New York, 606 7150*

Postage stamps
John Michael *London, 408 5223*

Pre-Columbian art
Stacy Goodman *New York, 606 7330*

Prints
Susan Pinsky *New York, 606 7117*
Ian Mackenzie *London, 408 5210*
Ruth M. Ziegler *Tokyo, (212) 606 7112*

Silver
Kevin L. Tierney *New York, 606 7160*
Peter Waldron (English) *London, 408 5104*
Harold Charteris (Continental) *408 5106*
Dr Christoph Graf Douglas *Frankfurt, 49 (69) 74 07 87*

Sporting Guns
Adrian Weller *London, 408 5319, Sussex (0403) 783 933*

Tribal art
Dr Bernard de Grunne *New York, 606 7325*
Sabine Dauwe *London, 408 5115*

Twentieth-century applied arts
Barbara E. Deisroth *New York, 606 7170*
Philippe Garner *London, 408 5138*

Vintage cars
Malcolm Barber *London, 408 5320*
William F. Ruprecht *New York, 606 7165*

Western manuscripts
Dr Christopher de Hamel, FSA, *London, 408 5330*

Wine
David Molyneux-Berry, MW, *London, 408 5267*

Contributors

Tim Ayers has edited a variety of books for Philip Wilson Publishers, including *Art at Auction*. He has worked as a cataloguer for Sotheby's European sculpture and works of art department in London, and was for several years editor of Sotheby's *Preview* magazine.

Peter Cannon-Brookes studied and taught at the Courtauld Institute in London, and has been Keeper of the Departments of Art at the City Museums and Art Galleries in Birmingham, and the National Museum of Wales in Cardiff. He is a regular contributor to *Apollo*, the *Art Bulletin*, the *Burlington Magazine* and *Connoisseur*.

Stefano Carboni and **Anna Contadini** graduated in Arabic and Islamic Art at the University of Venice. They are presently researching their Ph.D in Islamic miniature painting at the University of London School of Oriental and African Studies. Their interests also cover other aspects of Islamic art and civilization (glass, leather, chess and gaming pieces, the relationship between Venice and Ottoman Turkey) on which they have published several articles, and given papers.

Professor John Carswell is Director of the Islamic art department at Sotheby's London, and was formerly director of the Smart Gallery at the University of Chicago. He is the author of numerous articles and papers, and his books include *Kutalya Tiles and Pottery* (1972), *Islamic Bookbindings and Bookmaking* (1981) and *Blue and White: Chinese Porcelain and its Impact on the West* (1985).

Julia Clarke joined Sotheby's in 1972, where she specialized in nineteenth-century objects of vertu at Belgravia. In 1974 she became responsible for eighteenth-century vertu, gold boxes and English enamels. She has been involved with starting sales in Zurich, Monaco and Geneva.

John Culme joined Sotheby's in 1964, and is a member of the London silver department. His publications include *Nineteenth-Century Silver* (1977) and *The Jewels of the Duchess of Windsor* (1987). He has also compiled *The Directory of Gold & Silversmiths, Jewellers & Allied Traders 1838–1914* (1987). He is a liveryman of the Worshipful Company of Goldsmiths.

Jay Dillon is a Vice President for the department of books and manuscripts at Sotheby's New York, where he has been responsible for many famous sales including the Webster copy of Shakespeare's First Folio, Einstein's earliest surviving manuscript on relativity, and the collection of The Garden Ltd.

Philippe Garner joined Sotheby's in 1970. He is now a Director, responsible for sales in applied arts from 1880. He has written extensively on the decorative arts, and is the author of *Emile Gallé* (1976, revised 1990). He edited the *Phaidon Encyclopedia of the Decorative Arts 1890–1940* (1978) and has recently revised and edited Martin Battersby's *Decorative Arts of the Twenties* and *Decorative Arts of the Thirties*.

Wendell Garrett joined Sotheby's in April 1990 and is a Senior Vice President of the American furniture and decorative arts division. He has been editor and publisher of *The Magazine Antiques* since 1972 and is the author of a number of books including *Arts in Early American History* (1965) and *The arts in America: the nineteenth century* (1969).

J. A. Gere was for nine years Keeper of the Department of Prints and Drawings at the British Museum. His publications include *Taddeo Zuccaro: his development studied in his drawings* (1969) and *Italian Drawings in the British Museum, Vol. V: Artists Working in Rome c. 1550–c. 1640* (1983).

Hayden Herrera is the daughter of two painters, and spent much of her childhood in Mexico. She received a doctorate in history of art at the City University, New York, and has since contributed numerous articles to scholarly and popular publications. She is the author of *Frida, A Biography of Frida Kahlo* (1989).

Lars O. Larsson is the author of *Von Allen Seiten Gleich Schön* (1975), a study of sculptural aesthetics from the Renaissance to the eighteenth century. From 1971–72 he was a Fellow of the Harvard Institute for Renaissance Studies at Villa *I Tatti* in Florence. Since 1980 he has been Senior Professor of the Institute of Art History at the University of Kiel.

Ian Mackenzie has been a Director of Sotheby's print department in London since 1983, where he specializes in contemporary and modern prints. He is the author of *British Prints* (1987).

David Molyneux-Berry joined the wine trade in 1964, working for John Harvey & Sons Ltd of Bristol. He joined Sotheby's in 1970, when the wine department was first established, and became a Master of Wine in 1979. Having been Head of the department, he is now a consultant, and is also Chairman of the International Wine and Spirit Competition. He conducted the first auctions of wine to be held in Thailand and Japan, and is the auctioneer for the New World Wine Auction.

Susan Morris has recently completed a doctorate on the English watercolourist Thomas Girtin, at the Courtauld Institute in London. She was a Mellon Fellow at Yale University where she curated an exhibition on Thomas Girtin, and is currently writing for the *Antique Collector*.

Tamara Northern is Senior Curator of the Hood Museum at Dartmouth College, and the author of *The Art of the Cameroon* (1984) and *Expressions of Cameroon Art: The Franklin Collection* (1986).

David Park joined Sotheby's in 1975, after eight years in the book trade. He is now a Director in the London books and manuscripts department, specializing in atlases, maps and travel books.

Nicholas Rayner is a senior Director of Sotheby's, and a Group Expert for jewels worldwide. He opened Sotheby's Geneva office in 1975, since when sales there have become established as some of the most important of their kind. He conducted the sale of the jewels of the Duchess of Windsor in 1987.

Stephen Roe is a Director of the books and manuscripts department in London, and is responsible for the cataloguing of music manuscripts worldwide. He is the author of *The Keyboard Music of J.S.Bach* (1989).

Timothy Sammons is a Director of Sotheby's London, heading a department that arranges private treaty sales to the nation and offers in lieu of tax (Heritage sales). He is also an expert in Chinese art, and is a Director of Sotheby's Hong Kong.

John Stuart studied icon painting and restoration at the Grabar Central State Restoration Workshops in Moscow, under Adolf Ovchinnikov, a leading authority on East Christian art. In 1977 he set up the Russian department at Sotheby's, where he is now a consultant. His publications include *Ikons* (1975), and he is co-author of *St Petersburg* (1990). He is currently helping to organize a major exhibition from the Russian Museum in Leningrad, to be held in America in 1991.

John L. Tancock is a Senior Vice President and Director of the department of Impressionist and modern paintings at Sotheby's New York. His publications include *The Sculpture of Auguste Rodin* (1976), and *Multiples: The First Decade* (1971).

Ronald Varney is a Vice President in the marketing department of Sotheby's New York. He has written widely on the arts, for *The Wall Street Journal*, *Esquire* magazine, *Smithsonian* and *Connoisseur*.

Nicholas Wadley is an art historian specialising in late-nineteenth-century French art. He was head of the Art History department at Chelsea School of Art in London from 1970 to 1985, and since leaving has published *Noa Noa: Gauguin's Tahiti* (1985), and an anthology of writings on Renoir (1987). He is currently working on a study of *Impressionism and the Art of Drawing*, to be published in 1991.

Elizabeth White is Vice President and Director of publications at Sotheby's New York. Before joining Sotheby's in 1981, she was an editor at the Philadelphia Museum of Art.

John Wilton-Ely is Director of Sotheby's educational studies in London, and Professor Emeritus of Art History at the University of Hull. His publications include *The Mind and Art of Piranesi* (1978). He has explored Palladio's influence on British architecture through two pioneering exhibitions, *Lord Burlington and his Circle* (Nottingham, 1973) and *William Kent: a Tercentenary Tribute* (Hull, 1985).

Index